If You Print This, Please Don't Use My Name

Questions from Teens and Their Parents About Things that Matter

compiled and edited by Nancy Keltner
illustrations by Gina Coffman

Terra Nova Press, Davis, California

IF YOU PRINT THIS, PLEASE DON'T USE MY NAME
Questions from Teens and Their Parents About Things that
Matter

compiled and edited by Nancy Keltner
illustrations by Gina Coffman
cover photograph by Barbara Cheney and Todd Hammond

Published by: Terra Nova Press
                  1309 Redwood Lane
                  Davis. CA. 95616. U.S.A.

Copyright © 1992 by Nancy Rickey Keltner
Printed in the United States of America

Library of Congress Cataloging-in-Publication Data

If you print this, please don't use my name : questions from teens and their parents about things that matter / compiled and edited by Nancy Keltner ; illustrations by Gina Coffman.
        p.   cm.
    Compiled from the newspaper column "FYI," which has appeared since 1985 in Davis, Calif., newspapers.
    Includes bibliographical references and index.
    Summary : Questions and answers explore areas of interest to adolescent boys and girls, including love, drugs, family life, and sex.
    ISBN 0-944176-03-8
    1. Adolescence--Miscellanea. 2. Teenagers--United States--Miscellanea. 3. Parent and Teenager--United States--Miscellanea.
    (1. Adolescence--Miscellanea. 2. Questions and answers.)
    I. Keltner, Nancy, 1940-   . II. Coffman, Gina, ill.
HQ796.I24   1992
305.23'5--dc20   91-36306
                                                      CIP
                                                       AC

This book is dedicated to Herbert Bauer, student, teacher, physician, counselor, friend. He has always been there, for me and for FYI, supplying wisdom and humor... and a steadying hand.

WHERE TO GO FOR HELP

"White pages" refers to front pages of phone book --community services
    section).
* AIDS: hotline: 1-800-342-AIDS (English); 1-800-344-SIDA
    (Spanish).
* Alcohol Abuse: call Alcoholics Anonymous.
    (also Alanon/Alateen/Ala-Preteen/Alanon Adult
    Children of Alcoholics).
    National Council on Alcohol and Drug Abuse: 1-800-622-2255.
    National Institute on Drug Abuse (information and
    referrals to alcohol and drug-abuse treatment programs): 1-800-
    662-4357.
* Child Abuse: call Children's Protective Services. National Child Abuse
    Hotline: 1-800-422-4453.
    Parents Anonymous: 1-800-421-0353 for crisis or
    referrals.
* Domestic Violence: call 911 or "0" for operator, or call local police
    department.
    National Coalition Against Domestic Violence hotline: 1-800-
    333-7233.
* Drug Abuse: see "alcohol and drug abuse" in white pages.
    National hotline: 1-800-852-5209 (information and
    referral).
* Missing Children: National Center for Missing and Exploited
    Children, hotline: 1-800-843-5678.
* Poison Control: national hotline: 1-800-342-9293.
* Pregnancy: Planned Parenthood listed in white pages, or
    national number: 1-800-777-1740.
    National Right to Life Association: 202-626-8800.
* Rape: look under "rape and sexual assault" in white pages.
    National Organization for Victim Assistance: 202-393-6682 (will
    give information on nearest rape crisis center).
    National Coalition for Sexual Assault: 618-398-7764.
* Runaways: National Runaway Switchboard: 1-800-621-4000.
    Greyhound and Trailways Home Free hotline 1-800-448-4663
    (1-800-HIT-HOME).
* Smoking: call nearest Lung Association if listed in phone book,
    or 1-800-4CANCER.
* Suicide: call nearest Suicide Prevention or crisis line listed in white
    pages.

CONTENTS

INTRODUCTION

This book owes its existence to a newspaper question-and-answer column for teen-agers and their parents. Called "FYI" (For Your Information), the column debuted in *The Davis Enterprise* (Davis, CA.) in 1985, and expanded to *The Daily Democrat* (Woodland, CA.) in 1987.

Being - or parenting - a teen-ager comes with many challenges. FYI filled a void and became very popular.

With *If You Print This, Please Don't Use My Name,* we have compiled questions and answers from "FYI." Some concerns are pretty basic: "How can I get others to notice me?" Others are tough: "Both of my parents drink. What do I do?" And some are dead-serious: "I have a friend who does drugs. What will happen to him? How can I get him to stop?"

While this book does not attempt to be a "complete text" of dealing with teen-age and parenting problems, it does let young folks and their parents know that they are not alone in their daily, seemingly unique, struggles.

This book is not designed to supply all the answers: we don't have all the answers. We just hope it is a starting point for the tough problems. We know it's a quick reference for the easy ones.

ACKNOWLEDGEMENTS

I would like to thank the people who made *If You Print This, Please Don't Use My Name* a reality.

Without the initiative of Sue Curry, publisher, Terra Nova Press, this book would not exist. She skillfully edited and organized volumes of material and firmly but graciously kept the project on schedule. She had the wisdom to allow us to occasionally misplace, but never lose our impetus.

Bruce Gallaudet brought verve, dedication and a wealth of knowledge and ideas to the book. His skills in editing and formatting gave the manuscript a clear and lively form.

The reviewers who offered many helpful suggestions were: Lynn Zender, Ann Hallisey, Susan Lohse, Gretel Wandesforde-Smith, and Michael Chulada. And special thanks to Craig Kubey for his help.

I am enormously grateful to the people who supported the FYI column over the years, laying the groundwork for the book.

The column was born out of the haunting challenge of high school English teacher Linda Vanderwold, who said: "I know from (what they write) that a lot of these kids are - among other things - anorexic and angry and depressed enough to be suicidal. What are we doing for them?"

It was the daring of Debbie Davis, editor, *The Davis Enterprise,* that launched the column. She took a chance on it, and on me. Her constant approval and support allowed it to evolve and flourish.

Cheerfully spreading its broad umbrella, the Mental Health Assocation of Yolo County co-sponsored the column and adopted it as an official program.

Dean Alderman, chief probation officer of Yolo County, gave the column public support just as it was getting its sea legs. This vote of confidence was greatly appreciated.

The Yolo County Alcohol and Drug Program awarded a mini-grant to enable the column to be disseminated throughout the county.

The early and on-going support of family life teacher, Grace Kim, provided the column with a breadth and depth it could not have otherwise attained. Her love of and concern for teen-agers has been a source of inspiration for many.

The teachers were our silent contributors, urging entire classes to write and participating in our yearly surveys of students. They enthusiastically posted and distributed the column in classrooms and championed the idea of the column becoming a book.

Often working against tight deadlines, the experts, from diverse professional backgrounds, lent their expertise with assurance and compassion.

Finally, my husband, John, whose well of patience, love and support never runs dry, encouraged my work on the column and book with his usual enthusiasm.

Nancy Keltner.

1

Who said this would be easy?

Dating and relationships. Seems harmless enough. Boy asks girl to school dance. They have a good time, start seeing each other on a regular basis and suddenly they're a steady item.

Piece of cake...

Hello, McFly? Reality check.

Dating and relationships. The bittersweet part of teen life. What seemed like the greatest moment in your life on Saturday night can turn to long- or short-term disaster the following week.

Dating and relationships. Not always what they should be; not always as difficult as we might fear.

Got your ticket? Get ready for this emotional rollercoaster ride...

Dear FYI: I'm a 16-year-old girl. I've accepted the fact that having a physical relationship doesn't mean the other person really cares about you. That's just life. But it makes me really angry when people use words like "I love you" when they don't mean them. I wish at least that was sacred.

Furious

Dear Furious: Your assertion raises some important questions. Many teen-agers share your concerns.

The teen-age years can be a confusing time of life. Sorting out the messages of sex, friendship and love are a major part of the confusion and increase the chances of getting hurt. Having sex without caring sounds pretty unsatisfactory and anxiety-producing to me. If one doesn't feel cared for it's hard to feel good about oneself. And it doesn't work to think one can trade sex for love.

"I like you," "I love you," "I want to have sex with you" are statements about three different feelings.

But it's easy to mix them up. It's important for you to know which you feel and what you want to do about it in any situation.

1

Teen-age years are a time of exploration of feelings and your chance to ask yourself: how will I know what love looks like? What kind of love am I looking for? Is sex without love OK for me? This is how we all begin to know ourselves and perhaps to be able to choose partners with whom we can build lives that include both caring and sex.

Edith Rothchild, MSW & LCSW
Psychotherapist

Dear FYI: My daughter has been going with a guy for almost two years. He is exceptionally clean cut, a "mother's choice" type kid for her daughter, but the two of them have totally different backgrounds and religions.

She's 16, he's a few years older. I never really thought anything about this dating, but when they start talking about raising kids and how "in love" they are, it scares me.

There is no way it would work. Their statement "love conquers all" is my worry.

My daughter tells me that "we do not have sex and I would not allow it to happen, and I've told him I wouldn't and that's OK with him." She says they don't have to use birth control because it just won't happen.

At first I told her she couldn't see him as much or talk to him every night on the phone. She could see him, but not so thick. Then I got mad when her boyfriend asked "who do you think you are -- interfering in our lives?" Anyway, the outcome was we told our daughter "go ahead and have your way, but remember if you screw up your life it's a hard, hard emotional sad life".

I am so upset. I can see her getting pregnant and having their little kids so confused between lifestyles and I'm sure there will be a lot of fighting. I'm not opposed to him, it's the entire picture of a non-workable situation. What if he did change or she did change (which she won't, she says) and she ends up pregnant?

Upset Mother

Dear Mother: Being a good parent, you wish for your daughter a carefree and risk-free life in which nobody makes any mistakes and in which there is always a happy ending. This is simply not in the cards and taking some risks is part of normal human life.

There are two things you can do as the good mother you are.

First, you can set a model by living the kind of life that you would like your daughter to emulate (which I'm sure you have tried to do).

Secondly, you must develop some trust in her and give her a chance to do some things to the best of her abilities. In this respect, you may have to do a bit of practicing.

In fact, you set the stage with a single sentence in your letter by saying "there is no way it would work." You may not realize that this very attitude will actually help it not work. It is often such a prophecy that determines the outcome.

What can be done about it?

Two things, I believe, may help.

First, keep expressing your love and concern for your daughter, but make it clear to her and to yourself that in the end it will be she who must decide how to organize her life; you no longer can regulate her lifestyle, nor should you.

> **Professional help is often a good approach for very tough problems**

Secondly, I think that emotional support for you would be beneficial for those concerned.

Try to find some professional person whom you can trust and who, in turn, may help you to abandon your fatalistic attitude. None of us can predict the outcome of a human relationship, no matter how involved we may be. At your daughter's age, there has to be a definite line where you end and she begins, and vice versa. You may need some help in drawing this line. It will be extremely difficult for you to do that all by yourself. Please see a counselor, it will be good for all of you.

Herbert Bauer, M.D.
Psychiatrist

Dear FYI: Our son is in junior high. We have been going crazy with calls from girls for him. At first he was flattered and now he is annoyed, which the rest of the family has been all along. Do you have any suggestions for tactfully turning these calls off? He isn't anxious to listen to any of *our* suggestions.
Wishing For Quiet

Dear Wishing for Quiet: Your son's annoyance (if he is genuinely annoyed and not bragging or seeking attention) is a good opening for a family discussion about how various members have dealt with similar problems. It is also a chance to encourage your son to work out his own solutions in dealing with folks who pursue him when he does not wish to be pursued.

Have you modeled appropriate ways of handling comparable situations, or have you allowed yourself to be a doormat? How do you respond to intrusive phone calls? Are you able to say "no" to your son, your spouse or your friend when you prefer not to give them your attention? Are you able to assert the right to do what is important to you rather than automatically indulging the demands of others so they don't dislike you?

This complex situation creates an opportune time to explore the intricacies of social relationships, and to develop the skills which we need throughout life.

Beulah Amsterdam, Ph. D.
Psychologist

Dear FYI: I have a son who has just turned 14.

I am in search of a reference resource to guide me in broaching a personal subject with him and I hope you can point me in the right direction.

Although he has a pretty solid understanding of the biology of sexual function, I'm not certain he is well grounded in the ethics and etiquette of relationships with girls and women.

I want to encourage him to view women not with wonder and mystery and lust, but with understanding and admiration and friendship. I don't want him to develop the kind of warped misunderstandings that locker room talk can breed. I don't want him to learn to equate masculinity with dominance.

I would like him to learn to be friends with, rather than fear, women. And I want to instill in him an understanding of the principles that some men never seem to get: that women, quite simply, deserve to be treated with no less than common courtesy, honesty, trust and genuine respect.

I would prefer that you not mention my name because I don't want to unnecessarily embarrass my son. But I would very much appreciate your advice -- and so would, I suspect, other fathers of teen-age sons.

A Father

Dear Father: Most reference material on this subject will tell you and your son all about anatomy, physiology and the psychology of sexual behavior -- things

> **When all is said and done, parents remain the best role models for their children... In other words, parents will lead by example**

which you know and your son at 14 should know. But the most important reference of all is your own honesty and decency in man/woman relationships. To model your own attitude is by far the most valuable reference for you to offer and for your son to adopt.

At 14 he will be influenced by peer talk and will need to feel vastly superior to any woman who ever lived. Don't let that worry you, nor need you be upset in case his sexual vocabulary contains words which have fewer letters in them that you would like. All this is part of growing up. At 14, your son is not likely to express appreciation for the kind of father he is lucky enough to have, but in the end his lifestyle will show the result of your upbringing.

Herbert Bauer

Dear FYI: There is a guy I care about a lot and I think I like him, and he knows it. He wants a relationship, but the word "relationship" scares me away. But I love to be with him! What should I do?

Confused

Dear Confused: If you can, talk with the guy you care about and let him know your reaction to the word "relationship."

Tell him what scares you and what you would be comfortable with at present. Then take things as slowly as you need to. Don't let yourself get involved faster than feels safe to you. It is OK to say "no" to anything that makes you feel unsafe.

Nancy DuBois
Psychologist

5

We polled 51 high-school students on the question of attraction to others. Many who mentioned physical appearance apologized for thinking it was important. Interestingly, height, weight and breasts were rarely mentioned...

The most important quality? Both guys & girls rated sensitivity first...

A girl needs that air of kindness that lets you know she's nice, before even saying a word. Sensitive but honest, funny but not silly. I would want to be able to confide in her, for her to be my friend.

I like guys who are generous, humorous, friendly and respectful. I don't like guys who leave people out.

I want a guy I can be comfortable with.

It wouldn't be bad if she came with a car.

I look for a boy with a great smile and a glisten in his eyes. He has to be sensitive and funny, and have a good loving heart, be adventurous and take risks and have fun on a date and not be all over me all the time.

If I'm going out with a girl who agrees with me on everything I might as well be dating myself. Oh yes, manipulation is a huge "NO."

I hate to say it, but looks and body do count. They are not the overriding factor, but they are the first things you see.

What attracts girls to guys -- and vice versa?

While it may seem shallow, one of the qualities I look for in a girl is looks.

But what constitutes good looks? There were orders for black flowing hair (on a guy); sexy feet; eyes of teal, blue, green, brown, and grey-blue; rosy cheeks; "nice butts;" firm and muscular behinds; blonde brown golden hair; athletic legs; feminine but strong hands; a "pretty" face; nice firm toes; and even a "well defined" Achilles tendon. But hands down the top priorities in the appearance category were "nice" smiles and eyes.

I look at how he treats other people. Chances are if he treats his friends well, he'll do the same for me.

Since I like sports and they take up a lot of my time, I find that guys in sports can understand the importance of time in my life (echoed by guys).

Caring. He's got to be romantic.

A good sense of humor... he can't act all macho around his friends.

I hate it when guys are very chauvinistic and believe that their "w o m e n" should abide by their rules and be at their beck and call.

I want him to be my best friend. He doesn't have to be incredibly good-looking, he just needs to be him. He must be loyal, honest, spontaneous, eccentric and have a good sense of humor.

She must have a great sense of humor and a nice smile, good-smelling breath.

Dear FYI: What if you're too shy to ask a girl out?

Dateseeker

Dear Dateseeker: At the root of shy feelings is a fear of being embarrassed, not respected, or not being accepted. There is too much looking to others for approval, rather than focusing on what's right for you. When people give in to shy feelings and retreat from others, no one learns comfortable social behavior. So you have to challenge your shy feelings and give confidence a chance to grow. Here are some suggestions:

1. Practice what you initially want to say before you make contact. Write down some topics to talk about if you're anxious about the conversation lagging. Once the ice is broken, you will probably forget the "agenda" and the conversation will flow naturally.

2. Try to shed your own self-consciousness by showing interest in and focusing on how things are going with the girl. Ask her about school matters, vacation plans, how she feels about whatever is happening in your peer group, and so on. And then really listen to what she is saying! Don't get stuck just asking questions; after a while begin making statements about your life and beliefs. That is the only way people get to know each other.

3. At first, make contact with her in easier, low-risk situations. The important thing is to get started. A small chat in the hallway is good practice for a more formal date later.

4. Don't criticize yourself if you aren't initially successful. Being turned down may have nothing to do with you, and it isn't the end of the world. Maybe she struggles with shyness, too -- or really has made prior plans. Above all, don't continually label yourself as "too shy"; it can be a crutch for no action at all.

Remember that shyness is seldom permanent. Be gentle with yourself, but take some risks. Go for it!

Sumner Morris, Ed. D.
Counseling psychologist

Dear FYI: I'm having trouble communicating with girls when I'm going out with them. What should I do?

Hopeless

Dear Hopeless: Communication is a very big subject. It may help to remember that it's impossible *not* to communicate -- even if you don't say a word! I imagine you would like the communication to be easier, more sponta-neous, and more direct.

Any time you can identify how you're feeling and say so plainly, you are

> **At the root of shy feelings is a fear of embarrassment or not being accepted or respected...**

> **Sure, sometimes there are risks ... but that's part of the fun of living!**

paying the other person the honor of being real with her. She also is possibly feeling tongue-tied and awkward. If you tell her what's important to you -- interests, beliefs, politics, school activities or whatever -- and ask her about her feelings and opinions, I think she'll be pleased and responsive.

Remember practice makes perfect, so don't withdraw from social activities. Good luck!

Nancy DuBois

Dear FYI: Is there a cure for clammy hands?

Afraid to Hold Hands

Dear Afraid to Hold Hands: Are you afraid to hold hands because you feel clammy, or are you clammy because you are afraid to hold hands? If by clammy you mean cold -- the cure is simple: put your hands in your pockets, sit on them, or put them around a cup filled with a hot drink.

The best cure of all? Grab hold of the hand you would like to hold, hang on to it, and if the owner complains about the temperature difference, simply say, "That's why I hang on to you, because you are so nice and warm".

True, it's a risk, but so is everything in life ... and that's part of the fun of living.

Herbert Bauer

Dear FYI: I have a girlfriend and I haven't kissed her yet. I'm afraid to. She wants me to, but I don't want to rush things. What should I do?

Help

Dear Help: No one should be rushed into any situation or action he or she is not comfortable with -- no matter what someone else wants. People's sexual choices are unique and purely their own. Maybe you would find it helpful to talk

9

this over with a trusted older person and learn to accept yourself more comfortably.

Nancy DuBois

Dear FYI: I like this boy a lot and my best friend says she heard he is going to ask me out. I have never been out on a date and don't know if I am supposed to pay my way or not. Can you help me?

Excited But Scared

Editor's Note: We polled a high school English class, planning to run a sampling of replies. However, this one letter seemed to "say it all."

Dear Excited But Scared: The dilemma you face is not uncommon -- you are not alone.

My gut feeling about your situation is if the young gentleman asks *you* out, he will probably pay. Unless, of course, he is rude, in which case he would ask you out and then expect you to pay. Nice guy. However, this shouldn't happen unless you develop a long, meaningful relationship (about two weeks!). Seriously, I would think that if you feel uncomfortable about the situation, you could at least offer to pay, out of courtesy if nothing else.

By the way, there is another option. If you get sick and tired of waiting around for him to ask you out (guys can be soooo slow sometimes), you could ask *him* out (surprise). In this case, you would probably feel you should pay although he may offer. Another option is going dutch, and this way you don't feel obligated or uncomfortable, and neither does he.

Whatever you decide, take some cash in case of emergency -- like if he leaves his wallet at home, or some such crisis. Try to do whatever feels comfortable for both of you, otherwise you will both be miserable and won't be able to concentrate on having *fun* -- which is what you should be doing.

So, good luck with your guy and remember to be comfortable, prepared and most of all, be yourself! If the guy is really worth it he will understand the situation no matter what happens. Get out there, be confident, and just plain *enjoy!*

Female (thank goodness)

Editor's Note: Several writers suggested splitting the cost for the evening. For example, he pays for dinner, you pay for the movie.

Dear FYI: I am having trouble because I still have some old-fashioned feelings toward relationships. Is it wrong to want the guy to make the first move and ask you out?

Old-Fashioned

Dear Old-Fashioned: You describe yourself as "old-fashioned", but you have a lot more company than you realize. No feeling in itself is wrong, any more than sneezing is "wrong," but when social customs are changing rapidly it's hard for everyone, adults too. If a man offers a woman his seat on the bus, will she accept and appreciate it, or will she be an offended feminist? It does cause confusion! If you let it be known that this is your style, boys will know that you're not turned off by them, but just being conservative.

Nancy DuBois

Dear FYI: I'm 15. My question is, is it proper for a girl to ask a guy out for dinner or something?

Thinking About It

Dear Thinking About It: There would seem nothing improper about a girl asking a guy out. It is risky, you might get turned down. But, you might begin something fun. Most guys would probably be flattered and relieved not to have to do the asking for a change. There may be a few "traditional" guys who would feel you are being too "forward" or might be threatened. So, think about how "traditional" the guy you like is -- and if you are prepared to hear "no." If he's not too traditional, have fun!

Nancy DuBois

Dear FYI: I know a couple who have been going together for a year now. All they do is fight. Should they keep at this relationship or break up and go out with other people?

Their Buddy

Dear Buddy: If this couple has been fighting for a year, while going together, it would appear to me that:
-- They are not getting anywhere in solving problems;
-- Their mutual needs in the relationship are probably not being met;
-- There has not been a level of mutual trust established in the relationship;
-- They may need a third party to mediate their fights -- such as a mutual friend, a helpful parent or counselor;

11

-- They may well need a break from each other to be with other people for a while.

Not all relationships work, and we simply are not going to "connect" or form friendships with everyone we meet in life. If third-party mediation or taking a break from each other does not help patch things up, then perhaps they should move on to other relationships. An unsolved relationship is not necessarily a failure. It just means that it did not work out, and does not have to mean the end of the world.

William J. Treguboff, MFCC
Family & marriage therapist

Dear FYI: I am in high school. I have a boyfriend that I really care about, and recently I cheated on him. It was just a one-night thing and after I realized what I was doing I felt extremely bad. The problem is that I do not know if I should tell him and risk losing him. If I don't tell him and he finds out, it will be a lot worse. The chances of him finding out are quite slim. Only a few of my friends know, but it could always get out. Should I tell him or keep it a secret?

Guilty Conscience

Dear Guilty Conscience: When someone leaves a relationship with a person they care about -- even if only for a night -- it often happens as a result of something being not quite right about the relationship.

It can mean that the relationship has been too confining for you and that you would like to broaden your experience with the opposite sex (which would be a very natural need for someone your age, especially if the relationship is long-standing).

What you call "cheating" can mean, further, that one or both people are not being very honest with one another about some of their feelings, particularly their resentments. It may be that the issue is not so much whether you tell your boyfriend what you did but that you sit down, first with yourself, later with him, and confront what it is you do and don't like about the relationship.

Being honest about the things in the relationship that make you unhappy or frustrated does not mean that the relationship is bad and should end.

Sometimes it is necessary to bring out into the open with a boyfriend or

12

girlfriend what it is that displeases you. This can be especially hard if you feel guilty about saying what it is you don't like about the other person's behavior or about the relationship. But at the same time, this can make the relationship stronger. At the very least, both of you, whether together or apart, can learn something valuable and be more satisfied.

Kent F. Bennington, Ph.D
Psychologist

Dear FYI: I'm too jealous! Whenever my boyfriend goes out I worry about him finding someone better. I know it's wrong but I can't help it. We have been going out for a year and a half and it seems to be getting worse. He did once cheat on me and now it is always on my mind. I'm afraid it will happen again.

I wish I weren't so jealous.

Why can't I forgive him?

Too Jealous

Dear Too Jealous: All of us feel occasional pangs of jealousy as we dream of being the one and only companion to someone. Yet, when we become consumed by jealousy it means that something is missing in our self-esteem. Having to "own" someone often comes from fears that we may not measure up.

Every relationship needs a contract between partners, a contract that must be worked out and is acceptable to both partners. A contract that keeps one or both partners from relating to outsiders leads to a diminishment. Love and friendship need to be an augmenting, growing experience.

If you can, speak to your boyfriend, tell him your feelings and allow the two of you to explore the relationship together. Also, speak to your friends (don't just complain). If your pain is intense, seek out a counselor to deal with your feelings of adequacy and self-esteem.

Hanna Bauer, Ed. D.
Psychotherapist

Dear FYI: There is a guy who I really like. I don't know how he feels about me. It seems like he only pays attention to me on the weekends when we are drinking and at a party. I want someone who is more interested in me every day and not just for sexual reasons. What should I do? Talk to him? I am very sexually attracted to him. If I have sex with him will he just forget about me? Or will he be closer to me?

Unsure

Dear Unsure: Your letter suggests that you have given a lot of thought to this situation and that you are genuinely frustrated and confused. The frustration results from not getting something you need or want, and the confusion is coming from not being sure how far to go to get it.

You need some clarification from this young man about his interest in you, and what his party behavior toward you really means. Maybe it's a matter of having different definitions of what a relationship might be. He could be perfectly happy with the current set-up or simply be unaware that you need more interaction between parties.

It is very easy to get mixed messages when alcohol is involved in social situations. You need to carefully consider how alcohol influences your own behavior and what messages you may be sending him. It is possible that he is also confused about this situation.

Sexual attraction is a physical and emotional reaction and should not be confused with love and affection. Using sex to find out if someone really likes you is a big mistake. This approach may be a test of the other person's sexual curiosity, but it is not an indicator of his affection and caring for you as a person.

It seems that what you really want is a feeling of closeness and belonging. These feelings come with honest and open communication between two people who respect each other's needs, share a special feeling for each other, take mutual responsibility for what is happening in the relationship and understand each other's expectations. Sexual familiarity is not the same thing as emotional intimacy.

> *It is very easy to get mixed messages when alcohol is involved in social situations.*

My suggestion is to approach this young man at school and in your own special way let him know that you find him attractive and interesting. Explain that you would like to get to know him better and suggest doing something that doesn't include alcohol but does provide an opportunity for talking. Relationships start with sharing simple things together.

Judith Buchholz,
School counselor &
Sex education teacher

'*I love this girl, but don't know how to tell her. What do I do?'*
— **Desperate**

'*How can you tell a guy how you feel about him without scaring him off?'*
-- **Undecided**

'*What's the best way to get a guy?'*
-- **Not Outgoing**

Dear FYI: I have a friend who is madly in love with a girl. The problem is that he doesn't know how to tell her. So, how can I advise him? Is putting a love letter in her locker all right (that was one of the ideas I gave him)?
A Good Friend

Dear Good Friend: What a good friend, indeed. We loved your letter and though it would be fun to ask a whole high-school class for suggestions for your friend.

P.S. -- The love letter sounds good!

Maybe your friend can try some of these little gems...

1. Have a friend tell her that you like her.

2. Give her a little present (if you can, make something for her).

3. Cards can sometimes say what you can't Find a special one and mail it.

4. Ask for help in a subject at which she is particularly good.

5. Think of something special about her -- and tell her.

6. Leave a flower on her car window.

7. Invite her to a movie or dinner.

8. Ask her for a lunchtime walk.

9. Ask your Dad what he did to get Mom's attention.

Editor's note: Girls -- remember, these will work for you, too!

'*Can you suggest some right moves to get a girl to see that you're alive?'*
— **Shy One**

'*I don't have the nerve to talk to this boy I like. I'm sure he thinks I'm quiet and wimpy. I'm just petrified...'*
-- **Need Guts**

'*...and by the time we meet, we'll both be in our 90s. I need a bold plan -- and quick!'*
-- **Getting Old**

Dear FYI: I seem to be attracted to guys who are very stuck on themselves -- it has always been that way. I am sick of liking guys like that, but I always do. Why?

Annoyed

Dear Annoyed: You have taken the first, biggest and most important step already in realizing that you pick people who you really don't want to be with.

It might be interesting to go on a big psychological hunt and find out why this is, but in the meantime, it may be helpful to look at your attraction to these "giant egos" as a sort of addiction, like chocolate, junk novels or whatever you might find yourself drawn to even though you had made a conscious decision to give them up. Sounds like going on a diet, doesn't it?

Do you have a good friend who can help support you when you feel that old magnet working on you and remind you of your resolve?

Do you have a good friend who can help support you when you feel that old magnet working on you and remind you of your resolve?

It might help, too, to make a good list of pros and cons. For example, "giant egos" often are looked up to by the crowd because they seem so self-assured, to have lots of questions answered and so on. On the other hand, they often do not have lots of time or attention to really listen to you. You might look back on your life and see if there are any people who remind you of these guys.

Or maybe the compassionate side of you is responding to the part of the "giant ego" that really is a scared little boy whistling in the dark. You're the best judge!

Nancy DuBois

Dear FYI: I have been dating a guy for a little over a year. I'm 19 and he's 18. I have no freedom. He wants me

16

to be with him all the time.

I suggested that we take one night a month to be with our friends, he says "no".

Then he goes to his friends and I don't know where he is. I worry myself sick thinking he's been hurt or something. Then he comes over later and says he went to a friend's house, but he doesn't want me to leave the house. He says, "I'm afraid someone will pick up on you, so you have to stay home unless you're with me".

I do not want to end our relationship; I just need some suggestions on what to do.

Sick of Staying at Home

Dear Sick of Staying at Home: Your boyfriend sounds like he feels insecure about your relationship. There may be different reasons for his insecurities. Have things happened in your relationship to increase his insecurity about you? Has he had poor relationships with previous girlfriends?

Does he lack self-confidence? Is he afraid that people wouldn't want to be with him if they had the chance to be with others? Does he come from a family where there is little trust in each other?

The only way you'll find out why he is so unsure of your relationship is to talk with him about it. Tell him you need boundaries so you can maintain your own individuality. Also, talk about your need to be with friends. It is healthy for relationships when each partner has friends. Plus, the chances of the relationship lasting are greater if each of you can pursue your own interests.

Without individual interests, the relationship will feel more like a jail where you are the prisoner and he is the jailer. It is difficult for love to survive in those conditions. You will soon find yourself feeling bored and resentful.

So, talk with him, listen and understand. Reassure him of your feelings for him, but do not allow yourself to become his prisoner.

Nancy Chadwick, LCSW
Psychotherapist

Dear FYI: When my boyfriend and I first got together he treated me real good and with a lot of respect, but after a few months went by he started hitting me around and accusing me of seeing other guys every chance I got, which wasn't true at all. I was always honest with him and I never felt like I gave him reason to think that stuff.

We've been going out for two years, and in that time I've left him four times and gone to my parents -- 1,000 miles away -- but I always go back to him. I've tried everything to get him off my mind, but it doesn't work.

I've been back home for one month, and I'm so unhappy without him. He was

17

like a part of me and without him I don't exist. I'm afraid to start a relationship with another guy because I'm still in love with him and if I see another guy I would expect him to replace my ex-boyfriend and he wouldn't be able to.

I'm real confused and need some good advice. What should I do? He always promised he'd change, but he never did. He always begged me not to leave him. Help me please. Please answer my letter soon. I need advice before I lose my mind.

Confused Cal

Dear Confused Cal: Confusion often results when the passions of the heart conflict with the rational thinking of the mind. Fortunately in your case, good judgment has won out. No one deserves an abusive relationship.

Patterns are often established early. Your boyfriend has been abusive and both of you know it is wrong. Terminating a relationship as you have done is the only logical option. He may change as time passes, but there are no guarantees. Often in abusive relationships, abuse continues after feelings of love subside.

Human relationships are extremely complicated and we typically bring both the heartaches and rewards of past major relationships into current ones. Your boyfriend probably genuinely cares for you with no intent of upsetting or harming you.

Despite this, past relationships may have been troubling for him. He appears to harbor unjustified anger and suspicion, which become readily triggered when he questions your loyalty. You describe yourself as an innocent victim, and I trust you did nothing to provoke his behavior. If you did, you should question your motives so your behaviors do not continue.

A healthy approach for you and your boyfriend would have been to openly discuss your concerns with each other, while realizing that false accusations and physical abuse do not solve problems or help relationships. Apparently you tried this approach with varied success.

Troubled relationships can also be helped by counseling, but both parties must agree to contribute and change.

You should remember that a period of grieving often follows romantic breakups, and is associated with feelings of loneliness, depression, anger and abandonment. We all need to be loved -- and there will be others with whom you can share your love -- but make sure you let some healing occur first (which could take a few months). Do not feel guilty. You gave him many chances to treat you with respect.

You are wise in holding off dating new boyfriends until your ill feelings have been resolved. People who rapidly move into new relationships before clearing troubled feelings from the past often find themselves in the midst of another romantic heartache.

Finally, I suggest that you discuss your concerns further with a trusted friend or counselor. Talking things out really works. Not only does it reduce ill feelings, it also helps outline healthy solutions.

> *P.T. Donlon, M.D.*
> *Psychiatrist*

Dear FYI: I have an ex-girlfriend who suggests getting back together every couple of months. So far we haven't. I think she just wants attention from me and I'm bothered by it. How do I tell her to bug off or tell me what she really feels?

Dear Disturbed: Since no one of us is very good at mind-reading, there is no guaranteed way to find out what she really wants or feels.

She may not even know herself.

That means you can concentrate on whether or not you want to get back together, and under what circumstances. Are the issues over which you broke up resolved ... and have either of you (or both) changed in any way that would make a better relationship a second time around?

As far as telling her to "bug off" is concerned, probably the most effective way is with kindness and firmness.

> *Nancy DuBois*

Dear FYI: I have a lot of guys who are friends (close friends), but when it comes to a serious romantic relationship it seems they overlook me. I have their respect but not their romance. Can you help?

> *Everyone's Sister*

Dear Sister: This is a very commonly asked question -- by guys as well as girls.

Dear FYI: What are some good things my guy and I can do to have fun? Movies are out.
-- *Getting Bored*

Dear Bored: We asked a high school journalism class for ideas. We hope you will dare to break the monotony by planning ahead and/or connecting with others. Have fun.

-- Do something off the wall ... go swimming at midnight.

-- Set a table in the park; add candles, flowers and your favorite fast food.

-- Do something that one of you is especially interested in. You'll know more about the other person.

-- Cook dinner for your guy, then go to the music shop and compare tastes.

-- During the day do some sport like tennis, basketball or even golf.

-- Talk about things in life, yourself and each other.

-- Get a two-person raft, stock it with munchies and head down the river.

-- Go out to dinner and walk through town.

-- Go to a baseball game or take a hike.

-- Bowling or shopping are fun.

-- Get intimate ... dance in the moonlight.

-- Go jogging, play cards or board games.

-- The ol' standby -- miniature golf.

-- Take your date on a walk-a-thon or a charity fun run.

So you are not alone in your situation.

It sounds as though you know how good it is to have close friends of both sexes.

Do you feel romantic toward one of your male friends?

If so, maybe you have to let him know that you are feeling something special. This is a risk; you may get ignored if he isn't ready, but if you want to find out, you may have to take this chance.

On the other hand, if you don't feel this way toward anyone right now, there is no need to push it. Enjoy your friends, because knowing how to make and keep friends will be the basis of all your ongoing relationships now and later.

Lots of people don't get involved in serious romantic relationships until their 20s or later.

Most people (at all ages) want a mate and it is scary to wonder if and when we'll find one.

Edith Rothchild

Dear FYI: Is it normal to have a secret crush on an older guy ... even if you have a very special boyfriend?

Wondering

Dear Wondering: In a word, yes! It is normal to notice, admire and often be attracted to members of the opposite sex while having a committed relationship with a special person.

What we decide to do with these feelings becomes the question.

In a truly committed relationship we often note the feelings as natural, then choose to let them go without acting upon them.

Marilyn Roland, Ph.D., FMCC
Family therapist

Dear FYI: I'm 17 and in love with a guy who is 23 and has his own apartment. He wants me to have sex with him. If I don't, I'm afraid I'll lose him. I know I need to think about birth control, but if I bring it up, I'm afraid I'll sound cheap. My parents don't know he's so much older, and if they did, they wouldn't approve. I really love him ... and it's making me miserable. What should I do?

Too Young to Love

Dear Too Young to Love: A teen can get into a real trap when she becomes involved with someone several years older.. While the attention and attraction are flattering, there is often pressure to do things you are not quite ready to do in order to keep the relationship going.

You have addressed many issues, most of which are related to honesty, responsibility and fear of loss. You must be honest with yourself first. What exactly do you want from this relationship? Love, acceptance, attention, experience or simple entertainment?

Are you clear about *his* intentions?

Regarding your parents, they deserve to know the truth about your friend's age and living situation. You're right, they may not approve -- for a variety of legitimate reasons which you'll want to discuss with them.

Your friend needs to be told about your concerns. Tell him just as you have explained here.

It is not cheap, but rather, responsible behavior to discuss birth control, sexually transmitted diseases and AIDS. In fact, it is critical to your lifelong health. What the relationship means to each of you needs to be clear before you move any further toward sexual activity.

Come to grips with what it is you are afraid of losing by not being up front and honest about your concerns.

It is possible to have a meaningful relationship without engaging in sexual intercourse.

Judith Buchholz

Dear FYI: I am a 15-year-old girl. I consider myself attractive and I am friendly. However, although I am interested in boys and would like to begin dating, I have not yet been asked out. Am I sending out some sort of message that I'm not aware of?

Late Starter

Dear Late Starter: There is not a fixed calendar date when beginning to date is "right" or when one is necessarily ready. Can it be that as much as you may want to date, a part of you is not yet ready? What signals would you like to send?

For example, if you like someone, how do you let him know? Since all your peers are also new at this, try practicing with a friend. Perhaps you're missing positive return messages.

Do what interests you so that you meet people who like to do the things you like. That also means being in places you really want to be — so that you meet the kind of people you want to be around.

Go out with a group rather than waiting to be asked out. You may extend an invitation to one person or plan to do something with friends (include new friends).

When you do meet one special person, aim for friendship first. If romance follows that will be great, and you will have had time to ready yourself for dating.

Guille Libresco, Ph.D., LCSW
Psychotherapist

Dear FYI: I am a girl who is 12 and wears glasses. If possible, would you tell me why this one boy in class makes fun of me and calls me names because of my glasses and how smart I am? If answered, this would help because my teacher doesn't help and I am getting sick of his teasing.

Thoroughly Confused

Dear Thoroughly Confused: There are two ways for this boy to get your attention, a nice one and a silly one.

The nice way would be to tell you how pretty you look with your glasses on, to offer to carry your books, perhaps to ask you for a date.

The silly way is to tease you and make unpleasant remarks about your glasses.

But the main thing to remember is that both methods have exactly the same purpose, namely to attract your attention.

What you need to do is to decide if you want to return his attention or not. If you don't, all you have to do is to do nothing. Don't look at him, don't talk to him, don't answer him; sooner or later he will realize that the game is up.

If you want to respond to his approach, you may tell him that you have put him on probation for a whole week. If he continues to act silly, that will be the end of your even noticing him.

If he can behave himself during the entire week, you may reward him with a smile (if even for a brief moment).

But always remember, you yourself are in charge of your feelings -- not other people.

Nobody can make you "thoroughly confused" unless you allow him to influence your feelings. As long as you like your glasses, that's all that really matters.

Herbert Bauer

Dear FYI: I don't know what to do! I'm a sophomore in high school and every day I find myself going out of my way to make friends with seniors.

I'm going out with a senior but that just doesn't seem to be enough. I feel like I have to have all the seniors know me and talk to me.

I've noticed that every day I take longer and longer to get ready for school because I want to be sure that my clothes and hair are perfect. I know it is awful, but lately I have been listening for gossip about people just so I have a reason to talk to them.

Is this normal? Will I get over this?

A Mess

Dear A Mess: I think you've already taken the most important step in realising that the rat race you're running, instead of making you happy, is making you feel even worse about yourself -- the "mess" of your signature.

I suggest that every time you catch yourself so furiously running, you stop and ask yourself -- just what is the point of all this?

So what if you succeed? So what if you don't? My guess is, too, that spending time just relaxing with and enjoying people your own age will boost your good feelings about yourself and the world more effectively than chasing seniors ever could.

To answer your other questions:

I think the hunger you show for approval and recognition by others, especially if those others seem somehow superior (as seniors seem to a sophomore), is a normal part of being human ... and a part that pushes especially hard in the early years of high school.

Chances are very, very good that as you get older you will feel less anxious to prove yourself worthwhile by measuring yourself by what other people think of you.

Bonnie Wilson, Ph.D.
Marriage, family &
Child counselor

Dear FYI: I have been friends with a certain person since I can remember. We both feel really close to each other and I want to get closer. I want to have an intimate relationship with my best friend and I think he does too. What can I do to get closer?

Confused Guy
(serious question, not a joke!)

Dear Confused Guy: To be friends with a person of the same sex, particularly during the teen-age years, is a perfectly normal, healthy and enjoyable thing to do. This is as true for boys as it is for girls. Such "couples" walk together, arm in arm, call each other by pet names, and have deep, dark secrets between them and the rest of the world. They share ice-cream cones, read books together they are not supposed to read and agree that their parents and teachers act as though they had never been teen-agers. Such pairs of boys and girls feel deep affection

24

for each other. If that's what you mean by being "really close," be assured that this is a normal and almost universal stage of teen-age development.

If by "getting closer" you mean sexual involvement, that's a different story.

It is not advisable for young people to start sexual contacts until their own sexual orientation is clearly established. This approach seems to be all the more sensible in the light of recent research which indicates that sexual orientation may be genetically determined. As you may know, most people, including those who had an experimental homosexual relationship "just to see how it works," later develop a consistent and enjoyable heterosexual lifestyle. Some, although we don't know exactly how many (10 percent is often mentioned), are and remain homosexual.

The days when homosexuality was considered "evil" or "sick" are fortunately gone, hopefully for good. Just the same, you have to find out in which direction you are going to go. Obviously, you don't know yet, or you would not be confused about it. You don't state your age, but chances are it may take a few more years.

You don't hop on a train before you find out where it is going. To take the right train at the right time, you need a timetable. Your personal developmental timetable has not come out yet, it is still at the printer. Be patient and wait until it is published, it will make some very interesting reading. Good luck, and happy friendship.

Herbert Bauer

Further Suggested Reading

• Comfort, Alex and Jane Comfort, _The Facts of Love: Living, Loving and Growing Up_. Ballantine, New York, N.Y.
• Johnson, Eric W., _Love and Sex and Growing Up_. Bantam Skylark, New York, N.Y., 1990 (for 10 to 12 year olds).
• Norwood, Robin, _Women Who Love Too Much_. Pocket Books, New York, N.Y. , 1985.
• Wolf, Tony, _I'll Be Home Before Midnight and I Won't Get Pregnant: Stories of Adolescence_. Vintage Books, New York, 1988.

2

So you think you're alone?

"I have no idea what Johnny sees in Laura. We've been going together for more than a year and suddenly...

"I can't eat or sleep. My schoolwork is suffering, and every time I see Johnny and Laura with each other ... it's like my heart stops."

Carrie said Johnny was the only guy in her life. She felt there'd never be another person like her Johnny. "My world is coming to an end," she thought.

Then this cute guy from Arizona checked into homeroom.

"I guess I'll be OK," Carrie thought, as she walked over to introduce herself to Curt...

Dear FYI: How do you get over missing someone?
Lonely

Dear Lonely: The easy answer to your question is "by the passage of time." But that doesn't help now.

The "missing" feels different if it is someone who has died (and whether that death was expected or not).

But if you're longing for a special friend who is no longer available, it is important first to know who or what ended the relationship.

Many feelings may be swirling inside you -- emptiness, grief, longing, jealousy, anger, a sense of unfairness and just undiluted depression. How do you get over these?

There are many ways, but the start is in acknowledging to yourself, and to someone you can confide in, exactly how you feel. Just wishing away the feelings does not work.

Another thing that will help you is to give yourself time. When you're bereaved, the process goes at its own pace ... and trying to talk yourself out of it is counterproductive, nor is there a "normal" time schedule for healing. Be gentle with yourself -- you need comforting.

Think of what you would do to help a friend who is in emotional pain. Sit down and write out a list of at least 10 things you would try that might help him or her.

For example, hug the friend, encourage him or her, listen respectfully to your friend's feelings... I'm sure you can make an inspired list if you think in terms of someone else. Now look at each thing and see how you can apply it to yourself, or ask for some of these things from friends. Most good friends are honored to be told "I need you right now."

Good luck. Everything you're learning now should be a great help to you when you have future losses; losses of hopes and dreams, of function, friends, pets, jobs and relatives. Each one helps you learn more about your inner resources and while the losses will be painful, I guarantee that with each "missing" you will find new strength.

I feel for you -- I'm still learning about coping with loss, and it's tough.

Nancy DuBois,
Psychologist

Dear FYI: My best friend is moving to Mexico this summer. We have been like sisters since second grade and she has been the closest friend a girl could ever have. She says she will miss me greatly but she just doesn't understand how hard it will be for me to go through my freshman year without a best friend or to go through high school either. What can I do? It will be so hard! Please help me.

Sad and Upset

Dear Sad and Upset: A best friend is that special companion with whom we feel safe and comfortable in being ourselves. You and your best friend have been tied together emotionally and in common interests and activities for many years. Her moving away is a great loss for you. In the process of grieving this loss, acknowledging your sadness and pain is OK -- in fact, necessary -- so healing can begin. I hope the two of you will stay in touch, despite the distance.

Although the transition to high school seems frightening when you consider making it without your friend, there is also the excitement and challenge of a new experience that awaits you. You have the advantage of having known through caring and intimacy what joys and growth friendship brings.

In your upcoming freshman year, by continuing to pursue activities that attract you -- and by exploring new interests -- you will have the opportunities to make new friends. It's important to maintain an open attitude: as you seek new friends, you will probably be drawn to those who like you, too.

While you most likely will never have another friend exactly like the one you have now, you will meet people whose friendships you can cultivate with time, energy and caring.

Elanna Panter Sherman, MFCC
Psychotherapist

Dear FYI: It seems that everybody in my parents' generation is telling me that these are the best years of my life and that I have no worries so I should really enjoy myself. Actually, I'm miserable most of the time.

I worry about a lot of things (grades, getting into college, dating, friends and having enough money). If these are the good years I don't think I ever want to be an adult. Am I the only one who feels like this?

Miserable

Dear Miserable: You're not alone at all. It's healthy to have some worries, especially about the things you mention. Adolescence is a time to start to work these things through. Few people have it all together by the time they're adults. You are in the majority. Your friends, male and female, may share a similar view. Don't sit on this and stew alone. Talk with them, informally or in a support group.

Also, I'd like to recommend you ask your parents, grandparents or a trusted adult to negotiate a time to talk seriously with you.

They may not have been aware of how many casual remarks about "the good years" they've made. In a serious setting they may be willing to respect your maturity and share with you some of the uncertainties, concerns and mistakes of their youth. This might be one of the best conversations of your life.

There are good times, hard times, growth and satisfaction in both adolescence and adulthood. By all means, enjoy what's worth enjoying now and look forward to enjoyment in adulthood, too.

Ted Hoffman, M.D.
Family therapist

Dear FYI: It seems that everyone at school is always happy, as if their lives were perfect. I am just the opposite. My life is not so perfect. Over the past year I've lost a lot of very special people. I'm very depressed and people think I'm strange just because I'm not *always* happy. I need help. What should I do?

Not Happy

Dear Not Happy: You may be right in believing that "everyone at school is always happy," but people, of course, don't always act the way they feel. The fact is that nobody is always happy, at school or at home -- nor do they need to be. Certain amounts of ups and downs are perfectly normal for all of us.

However, you seem to be particularly sad over the loss of some "very special people." What do you mean by "loss"?

Were they friends and are no longer? Have they moved out of town? Have they died? A feeling of great sadness over the loss of friends or relatives is normal and human, but such feelings of bereavement usually get better by themselves as time goes by, without any particular treatment.

What should you do about it? You have made a very good beginning by writing your feelings down on paper, your first step in letting other people know that you feel sad and lonely. You must not stop here.

It is of great importance that you share your feelings with someone you can trust: your parents, teacher, doctor, counselor or friends. By sharing your feelings it will be much easier to decide if you need more help than just talking about it.

Herbert Bauer, M.D.
Psychiatrist

Dear FYI: Lately I have been tired and apathetic. I've lost interest in my job, school work and social life. I find it almost impossible to stay awake in class. When I get home I collapse and can't get up for hours.

Also, I've been slipping into extreme moods of depression from trivial upsets or for no reason at all. When I'm asked out I say no, even though I know I'd have fun. At first I thought my mood change was because I was partied out and going non-stop. I changed my schedule to give myself a rest but it didn't work. I'm still extremely tired and depressed.

Why have I changed?

Have I forgotten how to be energetic?

Have I forgotten how to be happy?

Changed

Dear Changed: I'm sorry that you don't feel well and that your zest for life has been reduced. If your spark doesn't return in the next few days, I suggest you see your family doctor.

Fatigue, apathy and depression can have many causes. The first is that you might be ill -- anemia, lazy thyroid, infectious mono, things like that. Second, you may be going through a crummy period in your life and it has gotten you down. If this is the case, review your personal life -- family, school, friends -- and see what you can do to upgrade the situation. Third, you may be one of those people who get depressed from time to time for no apparent reason. Your doctor can help with this.

Life has its highs and lows, but symptoms like yours are a warning that something is wrong. Identify the underlying problems so that they can be corrected.

P. T. Donlon, M.D.
Psychiatrist

Dear FYI: I need your advice on how to like myself and be happy. I am so lonely, I don't have anyone to talk to. I have no friends, my dad is a drunk and my mom doesn't like me. I hate myself. I must be a bad person if both my parents don't like me. I don't want to die, I want to love and be loved. Is that too much to want? Please help me.

Unhappy

Dear Unhappy: No, it is not too much to ask that you be able to love and be loved. Most express that wish, but some people need extra help getting there. You are on the right track when you say you want to talk to someone.

You are in a situation that affects all too many teen-agers -- living with a parent who drinks too much. Many times this also means that the other parent spends a lot of time worrying about or trying to deal with the alcoholic one, leaving little time or energy for the children.

Friends can often help, but there are times when an adult with special skills is needed. There are several places that could offer you some help. Alateen, a group associated with Alcoholics Anonymous, is specifically set up to help teen-agers whose parents drink too much. Also your local Mental Health Association or crisis line (look in your phone book for number) can refer you to a person who can help you and deal with your family problems.

It is important for you to know that the drinking is not your fault, that you are not alone with this family problem and that there is specific help for you.

It may be frightening for you to make any of these calls yourself. If so, find a friend, teacher, minister or relative to help you make that first call. You took a good step in writing this letter; now try to get the help you need.

Cathy Neubauser, Ph.D.
Psychologist

Dear FYI: How can you get through great depression if you don't trust people except *very* close friends?

Depressed

Dear Depressed: The ability to trust probably develops in early childhood when we learn that loved ones, especially family members, are truly interested in our welfare. If the early years go well, our ability to trust moves into other relationships, including friends and worthy people.

Depression is a horrible disorder, and with it our ability to trust withers. It may be replaced by social withdrawal, suspicion and paranoia. We also become more sensitive and each slight may seem monumental. Also, we can lose trust in ourselves, wondering if we can serve our own interest.

By writing, you're reaching out for help. It's an important first step. Remember that severe depressions are treatable ... and that it is not fair to blame oneself for being depressed.

Severe depressions are best treated by a professional. You should strongly consider discussing your depression with trusted people who can help you find treatment if you do not want to inquire yourself.

Life is too short to experience persistent gloom. Once you get help for yourself your ability to trust and enjoy friendship will return.

P. T. Donlon

Dear FYI: I used to be a very suicidal person, so I sought help. I needed to talk to someone. The problem is that as soon as I got to the psychologist, I was told that everything I said was confidential except if I said I was going to hurt myself, someone else, or go against the law. Does that mean that if I told him how I felt about suicide he would tell someone, or does it mean that if I was on the verge of killing myself, then he would tell someone?

I was very confused, and that's why I went in the first place. It ended up not helping me, I helped myself. But if this happens again, what should I say to the psychologist?

Scared & Concerned

Dear Scared: You raise a very important point, and one which is frequently misunderstood: your therapist is here to help you, not to add to your distress. The only circumstances under which your therapist would betray your confidence are those special circumstances that are *required to be reported by law.*

For instance, if a patient reports that he or she is so angry at someone that there is an actual plan to hurt or perhaps even kill that person, it is obvious that the person in danger should be warned of the intended plot. I am sure you would do that, even if somebody asked you to keep it a secret.

Another instance would be a case in which somebody hurts helpless children or adults. Certainly those people need to be protected, regardless of what somebody may think.

With regard to suicidal thoughts, I can imagine that in the case of a young and immature child the therapist may find it necessary to talk to the child's parents in case it looks as though the child might really attempt suicide.

However, in the case of a reasonably mature person who expresses suicidal feelings, there would be no reason at all to go outside the boundaries of professional confidentiality ... and under no circumstances without the patient's knowledge. The exception to this would be if there were a life-threatening emergency which called for prompt intervention.

Suicidal feelings are very frequent among people of all ages, and it is most important to confide such feelings to a person of trust. To carry such feelings inside is painful and even dangerous. Therefore, should such feelings come to the surface of your mind again, speak immediately to a person you can trust: a parent, an adult friend, your school counselor or a professional outsider -- and do so with the assurance that no professional therapist will violate your confidence unless the situation constitutes an emergency and calls for prompt intervention.

Talk about your feelings before they begin to frighten you. Take good care of yourself, you need and deserve it!

Herbert Bauer

Dear FYI: Could you please devote a few words to how to deal with the "holiday blues?"

Just Curious

Dear Just Curious: The "holiday blues" syndrome, unfortunately, is fairly common. We experience it when our lives change with the loss of a family member, divorce, or when children grow up and move away. We experience it when we compare our painful childhood to the one portrayed in the commercials on TV, or when we rush around in a frenzy trying to do everything we think we "should" be doing while completely losing sight of what we "want" to be doing.

What to do about our "holiday blues?"

Begin by sharing your feelings with a friend or family member so you don't feel so alone. Chances are that they have or have had the same feelings. Next, give yourself permission to do things differently this year. What would you do (or not do) to make this season a happier one for you and your family? Some traditions need to change as our lives change -- or when the tradition becomes more drudgery than pleasure.

Also, try slowing down. The holiday season finds most of us rushing around. If we slow down, it's easier to hear our own needs and then begin to take care of ourselves. By slowing down we are more available for our friends and family, and if they slow down, they will be more available for us.

Take time this season to listen to yourself and really listen to your family and your friends. That's a great gift to give yourself and others.

Nancy Chadwick, LCSW
Psychotherapist

Dear FYI: Why are there so many suicide deaths of teenagers?

Very Concerned

Dear Very Concerned: "Why" is tough to answer when it comes to issues of suicide. While we struggle for an answer, here are some facts and interpretations that might shed some light...

On the positive side, teenagers have the lowest suicide rates of any age group studied (12.5 per 100,000 population for 15 to 24 year olds compared with 22 for 75 to 84 year olds). However, teens are significantly increasing their rate of suicide, the death rate growing 160 percent every 10 years over the last 30 years.

National statistics can give us a notion of the overall problem, but they cannot give us answers to questions surrounding the suicide of any specific individual.

Published research, as well as what we learn from young people who call the crisis lines of Suicide Prevention, reveals that feelings of depression, loneliness, and a sense of being isolated from friends and family are strongly associated with feelings of self-destruction.

We also know that talking about suicide, alcohol and drug abuse, running away and sudden changes in relationships or behavior are suicide danger signals.

Why are there so many suicide deaths among teen-agers?

There are speculative answers: the disintegration of the family, the availability of drugs and alcohol, the increasing stress of our technological age and the threat of nuclear war. Yet no one has proven a cause-and-effect relationship.

Gary McConahay, Ph.D.
Community health program director

Dear FYI: Do boys or girls commit more suicides?
Carolyn

Dear Carolyn: Suicide Prevention tells us that men *kill* themselves almost three times as frequently as women, but women *attempt* suicide about three times as often as men.
FYI editor

Dear FYI: When do most suicides occur? Is it in January?
Ivan the Inquisitive

Dear Ivan: Holidays and the dark, wintry period that follows them are difficult times for many people -- perhaps especially for those who have experienced a loss of a loved one to suicide.

However, most suicides occur in the spring (March and April being months of high suicide). Most people's spirits revive in the spring, but those who are truly depressed don't feel better ... they then feel hopeless and some could move toward suicide at that point.

FYI editor

Dear FYI: How would you prevent suicide ...especially when you don't feel like talking and you just don't trust anyone. Although there are a lot of people

35

around me, I still feel lonely and not loved. Sometimes I feel left out just because I'm me and if I can't be me why live in this world?

Alone

Dear Alone: Feeling isolated and misunderstood can be overwhelming. Adolescence is a time when you have questions about your identity, and part of growing up is discovering values and priorities. When you feel left out, unloved or alone, it gets tough to have a sense of who you are or how you are going to grow up.

Unfortunately, most seem to suffer in silence. They don't want to impose on anybody, or they don't feel their problems are important or of interest to anyone. Thus, they live their lives "left out," hoping someone will notice. What happens most of the time is that no one is aware of how bad someone else feels. People frequently assume that you are just quiet or not interested in them.

No one can prevent a suicide unless he or she knows someone is feeling down. You need to take a risk and trust someone enough to tell him or her of your feelings and concerns. Whether this is your parent, a teacher, your doctor, a clergyperson or a friend -- it's a start.

If you prefer someone anonymous, call your local crisis line (should be listed in the front pages of your telephone book). A trained volunteer can help you understand your feelings and help you to get help from the right folks.

Your local mental health program could also help. It does not matter who you start with, it just matters that you take that risk and tell someone what you are experiencing -- and do it now.

Just remember, nothing can change, nor can anyone help, unless you take the first step.

Stephen Mayberg, Ph.D.
Clinical psychologist

Why are there so many suicides among today's teen-agers?

In divorce, teen-agers are often left out. Their parents might marry again. Where does this leave the teen-ager? They feel alone...there is a feeling that nothing will get better.
Female, age 15

Drug and alcohol abuse.
Every age, again and again

My reason was depression. I attempted suicide four times. I thought that if I wasn't around things would be better.

I felt no one loved, let alone cared about me. I never had any of the typical signs. I never gave away my things, I kept my appearance up. The only thing I can say is to talk to someone and if you know someone who wants to commit suicide *listen* to them, don't interrupt until they are finished, then let them know you care. I'm glad to be alive.
Male, age 18

Stress. Parents are usually pushing for good grades, and a question commonly asked is: Where are you going to college? Maybe some students don't plan to go to college, or at least not right away.
Female, age 16

Pressure from teachers, parents and friends...
Every age, again and again

We are constantly reminded that we must do well and are pushed into things we may not want to do and don't feel right about. When we go out we are warned about a long list of dangers they don't think we are smart enough to avoid.
Female, age 14

They think that no one cares and they can't talk to anyone.
Female, age 13

Most teen suicides are due to deep depression. Fights with parents, girl/boyfriend breakups, their dog dies, little things like this can push someone to suicide or sometimes drugs. And, depending on how you look at it, doing drugs is just as bad as killing yourself.
Male, age 17

37

Dear FYI: I hope you don't think I'm a freak when you read this.

No one in my life would believe what I am feeling. I read all this stuff about suicide signs, and I realized I have every single sign. I don't mind, because I'm sick of trying. And no one knows about this, because I don't tell anyone.

I'm not afraid of death; I just want it to be quick and quiet. I would be dead now if it weren't for my religion, which stresses that I will go to hell if I take my own life.

I don't have *anyone* to talk to anymore, I mean *really* talk to ... and I don't want to tell my problems to a stranger (counselor or psychiatrist). Everything is piling up inside as I wear my heart on my sleeve. I feel like I'm just floating through life; just going through the motions. Everything is real bad, and I get sick to my stomach thinking about how much longer I have to live.

What do I do? If I'm gonna be around awhile, how can I pick myself up? It's not like I'm a social outcast -- I'm involved in many school activities, but our "group" (which I guess you could call the "popular" people) is very superficial.

I need a reason to live, and lately I haven't found one. I want someone to *care*. Please help.

Lifeless

Dear Lifeless: Lifeless, fortunately, you are not; depressed you may be.

You obviously are not lifeless, or you would never had the courage to write and express your feelings. Apart from that, you do not sound as though you would like to die, just that you don't want to live ... at least not the life you have.

Let's talk for a moment about what has happened to some people who feel like you. Some have had a catastrophic loss in their lives. Most of those recover from their grief after a few months, but need some treatment if it lasts over a year.

Others have had a series of disappointments which makes them lose self-respect and they go through life with an "it-serves-me-right-I-am-no-good" attittude. Often all they need is some encouragement and success.

Others come from a deprived or depriving family where nobody talks, nobody touches, nobody seems to care. Those folks need a different kind of intervention, mainly socialization.

And then there are a great many who suffer from a disorder called "clinical depression," which has to do with a disarrangement of their brain nerves; they almost always improve with appropriate treatment, often involving drugs prescribed by a physician. In other words, the question in your case is not if you need treatment, but what kind of treatment would be best for you.

I can understand your reluctance to talk to a stranger or a psychiatrist, but you can actually start doing what urgently needs to be done without saying a single word. Simply show this letter to your parents, your doctor, your counselor or your closest adult friend, and they will lead you from there.

You are far too young to feel about life the way you do. Your condition looks thoroughly treatable as soon as you tell someone, as you have told us, about your distress.

One last thing. By the time you have done that, if you have a minute to spare, would you drop us a line and tell us how things are going?

Herbert Bauer

Dear FYI: I just have to respond to the letter from "Lifeless." I am now 18 and I too went through a similar time. My depression started when I was 16 and lasted almost all through my senior year. I basically had no good reason to be depressed, but I was...

My life now has meaning and I have a reason to live. I had one then too, but was too depressed to see it ... I just wanted to write to tell "Lifeless" to just hold on ... before you know it your life will take on meaning.

Former Lifeless

Suicide Warning Signs
- Feeling very depressed
- Abusing drugs or alcohol
- Giving away prized posses-sions
- Doing poorly in school
- Increasingly isolated
- Talking about wanting to die
- Acting in a strange manner
- Threatening to actually com-mit suicide

Dear FYI: I show some of the "classic" suicide signs, but I don't feel the slightest bit suicidal and my life is great! As I took a family life class in school, I saw parts of myself in the "suicidal" category. Am I really a psycho, or just odd? I don't want to scare anybody, or alarm them. What's up?

A Nervous Junior

Dear Nervous Junior: Your letter brought back vivid memories of my own college days, when I saw myself in every diagnostic category in my first psychology classes. As you indicate, it was frightening. Join the club, I was questioning my sanity then -- what a scary feeling.

Fortunately, I've learned much since that time ... enough to assure you that you are more than likely a very OK kid. One of the most difficult aspects of warning signs of suicide in adolescents is that those signs seen *individually* reflect typical teen-age behaviors or characteristics.

I've heard many teens say, "What's so different about these signs? Lots of my friends show them and they are not suicidal." Although individual signs (see accompanying chart) are typical in many teens, when two or more of them are

39

seen in the same teen at the same time, we want to take a closer look at what is going on.

If a friend tells you that he or she is thinking about suicide:

1. Talk with that person;
2. Listen to what is said;
3. Ask questions about feelings;
4. Ask if there is a suicide plan;
5. Share your concerns;
6. Talk to a trusted adult;
7. Encourage your friend to get help, or call a crisis line for help.

It is very important to note, though, that even if you are showing these warning signs it does not mean you are "psycho." Many ordinary teens and adults occasionally get overwhelmed with problems and stresses in their daily lives, and at that time consider suicide as an alternative to the pain of living. Friends and relatives may show concern during these times, and their care and support are invaluable in helping to overcome the difficulties.

Carol Rodgers, MFCC
Alcohol & drug counselor

Dear FYI: My son's friend has committed suicide and I am finding it very difficult to know what to say. Any help would be appreciated.
Troubled Parent

Dear Troubled Parent: The grief experienced by a suicide survivor is distinctly different from a normal death caused by illness. Survivors often feel intense anger, severe guilt, shame, rejection and blame.

Feelings of anger can be directed outward in attempting to blame the victim for the suicide, or at others for not preventing it. The feeling of guilt can come from feeling anger at the death, being relieved by the death, or feeling responsible ("If only I had not left him/her alone...").

Shame is felt because suicide still is stigmatized in our society and is not seen as OK to talk about.

The feelings of helplessness and anger that occur right after the suicide may disappear and then return. Survivors often fear that others may abandon them in the same way or that they themselves may commit suicide.

The most common feeling that survivors of suicide have is depression. It is important to remember that depression is sometimes caused by anger which remains unexpressed and is turned inward. It is therefore important that your son find a listener for his feelings.

This support can come from you, a friend, a counselor, or from a support group of suicide survivors. Encourage him to talk, but remember that as a listener you do not have to "fix things." He needs an environment in which he feels safe to talk about his feelings.

Finding someone who will listen is a major part of being able to talk. Your son will need help in working out his own answers and sorting out his feelings, but each person grieves in his or her own way.

Bonnie Beffa, MSW

Dear FYI: Is it possible to be insane and not have it be recognized?
Concerned for a Friend

Dear Concerned: Your question is actually a fairly frequent one. There are certain mental diseases which are clearly recognizable to the outsider -- but of which the sick person is unaware. However, those are very serious diseases during which the patient loses touch with reality and behaves in an irrational way.

If your friend has such an illness there would be no question in your mind, and you would do your best to help obtain medical care. My guess is that there are times that your friend does or says peculiar things which worry you. Why not be open and say that sometimes you wonder if your friend feels OK and if you could be of any help. Perhaps your friend will shrug it off with "I'm all right, don't worry about me!" Should this be the answer, you have to be specific and tell your friend exactly what you have observed that makes you wonder about "sanity."

If you don't get anywhere, don't hesitate to talk to your parents, your friend's parents, your doctor or your school counselor. If any of them feel that your friend needs help, they'll assist in making it available. But if all of them assure you that your friend is all right, you can safely quit worrying. You are a good friend to show such concern.

Herbert Bauer

Dear FYI: I have a friend who becomes very depressed very often. I hate to see her that way and I would like to help her feel better.

The only problem is that every time one of her other friends or I try to help she just pushes us away.

What should I do, leave her when she gets that way, or continue to try to help and let her know I'm here if she needs to talk?

Pushed Away

Dear Pushed Away: When people are depressed they often feel irritable and withdraw from social relationships because they are more concerned about their own inner turmoil and pain. They may not feel they have the energy to respond. They may feel you will reject them if you know how discouraged they feel about themselves. I would offer these related suggestions:

1. Reassurance. Tell your friend you like her and would like to share her down times as well as the good.

2. Empathy. Explain to her that you know how painful it feels to be sad and that you will simply be with her -- in silence -- if she would prefer not to talk about it today.

3. Solidarity. If she walks away today, let her know that you are persistent and will still be her friend tomorrow.

> Suicide is a common topic among my closest friends ... (we) agree that it's the environment around us (especially parents) which makes us feel depressed.
> I come from an alcoholic home, and I'm an only child so it gets pretty lonely considering I don't want anyone to see my alcoholic mother. But when someone talks about suicide, just *shut up* and listen to them.
> *Female, age 16*

Remember, a friend is someone who likes you in all weather.

Captane P. Thomson, M.D.
Psychologist

Dear FYI: I have a cousin who calls me up every time she's mad. She says she is going to kill herself or take drugs or OD on some coke. What should I say or do when she calls me?

Worried and Wondering

Dear Worried and Wondering: It sounds as though you're feeling over a barrel.

Sometimes it takes a lot of energy to be around depressed people.

Maybe your cousin is looking up to you, but make sure you don't feel completely responsible for her. Your cousin apparently doesn't have many friends to confide in and finds your advice invaluable. It also sounds as though she is seeking your attention by calling you so frequently.

Your concern about her taking drugs or killing herself is justified and should be discussed with her. People don't make comments about hurting themselves without some thought behind it. As a matter of fact, making such a statement is one of the danger signs of a suicidal person.

Besides talking to your cousin about your reaction to her threats against herself, suggest that she seek help from an adult she trusts. You could say, "Next time I'm going to insist that we see X (clergy, teacher, counselor, etc.)."

Lynn Zender, LCSW
Pscyhiatric social worker

Dear FYI: I have a good friend that I'm worried about. She has been under a lot of stress lately with school and boyfriends and other activities. Her emotions seem to have changed drastically. One moment she is laughing, the next she is on the verge of crying. I am wondering what I can do to help her through this. Does she need counseling or some other help, or is this normal?

A Caring Friend

Dear Caring Friend: You are not only a great friend, but also a mature and wise person. You have correctly identified that stress can produce behavioral and emotional changes.

You realize that stress can be caused by troublesome life events (including romantic relationships and school), and know that help can result from discussing problems with friends, family members or well-chosen professionals.

However, sometimes knowing what the problems are and discussing them are not enough. Corrective actions may be necessary.

Adolescence can be a particularly difficult period of life as young people are faced with so many changes and challenges.

Decisions can have major, long-term effects. A healthy approach is to realize that life brings problems. Many of them can be prevented or made easier by coping with them early and appropriately. They can be learning experiences. You can help your friend by being a good listener and perhaps even providing advice, but don't hold yourself responsible for solving her problems. If her concerns are major and persistent, suggest that she talk to her parents or a school counselor about getting additional help.

You certainly are a special friend to express your interest and concern for her.

P.T. Donlon

Dear FYI: Is there any chance that someone who has tried suicide once will try it again?

A Best Friend

Dear Best Friend: Most people who attempt suicide once never try a second time, but a prior attempt is what professionals call a "risk factor."

If your friend's life circumstances do not change, chances are that self-destuctive behavior may recur. Try to help your friend if you can, but do not feel you have to do it on your own. Get a trusted adult involved, too.

Gary McConahay

Further Suggested Reading

- Elchoness, Monte, *Why Can't Anyone Hear Me?: A Guide for Surviving Adolescence.* Monroe Press, Sepulveda, Ca. 1986.
- Joan, Polly, *Preventing Teen-age Suicide: The Living Alternative Hand book.* Human Sciences Press, New York, 1986.
- Krementz, Jill, *How It Feels When a Parent Dies.* Alfred A. Knopf, New York, N.Y., 1981.

Kushner, Harold S., *When Bad Things Happen to Good People.* Avon Books, New York, N.Y., 1981.

- Manning, Doug, *Don't Take My Guilt Away: What to Do When You Lose a Loved One.* Harper and Row, San Francisco, 1984.
- Phillips, Ron and Dan Brewer, *Gem of the First Water: A Recovery Proc ess for Troubled Teen-agers.* Resource Publications, San Jose, Ca., 1990.

3

Illegal drugs: a matter of life or death

He was my friend. We were pals for 10 years. We always hung out after school, sometimes we studied together and we always played basketball in the winters. We were going to the same trade school next fall. We'd hit dozens of parties. No problem. But usually we played it straight. No drugs, no alcohol. Just serious, clean fun.

Then one Saturday night, Bryan went a little too far ... a "friend" convinced him to try some hard drugs at this party. I was there for him -- you know, if he got too high or something.

I didn't know a few big shots of that stuff could kill you. I wish I'd said something. I wish he didn't get caught up in the rush to be "cool." It's not the same without Bryan.

Dear FYI: Do mixing drugs and alcohol have a more lethal effect than just drugs or alcohol alone?

Tempting Fate

Dear Tempting Fate: Yes! While the effects differ from drug to drug, mixing any two chemicals is dangerous. Many times the effects of two drugs together are greater than the sum of the effects when taken separately. This is particularly true of alcohol or other depressant drugs like barbiturates, which can suppress vital body functions like breathing.

There have been many famous cases of people dying from overdoses of alcohol and pills. For example, mixing alcohol with marijuana is dangerous because marijuana suppresses the vomiting reflex. That can prevent the body from taking its natural protective reaction when someone has consumed more booze than it is safe to drink.

Dave Stoebel, Ph. D.
Prevention coordinator

Dear FYI: Why don't we legalize marijuana? If we do I believe fewer people would use it because there would be no risk -- or challenge.
Thinking

Dear Thinking: The notion that people would be less likely to use marijuana if it weren't "forbidden fruit," has been debated for the last 20 years. The truth is we don't know because legalization has never been tried in this country.

Something similar (though in reverse) has been done with alcohol.

Until recently, a few states had drinking ages that were lower than 21. However, most of them have now raised their drinking ages.

The number of teen drunken-driving accidents invariably goes down when that happens. Instead of stimulating teens to drink, making consumption illegal seems to reduce their consumption. All drugs have potentially harmful effects and that's why most are controlled by law.

If making marijuana illegal really does reduce its consumption, then the case for *keeping* it illegal can be made on medical grounds. While we don't understand all of its effects, we do know:

-- marijuana use can lead to psychological dependence;

-- marijuana users are more likely to use other mood-altering drugs (which also can be physically addictive);

-- marijuana can adversely affect the body's growth and reproductive mechanisms, making it particularly harmful during adolescence;

-- heavy marijuana users often suffer "amotivation syndrome," a condition in which they lose their ambition and drive to accomplish anything in life.

In light of these facts we can agree that marijuana is unsafe.

There will always be people who choose to act in ways that damage their health, but by having laws against marijuana we bring to our awareness the damaging effects of the drug -- and provide a greater motivation not to choose a self-damaging course of action.
Linda Tell, R.N., MFCC
Psychotherapist

Dear FYI: My mother says she would rather have me smoke marijuana than drink. Why would she say that?
Puzzled

Dear Puzzled: We don't know. Maybe she's seen the disastrous effects of alcohol in someone else's life and thinks pot won't do the same. If so, we're afraid she isn't aware of the fact that marijuana is addictive and can have serious effects on physical and mental health, too.

Your mother may also be unaware that the marijuana of today is many, many times stronger and more troubling than it was in the '60s.

Why don't you ask your mother why she says that? It might lead to an interesting conversation.

Dave Stoebel

Dear FYI: If you smoke pot on the weekends (every other weekend), how bad can it affect you?

Not Quite a Pothead

Dear Not Quite: Marijuana is known to cause psychological dependence (the need for a drug in order to feel good or "normal"). A person develops tolerance to a drug when his or her body gets used to it. This means a larger amount of the marijuana is required to get the same feeling a smaller amount used to produce.

Most people who smoke marijuana start out slowly and over time require more marijuana to feel better. When the marijuana doesn't seem to make sad feelings go away, relieve boredom or decrease pain or stress, the marijuana user often experiments with other drugs which can be physically addicting.

I think it is important for you to question what feelings marijuana changes for

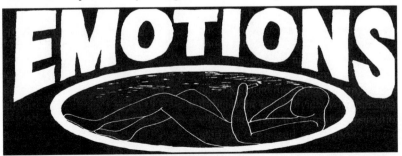

you. Feelings and emotions are good for us: even painful ones. They give us a signal that something is wrong inside. When we have stomach pains we go to a doctor to find out what is the problem. When we have emotional pain, we need to get outside help from a counselor so we can identify and fix the problem. If you are using marijuana (even on an infrequent basis), you could be ignoring a serious problem that needs the support of a parent or an experienced counselor.

Linda Tell

Dear FYI: Is eating marijuana less harmful than smoking it?
Afraid to Believe What I Hear

Dear Afraid: The tar content of marijuana is higher than that of ordinary tobacco.

Some studies suggest that pot smoking could be linked to lung cancer ... so eating pot gets around that danger. But by eating it you slow down the rate of absorption into the blood. Thus you may ingest more than you expected because you didn't feel the high until you had finished eating it.

In other words, by eating the pot you have less control over how high you get. When that happens, you run the risk of having an extreme anxiety attack or a bout of paranoia (these are fairly frequent occurrences with the new higher grade types of marijuana).

Dave Stoebel

Dear FYI: Where did drugs come from in the first place?
Baffled

Dear FYI: How did drugs get started?
Curious

Dear Baffled and Curious: Drugs are chemicals that change the way we think, act and feel.

Many of them are found in plants like the opium poppy and the psilocybin mushroom. People probably found out about the effects when they ate the plants.

For a long time, most cultures only used drugs as part of religious rituals, but in the last few centuries people started using drugs more and more for the "escape" they provide — the "high."

In this country most drugs were legal until 1914. By that time so many people had become addicted that the government decided to ban most drugs ... and to permit others to be used only for medicinal reasons under a doctor's supervision.

It is important to recognize that drugs themselves are neither good nor bad, but because they can be addictive and can have other harmful effects, their use needs to be tightly controlled for people's own good.

Dave Stoebel

Dear FYI: Can you die of withdrawal?
Puzzled

Dear Puzzled: Very few heroin addicts die of withdrawal. However, it is possible to die of withdrawal from other drugs such as alcohol, barbiturates and valium.
Linda Tell

Dear FYI: I heard that blue is a bad color for drugs. Is that true?
Cautious

> **The facts...**
> *Marijuana stays in your system a long time, is not a medicine and can cause infertility and miscarriages*

Dear Cautious: This is a new one to our drug experts. One possibility, however, is that since all drugs you buy on the street will be cut with things like sugar, talcum powder or cleanser, possibly some dealers have used the blue variety of cleanser.
Dave Stoebel

Dear FYI: People, magazines and books dealing with drugs usually only talk about how long it takes to have the alcohol cleared from your system and how much is the legal limit. Is there a scale or something that tells you how much of the drug in marijuana is in your system after inhaling it and is there a legal limit?
Progressive Thinker

Dear Progressive Thinker: Marijuana stays in your system a very long time. The half-life (the amount of time it takes for half of the drug to leave your system) is five days. Therefore, after five days, half of the drug is still in your system and five days after that, a quarter is still in your system ... and so on.

So you can see that if you smoke marijuana "just every weekend," for example, it will gradually build up in your system.

There is no legal limit because it is illegal to use marijuana.

Dave Stoebel

Dear FYI: Has marijuana been used in the cure of asthma?
Emerson

Dear Emerson: There is some research to show that one of the many chemicals in marijuana can open up the airways in the lungs. However, this does not mean that people with asthma should smoke dope.

Marijuana smoke also contains some not so nice things like carbon monoxide and a lot more tar than cigarette smoke.

If a marijuana component is ever approved for medical use, it will be the purified chemical taken as a pill or inhaler and not as a joint.

Dave Stoebel

Dear FYI: Is it true that regular marijuana use can make people more likely to have a baby girl than a baby boy?
Heard a Rumor

Dear Heard a Rumor: No, it isn't true. In fact, marijuana disrupts sex hormones and can increase the chances of infertility and miscarriages. Marijuana and other drugs should be avoided, but especially during the child-bearing years.

Staci P. Anderson
Outreach counselor

Dear FYI: If you are going to smoke marijuana (not that I *am*), how can you tell it if is pure?
Cautious by Nature

Dear Cautious by Nature: As with all street drugs, when you buy marijuana you do so with absolutely no guarantees about its quality or purity. It could be high-grade sensimilla, pot laced with PCP or chopped alfalfa. There is no way to tell for sure what is in it. Best rule? Don't buy it ... it's illegal and harmful.

Christine Cipperly,
Director, drug treatment &
Counseling services program

Dear FYI: Why do your eyes turn red when you smoke pot?
Bleary Eyed

Dear Bleay Eyed: Marijuana is a complex drug that contains over 400 different chemicals. These chemicals produce a variety of effects on the body, many of which are just being discovered. One of the effects is to dilate or widen the blood vessels of the eye, giving the eyes of the pot user that bloodshot appearance.

Dave Stoebel

Dear FYI: When I went to my brother's house in L.A. his roommates were smoking marijuana.

It was strange to see their reactions because one of his friends got really weird and would listen to music and move around really slow.

His other friend acted just regular and was not even affected it seemed. Is smoking marijuana hazardous to some and not to others?
Interested in This

Dear Interested: Marijuana can be hazardous to anybody.

As to why the two guys acted differently, we know that people's drug experiences are influenced by their expectations of how they will be affected.

Also, if the second guy was an inexperienced pot smoker, his lack of response may have been -- as is the case with many people -- that the brain has to be exposed to the drug a few times before the experience of intoxication can be felt.

Dave Stoebel

Dear FYI: All my friends -- no, just *most* of my friends -- drink or do drugs. Personally, it's up to them. I care for my friends, but doing drugs is their choice. I've done not-so-hard drugs, but some of my friends have done everything you can think of. I play sports, so I've tried to stop any kind of drugs.

My question is, how can I say no to doing drugs when I really want to say yes, but I'm afraid that my athletic skills will go to waste when I fry my brains out on drugs?

Damned

Dear Damned: Young people today are exposed to a variety of mixed messages about sports and drugs. It is good you recognize that use of drugs can impair your athletic performance. It also could get you kicked off the team, harm your health and get you into trouble at home, school or with the law.

How can you say no to drugs when you are surrounded by friends who use -- and when you're tempted to say yes?

Here are some suggestions:

1. Examine why and when you want to use drugs and look at possible consequences. Do you feel left out when your friends are using? Are you trying to run away from problems at home or school or trying to "fit in" with a certain crowd? What might you gain in the short run by giving in to the temptation? What might you lose in the long run if you start using again? You've already started asking yourself these questions -- that's a big start.

2. Ask for help in learning to say no to drugs. Contact your school outreach counselor. He or she can give you information to read on sports and drugs, talk with you about your concerns and perhaps put you in a support group with other students who are concerned about their own or others' drug use -- and want to learn how to have healthy, drug-free lifestyles.

3. Talk with your coach about your concerns. Maybe he or she could call a meeting with your team to discuss the use of alcohol and drugs at your school, the impact on athletes, and ways in which you can support one another in saying no to drugs and still have fun. As you know, it is against school policy for athletes to use alcohol and other drugs. By sharing your concerns and experiences with your coach, you will be doing everyone on your team a service.

4. Get involved with a group at school that knows how to have fun without using alcohol or other drugs. This could be an organized club or just some people you know who are trying, like you, to take care of their bodies and minds by getting off the drug-use treadmill.

5. Practice ways of saying no to drugs without losing your friends. Some examples: "no thanks," "not today," "let's play ball or go to the movies instead," or "sorry, I can't go with you today because you've been drinking or using". It is easier to say no to drugs if you have thought in advance about situations that might tempt you (for example, a party at a friend's house that is unsupervised,

> **Resist. It's for your own good and the good of those you like and love.**

cutting classes to get high with friends) and how you might handle them.

6. Find a good buddy who feels like you do. Make a pact with him or her that neither of you will use alcohol or drugs without first talking it over with the other person. Spend time together doing things you enjoy, working out and sharing what is going on in your lives. Pledge to try to stop the other if the urge to use continues.

It is hard to say no to drugs when everyone around you seems to be using, but you are not alone. There are a lot of others just like you. Resist. It's for your own good and the good of those you like and love. This is serious. Hang in there.

Christine Fry
Youth outreach coordinator

Dear FYI: I have a problem with drugs and I really want to stop so I can get myself together so that I can play my sports. The problem is weed and crank. I'm surrounded by it at my high school and don't know what to do.

If I don't do something soon I might do something I'll regret.
Really Afraid

Dear Really Afraid: As confused and anxious as you may be about your drug problem, there is one important way in which you are ahead of many others in your position...

You recognize that this is a problem that needs some outside help.

Recognizing this will make it a lot easier for you to take the next and even more important step -- picking up the telephone and making an

> **Recognizing the problem is an excellent start to getting straight.**

53

appointment with your local drug-abuse clinic.

Don't be surprised if they are not surprised to see you there. In fact, you might be amazed at the number of your friends who have used the services of your clinic. Your visit will, of course, be handled confidentially. If the counselors think that all you need is information and education, great. If you need more than that, treatment is available right there.

Whichever way it goes, don't let it slip for there's no need to feel helpless.

You are in charge of *your* life. Do for yourself what others cannot and should not do for you. Make an appointment now. Do what needs to be done to feel free again.

Herbert Bauer, M.D.
Psychiatrist

Dear FYI: I don't really know how to say "no" to drugs and alcohol. I think my friends would hurt me if I said "no". Should I arm myself for self-defense?
Not Sure

Dear Not Sure: I realize that saying "no" to drugs and alcohol isn't easy. It's much easier, however, once you have made a decision not to use them. The "no" answer should be delivered in a firm but non-threatening manner, so that the person offering the substance to you does not feel like you are making an accusation or passing judgment. As you learn to feel more comfortable saying "no," you will be more confident and less fearful.

I am deeply concerned about the thought of your carrying something for protection. A weapon can bring harm to you or your friends by making your "no" message appear threatening.

A weapon projects an inclination toward violence and is a violation of the law, which would only give you one more thing to worry about.

Sgt. Martin C. Ruiz
Police officer

Dear FYI: What exactly is acid?

H, T and J

Dear H, T and J: "Acid" is a street name for lysergic acid diethylamide -- simply, it's called LSD.

It is a potent, manmade hallucinogenic drug. LSD produces a high or "trip" that usually starts 60 to 90 minutes after ingestion, peaks in about three hours and lasts six to nine hours.

When under the influence of LSD, users experience a variety of sensory and perceptual effects including a scrambling of thoughts and sensations -- they may report "seeing" sound and "tasting" colors. Following the high, users experience a "crash" that may last a day or two.

Dave Stoebel

Dear FYI: How common are the so-called "LSD flashbacks"?

How much do people have to use it to begin hallucinating when they are off it? Do hallucinations really come several years later?

The Big C

Dear Big C: Your question about LSD and flashbacks comes at a very important time. There seems to be a recurring trend toward the use of this potent and dangerous hallucinogenic drug.

LSD is complex and little is understood about the properties and specifics of the drug.

However, it is known that hallucinogens work by temporarily "short-circuiting" the brain, affecting the balance of chemicals involved in relaying thoughts and feelings from one cell to another.

Effects are many.

They can be so strange that many people panic.

This is called a "bad trip."

Some users become so terrified that they fear they may never come down (and some don't, although most do).

Sensory input becomes so disorganized that the user can't tell sight from sound. A loss of sense of reality, distorted time and difficulty with concentration, coupled with an extreme preoccupation with philosophical ideas, explain why some users believe they have discovered great insights into themselves. However, these "discoveries" are often unintelligible to anyone not under the influence of LSD.

Flashbacks do happen.

They can happen without warning years after the user's first trip. They're a re-occurrence of LSD experience, but with no LSD in the body. Flashbacks frequently happen when a person is tired, scared or in a situation that triggers a memory of a prior "bad trip".

Flashbacks are scary because they're unpredictable and uncontrollable, which causes more panic.

Cheri McElwee
Chemical-dependency counselor

Dear FYI: Do many suicides relate to drug use?
Interested and Concerned

Dear Interested and Concerned: Your simple question cannot be answered simply ... as is often the case with the complex topic of suicide.

We know some facts about contemplated suicide. We know that drug overdose is the method of suicide selected most often by women, while men tend to choose the faster and more lethal means of shooting themselves (alarmingly, firearms are now the most common means used by both male and female teens).

> ## Drugs can be an effective coping strategy only as long as the high lasts.

No one knows what causes a person to commit suicide, but perhaps it results from increasing stress coupled with an inability to cope with that stress.

Drugs can be an effective coping strategy only as long as the high lasts, but they cannot remove the source of the problem, they can never "understand" you and they will always let you down.

Drugs can actively contribute to a suicidal crisis. Marijuana often cuts off communication and results in a feeling of isolation. Chronic use of cocaine (and relatively brief experimentation with "crank") can lead to what is called "substance-increased organic psychosis."

People who use speed, crack and coke have shared that the depression they feel when they stop using the drug is so bad they'd rather be dead.

> ## Alcohol leads to judgment errors, dangerous acts and tragedy.

Alcohol is a tricky drug -- a little bit can give the user enough false courage to overcome the taboo against self-destruction ... and a lot can lead to errors in judgment and dangerous behavior that still results in death.

There are many, many reasons for a person to feel suicidal, but it's no question that there is a strong relationship between drug use and suicide.

Suicide Prevention of Yolo County

Dear FYI: Can unintentional inhaling of paint, glue, etc., be harmful? For example: painting a house and involuntarily inhaling fumes.

Just Wondering

Dear Wondering: Under normal circumstances, the involuntary inhaling of fumes while painting a house or utilizing glue should not be harmful to those involved. However, it is important to make sure the area in which these substances are being used is well ventilated in order to minimize exposure to fumes.

Cynthia Reeves Tuttle, M.P.H.,
ACCE, health educator

Dear FYI: Do drugs intensify sex?

Studley Dudley

Dear Studley Dudley: That depends on the drug, but in most cases the answer is "no."

In many cases drugs diminish the experience.

Alcohol is probably the best example of that phenomenon. Because alcohol suppresses inhibitions, people who have been drinking often experience sexual attraction to others. Unfortunately, alcohol also is a tranquilizer that reduces the ability to perform sexually, especially for males.

In general, the same holds true for other downer-type drugs.

Marijuana and cocaine have been reported to enhance sex drive. However, if taken in larger amounts and/or for long periods of time, both tend to reduce drive. In India pot is used as a sexual suppressant.

"Poppers," or amyl and butyl nitrites, are sometimes used as a sexual stimulant, especially by gay people. However, there is some new research to suggest that these substances may play a role in causing AIDS by damaging the body's immune system. There is research which shows that they may also contribute to the development of Kaposi's sarcoma, a form of cancer that often occurs in AIDS patients.

Dave Stoebel

Dear FYI: Is there a drug that causes a guy to be infertile? My boyfriend told me I would be O.K. if we had sex while he was high. Is that true?

Uncertain

Dear Uncertain: It is not true.

Studies suggest that drugs impact reproduction in several ways, for example, they influence hormone levels, affect sexual performance and change chromosome structure. But they *do not* have contraceptive properties and should never be used with that expectation.

Be smart -- if you've chosen to be sexually active, practice "safer sex" by choosing appropriate, recommended contraceptives that are available to you. And tell your boyfriend the facts.

Barbara Colletto, MSC, MFCC intern
Drug & alcohol program intern

Dear FYI: If you are a drug addict and you become pregnant, what can you do suddenly to stop using drugs -- or will drug use already have hurt the unborn baby?

I.N.A. (I Need Advice)

Dear I.N.A.: You are very wise to want to stop using drugs so your unborn child will not be harmed. No one can promise you your baby has not been hurt, but I have seen teens who quit drugs have healthy babies.

The most important thing you can do is to get medical care quickly. Your obstetrical doctor will advise you on the safest way to withdraw as you and the fetus are carefully monitored.

Dr. Milton Lee of UCLA has demonstrated by his work with drug-using pregnant women that many potential problems can be detected and treated if good prenatal care is obtained.

Dr. Lee's experience is that the addicted mother who is a concerned mother can be helped to have an almost normal pregnancy. The addicted mothers who do not get good prenatal care are more likely to give birth to severely disabled children.[1]

While our bodies, which are larger and more fully developed, can withstand some abuse, the tiny, immature bodies of developing babies are less able to tolerate toxic substances such as alcohol, nicotine, LSD, crank, etc.

Often teens are afraid to talk to adults when they have problems.

If you go to an adult you trust (parent, teacher, school nurse or counselor), simply say, "I need help, I'm pregnant." You'll find understanding and assistance.

Jean Grandi, RN, PHN, SN
School district nurse

---

1. From a paper presented at a conference on Adolescent and Family Life, Los Angeles, 1987. Sponsored by the Department of Health Services, Sacramento, Ca.

Dear FYI: I have a friend who smoked marijuana through her pregnancy and still smokes while nursing the baby. Has she harmed the baby by doing this?
Frightened Friend

Dear Frightened Friend: For obvious ethical reasons, research into the effects of marijuana on the developing human baby is very hard to do, but according to Dr. Ethel Sassenrath of the UC Davis Medical School, animal experimenters have found some behavioral problems in monkeys whose mothers were given marijuana during pregnancy.

Doctors also have found that babies born to marijuana-smoking mothers are smaller and have smaller heads than babies born to non-drug-using moms.[1]

One thing we do know for sure is that the active ingredients of marijuana get into the baby's blood if pot is used before birth (or if the mother uses during the time she is nursing). Although we don't know for sure everything that exposure will do to the baby in the long run, it's not likely to be positive.
Dave Stoebel

Dear FYI: If your boyfriend takes drugs (not a lot, but some) and you have intercourse with him and get pregnant, can the drugs he takes affect the unborn child? Can it be transported in the sperm some way?
Wondering

Dear Wondering: Not all "social" drugs have been studied enough to give you a definitive answer to your question.

However, among the most-used street drugs today, marijuana is the one that researchers are most concerned about because of its potential for affecting generations. [2]

It is clear that pregnant females should not be exposing the developing fetus to any drugs during pregnancy.

In the case of the father, we know that marijuana causes increased abnormalities and decreased motility of sperm, as well as decreased levels of testosterone. In extensive studies in laboratory mice (where generation times are shorter and

---

1. *Effects of Maternal Marijuana and Cocaine Use on Fetal Growth.* B. Zuckerman, D. Frank, R. Hingson, H. Amaro, et al. New England Journal of Medicine 320 (762-768) 1989

2. Peggy Mann, *Marijuana's Effects on Sex and Reproduction: Male.* Chapter 13 in *Pot Safari: A Visit to Top Marijuana Researchers in the U.S.* Woodmere Press, New York, 1982. *Health Consequences Of Marijuana* in hearings before the Subcommittee on Criminal Justice of the Committee on the Judiciary, U.S. Senate, 96th Congress, 1980. Panel on Male Reproductive System, pp. 92-101. Serial 96-54 U.S. Govt. Printing Office, Washington 1980.

easier to study), it has been shown that exposure of the father only to THC and other components of marijuana can cause reduced fertility (fewer pregnancies per mating) and increased pre-or post-natal loss (babies dying before or soon after birth).

The surviving male babies also showed the same problems when they matured and fathered offspring, which strongly suggest genetic damage.

These studies were done in mice and are probably relevant only to heavy marijuana use in humans. But they do suggest implications for human use of the drug.

In human males, the effects on sperm abnormalities and chromosome changes have been confirmed. But since sperm regeneration is complete in three months, as far as we know now, staying drug-free for that period of time can reverse these drug-induced changes.

> **If a baby is born addicted to a drug, how long does it take for the baby to be "normal" again?**

Ethel Sassenrath, Ph.D.,
Behavioral biologist

Dear FYI: If a baby is born addicted to a drug, how long does it take for the baby to become "normal"? Please tell me there is some hope.

Another Curious Kid

Dear A.C.K.: That depends on a lot of factors.

If the mother has been using just prior to giving birth, and the baby still has the drug in his system, he will undergo withdrawal as the drug is broken down and cleared from his body.

However, because the baby's system isn't as well developed as an adult's, the withdrawal probably will take longer than it would for a grownup.

Beyond the initial withdrawal, we know that some damage is permanent.

Unfortunately, there aren't any studies that have followed babies born to addicted mothers through their entire childhood (we've only been aware of this problem for a few years).

The studies that are being done have found high proportions of kids with physical and psychological problems, and these problems often are permanent. Babies born to alcoholic mothers may be seriously mentally retarded, tend to be smaller and have smaller head sizes.

A 10-year followup on 11 children with these problems found that two had died and the others continued to have serious problems.

Children born to mothers who used cocaine or PCP during pregnancy are turning up with low IQs, learning disabilities, attention span disorders and tendencies toward aggression.

Some children born to drug users may appear to be "normal," but we can never know for sure if they are undamaged, or if the drugs' effects are slight enough not to be easily seen.

It can be very sad, can't it?

Dave Stoebel

Dear FYI: I heard that cocaine raised your I.Q. for a little while ... then it leaves you feeling low. Can you explain that?

Doubting Dana

Dear Doubting Dana: The second part of your statement is quite correct. One of the symptoms of withdrawal from cocaine or any other stimulant is depression, lethargy and a general sense of feeling down. This is sometimes called "Peruvian Flu". As to cocaine's raising the I.Q., that is quite unlikely although users may certainly think it does when they are high.

Dave Stoebel

Dear FYI: How long does it take someone to get addicted to cocaine?

Wondering

Dear Wondering: That depends on the person and the questions:

How long? How Much? How is it taken (crack versus snorting, shooting or smoking). It is variable, but since cocaine is extremely addictive, it could be one time.

Dave Stoebel

Dear FYI: What is the drug "ecstasy" and what are its effects?

AKA Curious

Dear AKA Curious: "Ecstasy", or XTC, refers to a set of hallucinogenic am-

phetamines. The most common are methylenedioxyamphetamine (MDA) and methylenedioxymethamphetamine (MDMA). The street names Adam and Eve have also been applied to these drugs.

Until 1985, ecstasy was legal. However, in July of that year it was placed in the same category as heroin and LSD. Manufacture, sale or possession of ecstasy is illegal.

Users say MDA and MDMA produce a euphoria that includes feelings of calm, heightened sensitivity and insight. Oddly enough, since it is a stimulant drug, physical effects include dilated pupils, dry mouth, grinding of the teeth and tension in the lower jaw.

Tolerance develops rapidly, meaning that more and more of the drug is required to produce the same effect in subsequent uses. Both drugs also produce a prolonged period of physical and psychological burnout following even moderate use.

There are other hallucinogenic amphetamines as well.

One of them, DOM, can trigger severe panic and anxiety and another, DOB, has been reported to shut off blood flow to the arms and legs.

Fortunately, these drugs are not readily available on the street, but as with any illicit drug, the buyer has no way of knowing if his purchase is what it is claimed to be.

Traces or even complete substitutions of LSD, PCP, caffeine and other adulterants have turned up in alleged samples of MDA or MDMA.

Dave Stoebel

Dear FYI: What are *shrooms?* How do they affect you?

Fungus Amongus

Dear Fungus Amongus: "Shrooms" is short for mushrooms and refers to any of several species of wild mushrooms that contain the naturally occurring hallucinogen, psilocybin. They are found throughout the world and are used by some Central American Indians as part of religious rituals.

Psilocybin produces a psychedelic high similar to, though usually shorter than, the high caused by LSD. Physical effects include muscle relaxation, coldness of limbs and dilation of the pupils. Psychological effects include hallucinations, mood changes and distortions of space and time perception. These effects depend greatly on the individual and the setting in which he or she uses the drug.

Like all hallucinogens, psilocybin tends to magnify the good or bad in any person's state of mind or situation. As a result, "bad trips" sometimes occur. Negative effects may include intense anxiety or panic, depression, paranoia, disorientation and an inability to distinguish between fantasy and reality.

On the street, psilocybin can be purchased as a dried mushroom or as the supposedly "purified" drug. In either case, "let the buyer beware" is a good phase to remember. Your local drug dealer has only one motive -- to make a profit. Thus a dried mushroom sold as one containing psilocybin may be the real thing or it could be the grocery store variety spiked with LSD, PCP, rat poison or anything else. The same holds true for the "pure" drug.

Another thing to be concerned about is the fact that many kinds of mushrooms, including some of the types containing psilocybin, are poisonous. At any time, determining the difference between

> 'Let the buyer beware' is a good phase to remember. A drug dealer has only one motive -- to make a profit.

edible and inedible mushrooms is a tricky business and should be left to an expert.

Dave Stoebel

Dear FYI: What is "crank"?

L.

Dear L: Crank is a street term for a variety of uppers. It may be amphetamine or speed, but like any street drug you buy it could be anything.

Dave Stoebel

Dear FYI: A friend of mine recently became addicted to crank. I am really worried about her. How can I get her off it without her hating me?

A Friend

Dear A Friend: First, let's get something clear. You can't "get her off" crank. Only she can do that. You can do something important, though. You can tell her how you feel about her using crank. When doing this, it's best to wait until she's straight. Tell her you're worried about her when she uses, and use examples of what you've seen her do when she's on drugs.

Most people on drugs don't know what their behavior looks like to others. Once they're hooked, they lie to themselves and everyone else -- and pretty soon they believe their own lies! This is called "denial:" "I'm fine, no problem, I can handle it ..."

If that's her response, back off a while.

In the meantime, don't be her "enabler."

Don't bail her out of messes caused by her drug use. Don't lie for her, make excuses for her, do her work, give her money or take over her responsibilities.

Tell her you don't want to be around her when she's high because you care about her and don't want to watch her hurt herself. Try to enlist other friends and relatives in this approach. Then wait a few weeks and confront her again.

There is also a process called "intervention". You gather all her friends, relatives, neighbors, teachers (everyone who cares for her) and confront her with her behavior -- all at once. This means major trauma time for your friend! But often it works! You'll need a professional counselor to guide the "happening" -- but they're available to work with you.

Meanwhile, good luck! Remember, only she can change her direction. You can't do it for her -- but good friends can make a difference.

Joan Parnas, director,
Alcohol & drug program

Dear FYI: Why do people always go in the bathroom and turn on the shower before they "shoot up"?

Perplexed

Dear Perplexed: Your question has us -- and our drug experts -- perplexed.

We hadn't been aware of this perception, however, it has been suggested that perhaps the bathroom is a good place to "shoot up" because it provides privacy. Some people may turn on the shower to give them an excuse to be in the bathroom.

It also could be that they think noise helps hide what they're up to. The fact is, people will find out soon enough. Eventually nothing can hide a drug user.

FYI editor

Dear FYI: What is this drug called ice? What can it do to a person? Why do people need to take drugs?

Bothered and Bewildered

Dear B. & B: "Ice" is a street name of a smokable form of methamphetamine or "speed." It's an upper drug that will cause the heart to race and blood pressure to rise as the user experiences a sense of euphoria and well being. Used in any form (smoked, injected, eaten or snorted), speed will cause a "crash" when the user stops taking it. The crash includes long periods of sleep and listlessness followed by anxiety, depression and/or paranoia.

If used in large enough amounts, the elevated blood pressure can lead to heart attacks or strokes and the user's behavior can be wild, unpredictable or violent.

The real danger in smoking "ice" comes from the fact that smoking puts the drug into the system very rapidly and in large amounts. Thus all of the effects described for speed are exaggerated with "ice".

As to why people *need* to do drugs, the short answer is *they don't*.

Unfortunately, some people think that it's neat to change their consciousness ... and a lot more people think they have to take drugs in order to fit in with the crowd.

Still others have so much emotional pain in their lives that they use chemicals because they think it will help them cope.

The truth is, that although sometimes people need outside help to learn how, anyone can live a happy and fulfilling life completely drug-free.

If you would like some of that help, call your nearest drug prevention program.

Dave Stoebel

Dear FYI: Can speed help you lose weight?
Clueless

Dear Clueless: Yes, speed can help you lose weight. It used to be legitimately prescribed in small doses (in diet pills and pep pills) for several months without apparent harm. But speed and whites can be very dangerous to your health.

Appetite is virtually non-existent when using speed, and it is almost impossible to eat solids.

Sleeping also is very difficult, if not impossible, during a speed "run." The body becomes very wasted and the liver and kidneys, which filter impurities from the body, are forced to overwork. This is like operating a complex water pump without water: it just burns up.

Because of the massive stimulation of the nervous system by amphetamines, and because appetite and sleep patterns are disturbed, an eventual state of toxic psychosis often occurs. This is usually characterized by hallucinations, tremendous panic and fear reaction, with added waves of dependency and depression.

During this period, it is extremely tempting to want to avoid the hard come-down, so the person usually shoots or drops more speed. By the third or fourth day of continuous use, the chemical starts taking over. People abusing speed often suffer an acute state of paranoia; the natural uneasiness and nervousness caused by the amphetamine is intensified by fear of getting caught or busted.

Most drug users don't notice the physical deterioration that this highly dangerous drug can cause because they have young, healthy bodies that can take a lot of stress and strain before they finally give in. Speed actually makes your body age and deteriorate years in a few short weeks or months.

Because speed activates the entire body and forces it to race at a high rate of speed for a long time, the larger the dose, the greater the strain. A lot of speed puts a great strain on the entire circulatory system and often causes aneurysm (ballooning) in the arteries and blood vessels.If one of these aneurysms bursts, it can be fatal. The final word is: don't use speed.

Carlos G. Matos, M.A.
Alcohol and drug counselor

Dear FYI: I am very concerned about a friend of mine who is involved with drugs. I know how bad drugs are for you, and I am worried about the long-term effects drugs will have on her health. I don't know how to approach my friend and tell her that she is ruining her life.

It hurts me to see her getting addicted more and more each day and not know how to help her, but I don't want my friend to think that I am interfering in her life and risk our friendship. What should I do?

Tongue Tied

> It hurts me to see her getting addicted more and more each day and not know how to help her, but I don't want my friend to think that I am interfering in her life and risk our friendship. What should I do?

Dear Tongue Tied: Your concerns about the potential dangers of drug use are correct, and your fears about the direction of your friend's life are appropriate. May I suggest to you three approaches in reaching out to your friend?

1 Be direct. In a caring way, tell your friend why you are concerned about her welfare. This is not "meddling" when we are expressing concerns about the behavior of others. "Meddling" is when we dogmatically tell others how to run their lives.

2.Be specific. Tell your friend what you have noticed in her behavior and lifestyle that worry you.

3.Be personal. Express to your friend how you feel about the friendship, and how you feel about her as a person, and how her behaviors and lifestyle with drugs affects you as a person.

All of the above involve some risk-taking on your part. That, in part, is after all what friendships are all about -- the freedom to take risks with each other in expressing personal thoughts, feelings and concerns. I appreciate your concerns and everyone wishes you well in your efforts to reach out to your friend.

William J. Treguboff, MFCC
Marriage & family therapist

Dear FYI: Can prescription drugs, like Dimetapp, kill you if you O.D. on them?
D.

Dear D: The answer is a definite "yes"! Potentially, *any* drug can kill if taken in excessive amounts.

We cannot tell from your question if you are just curious or if you are feeling suicidal. If the latter is the case, please share your feelings with a friend, family member, teacher or trusted adult. A call to your local crisis line number will enable you to talk to people who care very much about you and your future.
FYI Editor

Dear FYI: Can long-term prescription drugs cause addiction?
Always Curious

Dear Always Curious: Yes, a great many prescription medicines can be addictive.

The tranquilizers like Valium, sedatives and many pain killers have addictive potential.

That is why people should only take these medicines when there is a valid medical reason to do so, and only when under a doctor's care.
FYI Editor

Dear FYI: I am wondering if there was any way you could stop a drug user from using drugs without that person meaning to quit.

I come from a family with two parents and four children. My oldest brother has been using drugs since age 13. He is "hooked" on everything: cocaine, marijuana and speed. He mixes them all with alcohol. I love my brother dearly, but he says he is not addicted. He recently moved to L.A., "the cocaine capital of the world." He won't do any better there.

Please, what can I do to help him? It has gotten so bad he steals family belongings and sells them for drugs. He is totally isolated to all reality.

Help! Please publish this letter so I can show my brother I really care!
Worried

Dear Worried: It is quite obvious to me you care a lot about your brother. There are a number of things you can do to support your brother and help yourself, but you need to be aware that you cannot stop someone from using drugs when they are addicted.

One of the most helpful suggestions is often the hardest to follow -- being able to say "no" when it is appropriate. Saying "no" will begin the slow process of allowing the addict to feel the consequences of his or her use. This can only happen when the family and friends stop rescuing the user from difficulties relating to drug abuse.

This may feel uncomfortable, but the reality is that more harm is done if one continues to protect the user. This concept is referred to as enabling, and is an intricate part of the dynamics in a family with chemical abuse. That's why it's so important for everyone to understand and practice saying "no." The benefit is not only to the user, but to the self-image of the person who can say "no" when someone is taking advantage of him or her.

Here are some equally successful ways to help your brother:

1.Remember at all times that you are powerless over his behavior -- you cannot control him.

2.Tell your brother honestly that you love him, but you are not willing to watch him kill himself through chemicals. Express your feelings.

3.Don't preach or lecture. Do give information about chemicals in a caring, non-threatening way.

4.Get support for yourself in Al-Anon or Alateen in your local community.

It is important to remember what while your brother is "under the influence" of alcohol and/or other drugs, it is the chemical talking, not the loved one. Be supportive, patient, set limits of acceptable behavior, take care of yourself and pray that he finds help. Know that you have done all you can if you follow these suggestions.

Cheri McElwee

Dear FYI: People tell me I should not do drugs, but when I go to my dad's house he does them. What should I do?

No Name

Dear No Name: Since most adults tell you not to use drugs, it must be very confusing for you to go to your dad's house and have him using drugs. If you don't want to be around when your father is busy with his drugs, ask for help. You might consider talking to your mother or another adult about helping you to ask your dad not to use drugs when you visit. If he is unable to make that agreement, then perhaps you will choose not to see him for awhile.

As for using drugs, it is an important decision that you must make for yourself.

When you are growing up and learning so many new things, drugs interfere with your learning and growing. Sometimes people think they feel better for a short time when they use drugs, but in the end drugs always make things worse and keep you from learning what you need to know to be a successful person.

Joan Parnas

Dear FYI: Can you really get "brain-fried" from drug use?

D. From W.

Dear D: With most drugs (except for alcohol), the user's brain does not "fry" or "cook" in the sense that brain cells die immediately (except for alcohol). What does happen with drugs is the disruption or destruction of the chemical messengers from one cell to another. In this sense the chemical messengers are "fried." The end result is the same. When messengers "mess up," short-circuits develop, producing weird behavior and addiction.

Recently, however, research physicians have discovered a designer drug that was converted to nerve poison in the body. The poison killed nerve cells instantly. This was a new discovery which showed that some drugs can "fry" the brain.

Daniel Ferrigno., M.D.
Internist -- addictionist

Dear FYI: If you use drugs for a long time can it cause brain damage?

Freaked

Dear Freaked: Some drugs clearly do damage the brain. Alcohol is one. Many alcoholics exhibit Korsakoff's psychosis. These people have decreased ability to think abstractly, solve problems, express themselves verbally or accomplish motor tasks. In addition, alcohol can damage the liver, digestive tract, kidneys and heart. Using alcohol and tobacco has been linked to certain kinds of cancer.

Other drugs haven't been as well researched. We do know that some marijuana users develop what is known as amotivational syndrome. In other words, they lose their motivation to do much of anything except get high. Whether this is due to some form of brain damage is not understood at this time.

Looking at it from another angle, we damage ourselves any time we use a chemical in place of a skill. When we avoid the discomfort of not knowing how to do something, we lose the chance to perfect a skill that we may really need. If I take a drink to relax and unwind, I don't learn how to relax naturally. If I smoke a joint before going to a party so I won't feel shy, I don't learn how to handle my shyness and be with people.

Young people particularly risk damaging their lives if they do this. Teen-agers are constantly in situations that require them to perfect skills like solving problems, making friends or talking to people of the opposite sex. If they use chemicals in place of skills, they don't have a chance to learn things that they will need for their entire lives.

I think if there is any message from this, it is that there is still a lot to be learned about drugs. Some do cause brain damage, some we don't know about yet. Regardless of whether they do or not, however, we know of enough problems that they do cause to make them not worth using in the first place.

Dave Stoebel

Further Suggested Reading

- Donlon, Jane, *I Never Saw the Sun Rise: The Private Diary of a Fifteen-Year-Old Recovering from Drugs and Alcohol.* CompCare Books, Minneapolis, 1977.
- Maxwell, Ruth, *Kids, Alcohol and Drugs: A Parent's Guide.* Ballantine Books, New York, N.Y., 1991.
- Neff, Pauline, *Tough Love: How Parents Can Deal with Drug Abuse.* Abingdon Press, Nashville, Tenn., 1982.
- Schwebel, Robert, *Saying No is Not Enough: Raising Children Who Make Wise Decisions about Drugs and Alcohol.* Newmarket Press, New York, 1989.
- Seixas, Judith S., *Living With a Parent Who Takes Drugs.* Beech Tree Books, New York, 1979 (older but still very useful).

4

Family: differing & loving are compatible

Any ideas? I have a problem with my folks bugging me day and night about a couple friends I have. Sure, I've got a ton of friends that my folks like, but these two guys are different.

They like going to "strange" concerts, hanging with a different crowd than I'm used to and keep unsual hours (unusual for my circle of friends and parents, that is).

Anyway, they attend school, get passing grades and aren't into drugs or alcohol or anything. Simply because they're way different, my folks don't approve. Like I said, any ideas?

Dear FYI: I am an 18-year-old high school graduate. I have a full-time job and am living with my parents. I've been dating a guy a few years older and I'm feeling very happy being with him. I like to bring him home to visit with me and my mother and father, but whenever I do my mother acts kind of mean towards him, like sarcastic and cool. My boyfriend feels uncomfortable when she acts this way.

My mom also is making me feel guilty for going out with him so often. But she tells me that she thinks he is a nice guy for me to be going out with. So why is she acting this way and what should I do?

Feeling Guilty and Confused

Dear Guilty and Confused: Sometimes parents have a hard time when their daughters begin a significant relationship with a boyfriend; it can mean many things to your mother.

The relationship may be signaling your eventual leaving home. If you are the last child on the threshold of leaving home, she may be especially uncomfortable. If she senses an important relationship, she may be having feelings about the possibility of you being or becoming sexually active. If you are curtailing any important plans (like future studies) to be with your boyfriend, she may be worried about you sacrificing your plans for the relationship.

You are at an age when making meaningful relationships outside the family is part of what you need to do to mature and grow. It must make you quite sad for your happiness to be dividing you and your mom.

I suggest you do more talking with your mom. Both of you have complex feelings about this relationship. Sort them out.

Robert Ogner, LCSW
Psychotherapist

Dear FYI: My mother has always told me that when I decide to have sex to tell her and she won't mind as long as I use birth control. Now that it's come up she's mad at me and tells me I'm irresponsible (I'm 16 years old). Why does she do this? What can I do to make her see she's being unfair?

Getting Mixed Signals

Dear Getting Mixed Signals: The key to your problem with your mother is communication. There could be any number of reasons your mother is giving you these mixed messages, and the only way to really understand her is to confront her directly. Ask her to clarify what she means when she calls you "irresponsible." It is possible that your mother is being unsure or ambivalent about your becoming sexually active, rather than unfair.

She may be concerned about something such as your choice of partner or the potential exposure to sexually-transmitted diseases. Your mother needs to communicate her concerns openly. Maybe you could alleviate her fears by sharing who your partner is and how long you have been together.

Since your mother is concerned that you act responsibly, be sure you approach and speak with her in a mature and responsible manner.

For example, rather than becoming angry and/or calling her "unfair," ask if you can have a talk with her so you can understand what is behind her decision. Address any concerns she has. If you find it too difficult to speak with her openly, I would recommend family counseling to help you communicate, problem solve and resolve this conflict.

Becoming sexually active is an important decision to make and it is best made after obtaining information and considering all the possible implications. It would be helpful to take your mother's concerns into consideration before you decide what to do.

It sounds as if you have been unable to do this up to now.

Joyce Bezazian-Dovelli, MFCC
Marriage & family counselor

Dear FYI: It's hard to discuss sex with my parents because I think they would

> **'Don't forget parents were teen-agers and struggled with many of the same issues you are facing now -- dating, kissing, sex and all the rest...'**

not understand, and because I'm a little embarrassed. How do you think I should ask them about it?

> *Embarrassed*

Dear Embarrassed: You've already headed in the right direction. Sharing your feelings and thoughts with your parents is far better than living in a vacuum.

Sometimes we forget parents were once teen-agers and had to handle most of the same issues facing you right now -- things like dating, kissing and sex have been around a long time!

Sex has always been a troublesome subject, so your parents probably know the problems you are experiencing.

Tell your parents you want to talk to them about something important. Sit down together with no television blaring (these kinds of discussions need full attention), then tell them what's on your mind. It might seem tough at first, but your parents should recognize the trust you're offering and will be very attentive.

As for being embarrassed, it's a normal concern when you want to be taken seriously but are afraid you may not be. Don't let this feeling stop you from having this important conversation. Even some adults have a tough time talking openly about sex without some embarrassment or discomfort. You'll all get through that.

And don't forget, be as informed as possible about sex and intimate relationships. The library and Planned Parenthood are excellent places to find good information.

> *FYI Editor*

Dear FYI: Do you think a girl should talk to her mother if she is going to have sex?

> *Undecided*

Dear Undecided: By all means talk to her.

Let's hope your mom is someone you can talk to about other special people and events in your life. She may have some very good advice about how to know when it is the right time. Your mom may have some information about birth control, or she may tell you where to go for help.

It's hard for some people to talk to their moms, however.

If you try, you could be starting a very special bond between the two of you. If you can't talk to her, talk to someone -- especially someone older whom you trust -- so you can make the best decision possible.

Anne Seeley-MacLeod, M. Ed., BFA
Planned Parenthood

Dear FYI: How do I tell my mom that I made a really big mistake when she had a lot of trust in me? If I tell her, then she won't have trust in me at all.

Mistake City

Dear Mistake City: Your question reflects a terribly difficult dilemma for relationships of all sorts, whether the relationship is between parent and child, boyfriend and girlfriend, two friends, etc. When you care for someone and you feel you have made a mistake which would hurt them, or make them lose trust in you, the first temptation is often to keep the mistake a secret.

It's hard to tell the truth when we feel someone we care about would be hurt by it, but then the fact that you have written for advice suggests that you also feel burdened by keeping your mistake a secret from your mom.

Close relationships, because they are based on trust, prosper when both people are committed to telling the truth -- even when the truth is painful or disappointing to the other person. Keeping silent about your mistake will probably prolong your burden. Hiding a mistake also has a way of silently corroding trust in a relationship.

I get the impression that you care quite a lot about your relationship with your mother, so I would suggest approaching her with your mistake. She may be upset and disappointed at first, but it seems very possible that her trust in you may actually deepen when she recognizes how much thought you have given this matter.

John M. Meyer, Ph.D.
Clinical psychologist

Dear FYI: What can you do about over-protective parents?

Being Babied

Dear B.B.: First let's define over-protective parents.

I would say they are those parents who tend to be a beat behind in recognizing a teen's ability to cope with the world.

They are fearful of the dangers in society and unsure their children know how to take care of themselves. Certainly, everyone needs protective parents at times; however, over-protective parents deny a teenager the chance to choose and to make his or her own judgments.

What you can do is to sit down at a peaceful moment with your parents and begin to tell them about your need for greater independence. Then listen to their fears. This listening is the hardest part for both sides. It takes patience to hear your parents' worries because you know you need courage to face the difficulties that are bound to arise. It takes patience for parents to hear their teen's needs to be independent because they want to keep them safe.

The next step is to find a way to build trust. Start slowly with something you all can easily agree upon. Ask your parents to support you in going after your goals. Tell them you need them to believe you can do the things you aspire to and, of course, you need their support when you make mistakes.

By keeping your bargains with your parents you will teach them what you are capable of. You will begin to calm their fears, and you will feel very good about yourself. This is the dance that most parents and teens engage in, and it can have satisfactory benefits for both.

However, if you have followed this game plan and you still feel your parents do not appreciate the present level of your capabilities, then see if you can get a family friend or counselor to sit down with you and your parents to find what is needed for building trust and increasing freedom.

In all this, the important thing is for you to discover your own basic values. Once you have these worked out, you will have a foundation on which to establish your own independence as you grow to adulthood.

Edith Rothchild, MSW, LCSW
Psychotherapist

Dear FYI: Do you know of any way for me to convince my parents to let me go out with guys? They think I'm too young when I'm already in high school and turned 16 last summer.

Frustrated

Dear Frustrated: It must be frustrating not to be able to do what many of your peers can do. Although every family has different rules and customs, parents and their children usually can negotiate rules by offering gradual options.

Parents who prohibit "going out" often fear that the teen may abuse this freedom. Setting a plan that begins with a date at home with a gradual expansion to dates in agreed upon places at agreed upon times usually allays parental concern. If such negotiation is difficult, perhaps the help of a counselor, minister or adult friend may be helpful.

Incidentally, going out with "guys" sounds a bit unspecific -- like "going out with the navy" might be. I guess you really are concerned about going out with a specific boy -- and being more specific may also help your parents to grant the desired freedom.

Summer after next you will be 18 and emancipated. I wish you a less frustrating time until then...

Hanna Bauer, Ed.D.
Psychotherapist

Dear FYI: Why do mothers put extra pressure on their only girl? Why can't they live in the future and forget the past? We can't always be like them, so why don't they let us go a little? We'll still love them.

Pressured and Confined

Dear Pressured and Confined: It sounds like your mother cares a great deal about you and is having some difficulty in "letting go." Unfortunately, with all the current dangers facing young people these days, it may be especially difficult for any parent to resist the temptation to become overly protective or controlling.

Many parents also see their children as extensions of themselves. This can become dysfunctional in extreme cases (for example, if a mother overly invests in her daughter being "like her" and uses her own history as a yardstick to measure her daughter's growth).

A danger that arises from an unhealthy degree of investment in one's child is that the parent may be giving the child the message that she is not acceptable for who she is. Just as children need to learn and grow as they develop, parents need to evolve and learn how to "let go a little" in order to allow their children to grow into independent adults.

What you can do to facilitate this process of "letting go" is to demonstrate that you are trustworthy and able to make responsible choices. When your mother can see that you are able to function well independently, she may feel less of a need to influence, pressure, or hang on.

Joyce Bezazian-Dovelli

Dear FYI: Do you answer questions from confused parents?

I grew up in an alcoholic home.

Despite dire warnings from my parents against taking drugs -- and despite the example of what it is like to live as a practicing alcoholic -- I became dually addicted.

I'm recovering now through AA, ACA and Al-Anon. But one of my children exhibits the same behavior I did as a child; behavior I now know goes hand-in-hand with substance abuse -- denial, anger, emotional stoicism, fear and so on. How can I get across to him that he's hurting himself?

I feel that if I tell him of my experiences, he'll see only one thing -- "You took drugs and drank and you're still alive. It can't be that bad." I wasn't deterred by dire warnings because I knew people who used drugs and no one died (luckily). But do you see the logic I'm up against? So, should I tell my kids my experiences, my trip to the bottom? Will that just serve as an example that you can drink, take drugs and survive? Or will it help turn them around?

Before I "let go and let God," I thought I'd ask the earthly experts.

Anonymous

P.S. Although I've been addicted to drugs and alcohol, the externals of my life remained intact -- career, family, bank account. My hell was on the inside. So my kids don't really know what they stand to lose, or how it feels to live without hope.

Dear Anonymous: You ask if you should tell your children. The answer is an emphatic yes! However, the reason for my suggesting you "come out" is not to scare your children, not to teach them a lesson, not to save them from a grim fate, but simply to be the best parent you can be: give them yourself as an example that there need not be any deep secrets between parents and children.

They will love you for confiding in them, and your example will make it easier for them to level with you. That is as far as it goes. In the end, they will need to make up their own minds. Should counseling be needed, it will have to be done by somebody outside the family. You are their parent, not their therapist!

Congratulations on being alive and well after all you must have been through. I hope you can be as honest with your children as you have been with yourself.

Herbert Bauer, M.D.
Psychiatrist

Dear FYI: Parents teach their kids for years not to judge people by the way they look, and then they turn around and judge teenagers by their looks and dress. What gives them the right?

Angry

Dear Angry: Maybe you're asking why parents feel that they can dictate to their children what they are to look like.

If we think of this as an issue of either "having a right" or "not having a right" we will not get anywhere.

From an early age all of us are constantly influenced by our environment to judge and to feel judged.

We are bombarded by advertising that tells us how to dress and how to communicate.

It tells us that being different is bad.

These messages are hard to escape.

Often we will react by either doing as we are told, or doing the opposite which is, of course, also a reaction. To become really free we must learn to tune out much external pressure -- something difficult for both parents and teens.

Parents want to be accepted, and they want their children to be accepted.

It would be desirable for parents and their teens to sit down at a negotiating session and have each decide what they feel is the most important thing about looks and dressing. What are preferences, and what are basic requirements? In other words, what would they like and what would truly devastate them. Then parents and teens can negotiate in good faith.

If both sides allow themselves to listen, they will most likely be able to arrive at a mutually survivable solution.

Parents and teens learn and grow with conflict and conflict resolution.

They learn that difference is not "bad" and that differing and loving are compatible.

Hanna Bauer

'I have trouble telling my parents when I have done something wrong, that might get me into trouble.'

'I'm in high school. I have the most difficulty talking to my parents about grades. They'd kill me if I got a C.'

'I can't tell my parents that even though they are hard on me and strict on the rules, I am really thankful that they are my parents and I agree with most of their rules.'

Dear FYI: How come it seems that when society learns of a teen-ager committing a crime, teen-agers as a whole get the blame? Not all teen-agers are involved in drugs or gangs. Adults could try giving us credit for some of the good things we do.

Lumped

Dear Lumped: It has to do with a tendency by many people to make judgments about an entire group based upon information about one or a small number of that group. It is formally called stereotyping, and occurs when we don't take the time to get to know people as individuals.

Often, such judgments are inaccurate, and at the least, this is unfair to the group being labeled — and often leads to misunderstandings. Anyone who takes the time to get to know teens or members of the group they are stereotyping will come away with very different and often positive feelings about that population. They will find that the group is made up of individuals, each one unique.

When we don't rely upon ourselves to find out what people are really like, we rely upon other sources. It is often the media that does this job for us (and the media is notorious for sending out messages of a negative nature). If our only source of information about teens is TV, our viewpoints will naturally be biased in a negative manner. How often do you hear of the good things young people do on TV?

Parents and other adults should give teens credit for the multitude of positive things they do. The teenage years are such tumultuous years. Adults often get into the habit of looking only for the bad.

Try getting your parents more involved in what you and your friends are doing. Often, they do not come into contact with your positive behavior. If they are, and are just not seeing it, don't be afraid to toot your own horn. Once appreciated, let them know how good it feels to hear from them in such a positive manner. You might also try approaching this behavior in reverse. Relationships are a two-way street.

Kathy Blankenship
School outreach counselor

Dear FYI: I know kids are always writing to you guys about things like being pregnant or stoned or having dating problems.

You may think this is a dumb question, but it is important to me.

My mom is always screaming about my room. I tell her I'll be gone in two years and she won't have to worry. I also tell her that she's lucky I'm not on drugs. What else can I say to get her off my back?

Messy

Dear Messy: So many parents and teen-agers struggle over issues like messy bedrooms. Your mom, like most parents, wants to have some control while you are still living at home. You, like other teens, want to have more independence and freedom.

I suggest that you ask your mom if the two of you can have a talk (without screaming) to try to reach a compromise.

For example, if she wants you to clean your room every week, perhaps she and you can settle on every three or four weeks. Then you have to uphold your end of the bargain and she has to uphold hers (not to scream).

On the other hand, maybe the compromise won't involve frequency of cleaning, but rather some minimum standards, such as no food or empty food containers in your room in exchange for putting your clothes where you want (even on the floor). Learning to negotiate compromises is a skill you can use throughout your life.

Candice M. Erba, RN, LCSW
Psychotherapist

Dear FYI: My parents are strict and require me to be home by midnight on the weekends. My boyfriend does not have a curfew and stays out as late as he wants.

Why can't my parents trust me like his parents trust him?

Unfair Household

Dear Unfair Household: Your parents' curfew decisions aren't a statement about how trustworthy you are, but about what they see as the right way to parent and about their worries.

Many adults tell us that having had no limits set for them by their parents when they were growing up made them feel uncared for, even if it was handy at the time.

Perhaps when you can hear their rules as a statement about their concerns, not about you, you could have a discussion about how they choose curfew hours, at what age your curfew might change ... and if there is anything you can do to reassure them of your reliability and safety. Don't discuss this at a time when any one of you is angry!

If all else fails, a neutral person outside the family, such as a school counselor, might help all three of you to hear each other and learn about negotiation. At the very least, remember that when you are 18 and independent, you'll be making all the choices.

Nancy DuBois
Psychologist

Is it reasonable that a 15-year-old boy not need a sitter while the parents are out of town?

Dear FYI: My son is 15, responsible and a good student. Is it advisable to leave him alone in our home for three or four days while my husband and I are out of town? We would have a nearby neighbor play backup for us in the event of an emergency.

Concerned Parent

Dear Concerned: It is certainly reasonable that a 15-year-old boy not need a sitter while you are out of town. However, in deciding whether he stays by himself for the entire time, I would consider the following questions.

Will you be gone during school time or over a weekend? In the latter case, will he be left to his own devices or have a schedule to follow, including being with others? Are you comfortable with him not "reporting in" to someone, such as after school or in the evening?

Your son may be responsible, but what about his friends? Would they be able to convince him to bend your rules while you are away? While teenagers enjoy their freedom to be alone, they also need a structure for their protection. Be sure to talk over guidelines of behavior with your son before you leave.

Have you considered the possibility of having him stay with a friend's family overnight (you could reciprocate for them later) and yet be free to attend to his chores, alone and responsible at home during daylight hours?

You should communicate with him clearly regarding the expectations of both of you and explain why you might have him stay with someone or report in more often than in an emergency.

I congratulate you on not taking this lightly. This is a big step for you and your child as he moves toward adulthood.

Stewart E. Teal, M.D.
Child psychiatrist

Dear FYI: What do you do when your parents won't let you play tackle football? I'm 13.

Football Lover

Dear Football Lover: It is really a drag to know what you want to do and to be overruled by the authorities (in this case, parents). It might help you and your parents to try an experiment.. Some time when tempers aren't already high, see if they would agree to sit down with you ... with you playing the role of parent and them playing the role of you.

If each of you really tried to get into taking the opposing point of view, not only will you find out some interesting things, they may come to see your side of things ... or you may come to see theirs. Besides, it's usually fun to do something like this.

Of course you have many other options: sulk, pout, stay mad, be resistive, bad-mouth parents to everyone else, feel like a righteous victim or take up something they see as even more dangerous and get hurt. You make the pick!

Nancy DuBois

Dear FYI: How should you ask your parents for money?
Flat Broke

Dear Flat Broke: There's no easy way, no matter what age you are. Rolling on the floor kicking and sceaming might work simply because you're making such a nuisance of yourself, but it's not likely to make you a very popular person.

There are two key elements in successfully seeking money: the validity of your reason for needing the money; and the ability of your parents to give. After all, no amount of kicking and screaming is going to turn into cold, hard cash if the cupboard is bare.

My daughter, when she was about 4, would ask for money by letting her right shoulder droop toward the floor and putting on one of those shy, sweet, helpless looks no parent can ignore. It worked every time. Now that she's older and has a paper route, I'm having to ask her for money.

There are some basic rules for success:

1. Don't ask your parents for money on weekday mornings, when time is short and tempers shorter.

2. Don't ask for money on Saturday morning before your parents have had at least one cup of coffee and have been up for at least two hours.

3. Always have a "promise" ready to exchange for cash, such as cleaning your room, mowing the lawn, washing the dishes or taking that one-pound earring out of your nose.

4. Do not throw a tantrum. Your parents have all read Dr. Spock and they know

they shouldn't Give In To Such Antics.

5. Tell them you'll save half of what they give you. Until tomorrow.

Finally, every once in a while you should use the money your parents give you to buy them a little surprise, such as a bouquet of flowers from the grocery store or a little box of candy, depending of course, on how much they give you. Basically, though, anything cute and schmaltzy will do. In this way they'll be kept off guard, never knowing if your intent in asking for money is actually to buy them something nice. And once you get them thinking that way, they'll say yes every time.

Bob Dunning
Newspaper columnist

Dear FYI: I love my mother very much, but I have a very hard time expressing my feelings. Why do I feel like this, and how can I change?

Much Concerned

Dear Much Concerned: It is uncomfortable, even scary at times, when we cannot express our feelings. We react with such strong discomfort when we feel strongly and are afraid to express it. When we "love much" we tend to be afraid of showing something that might impair that relationship -- yet even "not" expressing is an expression of feelings.

Often we harbor feelings of approval and disapproval, of liking and not liking, which makes it so hard to express ourselves. Talking this over, perhaps rehearsing this with a friend or a counselor will help. And remember: expressing feelings is more than just words -- it is touch and gesture ... and how things are spoken.

Hanna Bauer

Dear FYI: I have a problem that's been upsetting me for a long time.

I have trouble expressing my feelings. It really shows now that I have a boyfriend . When we talk, it takes so long for me to get things out or to understand my feelings. My family is not super close.

It's pretty much a home problem; I guess it has to do with my parents. It's hard for me to say what I want to them because I'm pretty much talked at -- not talked to. I want to find some kind of counselor to talk to once in a while, who will give me ideas and ways to talk to my family and help me to understand myself more so I'll feel better about myself.

Locked Up Inside

Dear Locked Up Inside: You're not alone: communication on a feeling level is difficult. To help ourselves, we need practice. One way is with a counselor. Do call your nearest branch of the Mental Health Association for suggestions of available counselors.

Another practice is the "incomplete-sentence-exercise." Ask your boyfriend or your parents to share this exercise with you. Suggest that they listen as you give several completions of a sentence like "One thing that's bothering me is..." Give several endings, different each time, asking them to keep a list, but not respond. Then, ask them to do the same with "As I listen to you..." with you listening and listing. Use this to express love and appreciation, too, such as "One of the things I enjoy about you is..." With feeling communication, practice is important and basic.

Robert L. Neal, MFCC
Marriage & family counselor

Dear FYI: I want to be emancipated but my mother feels that if I was it would be solely because of her. This is wrong. I love her. How can I make her understand I want to do it for me. I love her more than anyone, but need to be on my own.

Distressed

Dear Distressed: We are assuming that you are using the word "emancipated" as in emancipated minor. An emancipated minor is one who, with some exceptions, has the rights and responsibilities of an 18 year old before his or her 18th birthday. Emancipation is a legal process with stringent requirements. It is by no means granted automatically, but once it is granted the parents of an emancipated minor are absolved from all responsibilities to their child.

In your case, perhaps you want to accept adult responsibilities and your mother thinks you are too young. Too young to handle them? Too young to know that to do and how to do it? And perhaps you want to make decisions about yourself and your life and to make them by yourself and you think that you are not too young to do a good job.

These decisions range from what flavor ice cream to buy to whether or not you live with your boyfriend, take out a loan to buy a car, get a certain kind of job and so on.

It is also probable that your mother is fearful that you will make some wrong decisions that will affect you adversely and give you pain the rest of your life.

You know that it's hard for her to see you leave -- she will miss you and worry about you. That's normal; and it's normal for you to be concerned for her feelings. She knows that you love her and that you're not wanting emancipation

86

because of anything she's done. I think that if you keep on being honest with her, keep showing her that you're trustworthy and can act responsibly and reliably, she is more likely to feel less insecure about you.

Joanne Evers, Ed.D.
Psychotherapist

Dear FYI: I want to get a motorcycle but my mom does not approve of it. She says it is dangerous to ride one, but I don't think it is so dangerous to ride a motorcycle when you've got helmet on. What do you think?

Annoyed With My Mom

Dear Annoyed: Let me give you the hard facts:

Statistically, it is indisputable that the No. 1 killer of teen-agers in our society is some form of traumatic accident. Motor vehicles play a dramatic role in these fatalities ... and motorcyle riders have a proportionately higher number of more severe injuries. It's no wonder when you consider the nature of the activity -- you are precariously balancing your unprotected body on top of a mechanical device capable of great speed.

When you are on the highway with much larger vehicles going great speeds, if one of them zigs when you zag, guess who loses the confrontation? You must also hope that a rock on the road doesn't cause you to lose your balance, dirt in your eyes doesn't temporarily blind you... Want more?

If direct impact doesn't harm you, the contact with the pavement, trees or other objects may cause you such bodily injury that you'll be laid up for the rest of your life.

Although today's helmets have had a significant impact on lessening the severity of some brain injuries, they are not guaranteed to prevent injury. And what about the remainder of your body? Do you plan to wear a full leather outfit including gloves and boots? Severe road burns are often more disabling than a broken bone. Do you have any suggestions for protecting internal organs? A suit of armor, perhaps?

(Continued on Page 90)

87

Communication: some advice worth saving

Dear FYI Readers: What keeps teens from communicating openly and honestly with their parents? The answer for many of them is really pretty simple: the costs are too high. It's too risky. They get punished or they get yelled at. Maybe they get belittled or made to feel guilty. They soon learn what to keep silent about and what to conceal. After all, who goes looking for punishment? Who wants to be yelled at? Who needs embarrassment?

Most teen-agers would like to be able to discuss things with their parents and certainly most parents would like to communicate with their children. Too often, though, the situation has deteriorated so far that both parties literally don't know how to do it. Old angers flare up. People get impatient. They start judging each other ("You're out of touch!" or "You're incredibly naive!"). Frustration sets in. Then silence and withdrawal.

One promising remedy is for both parties to relearn how to talk with each other about concerns that are sensitive.

A good way to begin the relearning process is for a parent and a son or daughter to talk with each other about the way they communicate (or don't communicate) with each other. They should talk about talking, apart from any specific incident or issue. In fact, bringing up old issues re-activates old angers and frustrations. This is not the time for rehashing some specific event in the past. This should be a discussion about how to begin to communicate once again.

Below are some guildelines to use in a talk about talking to each other. Both parties should try their best to follow them. You might even go so far as to read them aloud and discuss them as a way to get started.

1. Focus your attention on listening to and understanding the concerns being expressed. (All of these suggestions are difficult but this one may be the hardest for most of us. Many will admit that they ought to be better listeners, but they seldom do anything about it).

2. Find ways to show some respect for each other during this conversation. This, too, is easy to say and hard to do.

3. Show some patience. Resist the often natural urge to assume that you already know and understand the things the other person is saying to you.

4. Listen not only to the content of what is being said but to the feelings that are being conveyed.

5. Don't dismiss or invalidate a feeling or concern that the person is expressing. Something that doesn't look like a problem from your perspective can be a very big one from the other's point of view.

6. Show some more patience and respect. If you aren't conveying these two attitudes at this stage, there probably isn't any further communication occurring anyway.

7. Resist the automatic tendency to criticize and judge the position that the other person is taking. If you feel that you must judge, reserve your judgment until later in the conversation. Judgments have a way of stifling further dialogue.

8. Try not to equate your view of something that the other person does with your categorization of the whole person.

9. Recognize that understanding each other is a major achievement in many cases. Understanding each other is one thing, agreeing with each other is something else. You have to settle for understanding at the beginning. Agreement may require further work and, in fact, may not be possible at the present.

Communication between parents and their sons and daughters about their differing beliefs and priorities is hardly ever easy. It is seldom perfect or completely satisfying to both parties. If the costs are too high, it won't occur. If people honestly work at it, following some of the suggestions above, the rewards will outweigh the costs.

John Vobs, M.A.
Professor

88

I just turned 13. I can't talk about sex with my parents. Well, I can, but I never ask because I'm embarrassed and I think they will think I'm too young or a pervert or something.

What do you have the most difficulty discussing with your folks?

I have trouble discussing how much money I should get for an allowance.

My parents still live in the '50s. They think that $1 should last all week...

The issue which I have the most difficulty discussing with my parents is whether I should be able to go out and drink. I'm 18. Since my parents are divided on the issue it has led to some heated debates.

I'm 15 and female. I have a hard time discussing sexual matters with my father.

When I'm upset about a guy I like they try to tell me that he is not important enough to worry about. So when I'm upset I don't tell them anymore.

I have trouble with the discussion of sex. I have a boyfriend and my parents always hint how bad it is to have sex when you're younger.

I can't talk about girls. My parents needle me when I get a girlfriend.

Nothing really. My mom is very open and always there for me and all my friends (or whoever needs her).

The most difficult thing to discuss with my parents is how depressed and sad I am. It doesn't seem fair for them to come home and listen to me and my problems. When I tell them I'm down I feel guilty and I make my parents feel down.

I always have a hard time discussing my father's death with my mom. I am very sad that he died. I am afraid to ask my mom about him because she'll get sad. He always took me to movies and ice skating and I was very proud of him.

89

The personal message I can bring you from years of taking care of young people injured on motorcyles is this: "Even if you were right, you were wrong -- maybe dead wrong!" You will be wrong to think you won't get hurt in an accident that is someone else's fault. You may be right to think that riding only short trips around your neighborhood is reasonably safe, but wrong to think a serious accident can't happen around the corner. And you might think your parents are depriving you of some exhiliarating experience defying gravity and death, but you are wrong to think that they don't trust or love you.

Please consider it fortunate that your parents love you enough to advise you against this serious activity.

Michael H. Robbins, M.D.
Neurosurgeon

Dear FYI: My parents are divorced and now my mom has a boyfriend and my dad has a girlfriend. They are so busy making sure that their boyfriend and girlfriend are happy that they don't have time for me or my problems. I feel left out and in the way. Then I feel guilty for acting like a baby. Can you help?

Confused at 16

Dear Confused: What you are describing is an extremely painful and confusing situation. Sad to say, your experience is also increasingly common as the divorce rate continues to grow. You may or may not have wanted your parents to stay together. However, you certainly didn't expect to lose the attention of both of them, especially to new companions from outside the family. When this happens it is always easy to feel left out or in the way. Chances are that in your parents' minds you are neither. Rather, they see their new friends as additions to their lives rather than as substitutions for you.

As for feeling like a baby for wanting attention -- remember, we all need attention and affection in our lives and when we feel left out it is understandable to feel needy. This doesn't mean that we are babies, it means that we are human. These are needs your parents surely understand. Otherwise, why would they have sought out the attention of newcomers once they felt a loss of affection from each other?

Your feelings are understandable under the circumstances. If you have friends that you can talk to about your feelings, this may help. Above all, as with most problems, it is essential that you talk with the others directly involved -- in this case, your parents. Let them know that you need attention and affection too. Not telling them guarantees that they will not be able to help you.

Christopher Bauer, Ph.D.
Clinical psychologist

Dear FYI: My parents are divorcing and my dad has asked me to talk to my mother for him. He wants her to stop divorcing him. I feel stuck in the middle and don't know what to do.

Stuck in the Middle

Dear Stuck in the Middle: When parents divorce, they are often very involved in their own feelings. They may be less able than usual to give attention to the feelings of their children, forgetting that their children are going through an unhappy time too. Sometimes parents lean on their children for emotional support through this painful time. To a degree, this can be beneficial, allowing children to give and parents to receive in ways which create new kinds of closeness.

In your situation, however, it seems you are being asked to do something which is not and should not be your job. Being asked to carry messages between your parents is giving you additional burdens you do not need at this time. You might be worrying that you would hurt your dad's feelings if you told him you were uncomfortable in this role. This is probably a very lonely and stressful time for you.

I'd like to suggest that you tell your father that you love him and are worried about him, but that it hurts to be put in the middle. You may need someone else to talk to. Sharing your feelings with a friend you can trust, an adult friend, or a counselor at school can help you feel less stuck.

Robert Ogner

Dear FYI: My mom and dad have split. When I talk to my dad he always talks bad about my mom. How can I tell my dad this upsets me?

Miserable

Dear Miserable: Divorce is awful for everyone. Often parents go through a period of intensified hostility; they may seem cruel or hateful toward each other and have much to disagree about. They fight over money, property and child custody. Unfortunately, children are hurt by this fighting when, as in your case, your dad is so angry and frustrated he has lost sight of how voicing his feelings about mom is affecting you.

I am glad you are in touch with your feelings. Many children get too caught up in the hostile imagery of divorce. Not only do they experience the loss of the intact family, but they become seriously alienated from one or both parents.

Tell your father of your sadness.

Let him know that when he "talks bad" about your mom he is hurting you by devaluing the mom you love.

91

Ask him to keep his angry feelings toward your mom between him and her, and to try to spare you. Remind him that you love and need them both, now more than ever, and that you cannot stand to have your love and admiration for either of them damaged by, or during, the divorce. Tell him you should not have to take sides, and that you will not accept the idea that either one is bad just because of the divorce. I hope your father will respond with respect to your request. After all, you must assume that he loves you and does not intend to hurt you.

Keep in mind that this fighting phase of divorce will end eventually.

Meanwhile, try very hard to hold onto the best qualities of both parents, and do not let the hard times discourage you from the things you must do to further your own happiness and development.

Jay M. Feldman, M.D.
Psychiatrist

Dear FYI: I am constantly bothered by the fighting of my parents. They do it for hardly any reason at all and I can't do anything about it. Please advise me on what to do.

Bothered

Dear Bothered: When parents fight, children become anxious and concerned about their own physical and psychological well-being -- they feel vulnerable.

The child can feel responsible for the anger and unhappiness of the parent due to past associations with the parent being upset with the child's behavior. Although parents may say it doesn't involve the child, he or she responds to how the parent feels and acts, rather than what the parent says. When the problem persists the family may need professional counseling to resolve the issues.

There are several things you can do when your parents' fighting upsets you:

1. Tell your parents about your concerns at a time when they are not fighting.

2. Discuss the problem with a trusted family friend or relative who could relay the information to your parents.

3. If the above attempts have failed to help, seek a counselor or professional.

4. If either parent is in physical danger you should call the police.

You are not responsible for the resolution of differences between your parents.

Gordon Ulrey, Ph.D.
Psychologist

Dear FYI: I'm having problems at home. My parents' relationship is deteriorating and they have considered divorce before. I don't know what to do. They

92

will *not* listen to my feelings, and I can't talk to anyone else. I don't understand what is going on, because my mom says it's my grades that are bringing her marriage down. I get a B-minus average. I don't know who to talk to. Should I go to see a psychiatrist?

Sad and Mad

Dear Sad and Mad: A divorce is a very painful event for everyone involved. It is important for you for realize that you did not cause your parents' marriage problems -- whatever your mother says -- and that changing your behavior would not necessarily make the marriage OK again. Parents have the responsibility to manage their own marital problems, even if their child's behavior presents some difficulties for them.

Your signature indicates that you have identified two very real feelings that a person experiences when parents consider divorce, and you are on the right track when you look for someone to talk to about your feelings. A psychiatrist is one person who could help if talking with friends is not enough.

There are also many other possibilities: a teacher; school counselor; minister; social worker; psychologist; or marriage, family and child counselor. You might also encourage your parents to obtain some professional help in working on their marriage.

Cathy Neuhauser, Ph.D.
Psychologist

Dear FYI: I have developed an immense hatred for my father since he separated from my mother. Now I'm living with him, and I still hate him for what he did to my mother and my family. What should I do?

The Hater

Dear Hater: It is certainly understandable that you are feeling so miserable and angry. You have not one but at least two major pressures on you right now. First, you are angry about the separation of your parents, especially at your

93

father's role in the split. Second, you are now forced to make a life for yourself with someone you mistrust.

Let's deal with the first pressure. You need to find some way to feel accepting of your parents' differences. This is probably more easily said than done for now. However, the passage of time will help if you are able to talk with both of your parents about the reasons for their separation.

You may still end up feeling that your father was in the wrong; however, you may also begin to let your parents' differences be their problem and not yours. Even though you hate to see your mother being hurt, you cannot do her suffering for her.

Are you perhaps still angry at your mother for her inability or unwillingness to keep you from living with your father? This might be contributing to the anger that you now direct towards him.

There are no easy ways to deal with your second problem: having to live with your father. If talking directly with him cannot work out your differences, some form of joint counseling may prove helpful.

Christopher Bauer

Dear FYI: A few months ago my mom remarried. She and my new stepdad fight a lot, and I feel trapped. Mom and I used to have a great relationship, but not anymore. What should I do?

Trapped

Dear Trapped: It sounds as though you have had quite a change in your life this year. When a parent remarries and a new stepparent is brought into the household, the impact on everyone in the family is enormous. Wondering what you can do to make things better is an indication that you do not feel powerless.

When you hear your parents fighting, you do not need to participate silently by remaining near them. Do you feel the need to stay nearby to protect your mother in some way? Unless there is a possibility of physical violence (in which case an immediate visit to a counselor is in order), there is probably nothing constructive you can do by staying and feeling trapped.

I suggest you tell your parents when they are in a calm mood, how uncomfortable their fighting makes you. Add that after this you will go into another room when they fight. You might also ask if you can go to a friend's house for a short time. Remember as you leave the fight scene that you're trying to protect yourself (not to punish them) so retreat without fanfare.

Your changed relationship with your mother must feel like quite a loss to you. Does she know how you feel? Often the best way to improve a relationship is to share important feelings, though it is vital to do this in a non-accusing way.

94

Your mother may be caught up in her own turmoil right now, and you might be afraid that because of her new marriage she is lost to you. That does not need to be the case. You have a chance to take a somewhat grown-up role and work toward improving your relationship with this person who means so much to you.

> I really can't talk to my parents about anything. They are so old-fashioned. I ask them a question and they just yell at me...

Bonnie Wilson, Ph.D.
Marriage, family &
Child counselor

Dear FYI: I moved here in the summer to live with my dad. My step-mom and I used to have a pretty good relationship, but now sometimes she seems not to want me around at all. My dad and I don't talk much, and when we do not much is said. My step-brother and I don't get along well either.

Is it something I'm doing to cause this? I'm confused.

All Mixed Up

Dear All Mixed Up: The chances are very small that all the problems you've described are your fault alone. The fact is that settling into a new living situation with both a step-parent and a step-brother is really difficult for everyone. Each family member will, from time to time, feel hurt, angry, uncared for, and even long for the way things used to be before the separation or divorce.

Remember that your father and step-mother got married because they love each other and want their marriage, which includes you, to work.

Even though your dad finds it hard to talk, he cares about you and wants you happy; your step-mother wants you and her son to be happy too. Greater happiness for all of you makes it necessary that each family member talk more openly about feelings, disappointments, and what you want. Even though it's hard, let your family know about your confusion and concerns.

If you or your parents want or feel it necessary, contact a nearby therapist who has experience working with divorce and step-families.

Such a person could help each of you make changes so necessary and important to the family's happiness.

Jerry L. Plummer, MSW, MPA, BCD
Child psychologist

> I don't have any difficulty talking with my parents and I usually can talk to them about anything but sex.

95

Dear FYI: How would you feel if your mother was a prostitute?

(No Signature)

Dear Friend: If I thought or had heard that my mother was a prostitute, I would feel confused, angry, embarrassed, hurt and needing to talk about it to someone I could trust.

I think that we all want to look up to our parents -- and when a parent behaves in any way that others disapprove of or look down on, we feel a combination of shame and a wish to defend our parent that is very painful. We also feel angry at that parent for putting us in that position.

Although your question deals with prostitution, the broader question of parents and sexuality is there for everyone.

Certainly this area is loaded with feelings, ideas of right and wrong, fears and contradictions. Parents may want to protect their children from the burdens and hazards of early sexual relationships. However, parents are people with their own sexual relationships to work out, and watching this, a teen-ager might feel confused, angry at what might look like hypocrisy, or even feel fearful for the parent.

For instance, when a newly divorced parent begins dating again, it can be a shock and an embarrassment to adolescent children. In the situation where parents and kids are experimenting with new relationships at the same time, feelings can run high and it helps if family members can talk about their feelings with honesty and as much good will and even humor as they can muster.

Because we all want to love and respect our parents, we need to find out, if we can, who they are as people. As we do, we may find a way to forgive what we see as their faults and value their virtues. It is not possible to tell from your question exactly what your situation is, so I think it is especially important that you talk in confidence to a counselor and begin to sort out both the facts and your own painful feelings around them.

Edith Rothchild

Dear FYI: I am 15 and counting the days until I turn 18 so I can get a place of my own.

My step-dad is the biggest jerk you could ever believe. He is always telling me that I'm lazy, that I have a bad attitude, and that I'm going to grow up to be a "nothing" like my dad. My mom says she is tired of always being in the middle and doesn't want to deal with it.

Lots of times I sit in the park and wonder what it would be like to step in front of a car.

Despairing

Dear Despairing: You are caught in one of the most troubling of situations teens face: the blended family. No other generation of teens has had to face more divorce, remarriage, step-siblings, half-siblings and step-grandparents.

We are looking at family forests instead of family trees and the pain for all involved can be enormous. With time and maybe the help of counseling, blended families can become safe and satisfying places to be.

I am far more concerned, though, at this point, about the suicidal feelings you're experiencing. Persistent thoughts

> # No other generation of teens has had to face more divorce, remarriage, step-siblings, half-siblings and step-grandparents.

of this nature are a clear indication that professional help is needed. A counselor can help you to learn how to take a new look at your options, help you to see why the future holds promise, and how to handle the anger you have toward your step-dad.

I suggest presenting the idea of counseling in as non-threatening a way as possible. Let your mom know that you have been experiencing suicidal feelings. You might even add that you want to learn to be a more co-operative family member. This will advance your cause far more than saying you need counseling because your step-dad is such a "jerk."

Don't let cost stand in your way. Many fine services are based on one's ability to pay. For referrals to counselors see the front section of your phone book under crisis lines.

I will be with you in spirit as you go about getting the help that you very much deserve.

Kristine A. Rominger, M.S., MFCC
Licensed marriage, family &
Child therapist

Dear FYI: Everything I do seems to be wrong according to my parents. I feel I am a pretty good person, but they seem to find a lot of things wrong with me. I also have a little sister and they seem to like her a lot more than me. I get better grades than she does and I always do everything I'm told. When she's told to do something it gets done a week later.

97

Why can't they be proud of me? I just wish they would compliment me instead of saying that my attitude is terrible or that I don't do anything right. Please help.

Unwanted Teen-ager

Dear Unwanted: You're right. It's hard to feel OK about yourself when it seems like nothing you do is ever good enough. It's even harder when your parents give a lot more criticism than support. Your folks really need to know how sad and discouraged you're feeling.

First, try talking with them about how unwanted you feel. To improve your chances of being heard, pick a quiet moment, perhaps with just one of them. You might even show them your letter. If that doesn't work, talk with another trusted adult about how to get help for your family, for example a school counselor, favorite teacher, family friend or minister.

It may be reassuring to know that your feelings aren't unusual; many of your friends probably have similar feelings. Talking to one of them might also be helpful. You've already taken the first step with by writing. Now try the next step and reach out again.

Dale Blunden, Ph.D.
Psychologist

Dear FYI: If I ask my parents a question they just yell at me. How can I communicate with them? Why can't we get along? Why can't I talk to my parents instead of yelling too?

Yelled at and Yelling

Dear Yelled at and Yelling: Usually, yelling is a sign that the people yelling are feeling frustrated and angry that no one is listening to them. They yell to try to make themselves heard. The problem with yelling is that it makes the person being yelled at defensive. He or she wants to protect himself or herself rather than listen and understand what is being said. My guess is that no one in your family feels like anyone really listens to them.

Here are a few suggestions for you and your parents to try:

1. When someone is talking, listen without interrupting.

2. Let the person who is talking know you are listening by giving signals such as nodding your head, saying "uh-huh," "oh," "I see," and looking at them while they are talking.

3. Ask the other person what they think about what is being said and then listen to them when they answer.

4. To make sure that you understand what the other person is saying, say back to them what you heard them say in your own words, and ask them if that is

correct. If you didn't hear them correctly then ask them to explain it in another way because you want to understand.

5. Send "I" messages, not "you" messages. This keeps people from feeling attacked and defensive and makes it easier to listen and understand. For example, instead of "*You* stop yelling at me. Why don't *you* ever listen to me? *You* always yell..." you might try "I feel really upset when you yell at me. I need to talk with you about it."

These techniques in communication are from a book by Dr. Thomas Gordon called "P.E.T. (Parent Effectiveness Training) in Action." These techniques are good for all members of a family to use to improve communication, not just parents. P.E.T. books can be found in libraries and bookstores.

Maybe you could suggest to your parents that you have a special family meeting just to discuss ways you all could improve communication so everyone would feel listened to.

Nancy Chadwick, LCSW
Psychotherapist

Dear FYI: I'm sick and tired of having my dad always tell me how stupid I am. I know you can't help me, but I feel better at least writing this.

Sick and Tired and Sad

Dear Sick and Tired and Sad: I can understand why you signed your letter the way you did. All of us want to please those who are important to us. It hurts when you are made to feel you are not worthy of your father's praise and support.

Through the experiences that we share, images of our fathers are formed in our minds, and these images of smiles and frowns or of harsh words or praise have a strong impact on our minds, an impact that creates feelings of sadness or joy, self-worth or worthlessness. These feelings stay with us throughout our lives.

This is an important issue -- one which is worth the effort and patience it can take in trying to change this destructive pattern that is being formed with your father. Perhaps through carefully recalling what's been happening in your thoughts and actions you will be able to determine a pattern in your own life that seems to trigger your father's reaction and negative remarks.

Sometimes it's difficult to communicate, and forming a means of understanding can be equally difficult. Your mother, brothers, sisters, friends and counselors can often help. Perhaps with their support and guidance you and your father can discuss these issues together.

Let him know how you feel, don't assume that he knows you are upset and saddened by his remarks. Someone needs to make the effort to get the lines of communication flowing. If you can initiate this you should, don't wait for your father to do it.

Sometimes a father finds it very hard to say "I'm sorry, you're not stupid, I really meant to say that I'm bothered by..."

Professional counselors frequently can aid in these situations.

Your relationship with your father is one of the central issues in your life. It is vitally important for you, and I might add, for your father as well, that the two of you put in some effort so that you might enjoy one another and mutually profit from your relationship.

K.H.Blacker, M.D.
Psychiatrist

Dear FYI: How can you stop a person from feeling like they're stupid and dumb if their parents constantly tell them so?

Discouraged

Dear Discouraged: What if your parents, instead of calling you stupid and dumb, said "Sorry you seem to be having trouble with this, let me help you," or "I think that's a mistake, let me show you how to do it better," or even "Look, kid, you are almost as stupid as I was at your age!"

Wouldn't that sound a lot nicer?

Well, I have a hunch that that's really what your parents mean to express, only (and unfortunately) they do it in a way which hurts you. Chances are that is the way their own parents talked to them, and maybe there are other reasons which keep them from expressing their affection in ways that could make you feel better rather than worse.

Do they have any sense of humor? What would happen if, next time they ask you why you are so stupid, you answer, "Because you have so much power over me, that when you call me stupid I just act that way."

I would suggest three steps.

First, try humor, and I hope that's all it takes. If that does not work put this question and answer on the dinner table at dessert time. If nothing helps and they keep putting you down, talk about it with your teacher, counselor or school psychologist. You have a right to be respected as a person and to be treated as such.

Lastly, and most importantly, the fact that you are sensitive enough to be hurt, had the courage to write, and a plan to do something about it proves one point -- you are *not* stupid.

Herbert Bauer

Dear FYI: How do you tell your family to please get along with one another? I am really afraid of my dad when he gets mad. He has a bad temper and how do I tell him without him getting mad to stop and think it over before he hurts someone?

Really Afraid

Dear Really Afraid: As much as you want to do the right thing, it is not your responsibility to solve your father's temper problem ... or to assume the family leadership role. If you get in the habit of assuming responsibility that is not yours, it will be continuing source of confusion for you in future relationships.

The reasons an adult loses control of his or her temper range from personal loss or life crisis to alcoholism/substance abuse, to a childhood history of abuse, to mental illness. You did not cause your father's problems.

Let others know about your situation and your fear. If immediate family members are unavailable, approach your clergyman, school counselor, teacher, a family friend or local crisis intervention agency. Keep trying until you find someone who listens and offers help.

Trust the adults to whom you have gone to determine the appropriate course of action. You have a right to a childhood free from fear of adult (physical or emotional) violence. Seek help! People care and will help you to find a solution.

Jay M. Feldman

> # How do you tell your family to please get along with one another? I am really afraid of my dad when he gets mad.

Dear FYI: My sister and I are always in conflict. I just cannot seem to get along with her. It is as though she is ashamed of our family, especially me. She constantly criticizes me and other members of the family. It seems as though she does not like to be seen with us. I try to get along with her, but she never tries to get along with me. Is there anything I can do to improve my relationship with her?

A Concerned Brother, Grade 11

Dear Concerned Brother: First, try to understand her point of view, maybe by talking with her or your parents. Try to find out if you are contributing to the problem in some way. Is there a grain of truth in her criticism?

(Continued on Page 103)

How do you help parents who are stressed out by their jobs or family situations?

Dear FYI: My father is the best, but his job sometimes stresses him out. I try and stay on his good side, but once in a while he just blows up. He has never beaten me or anything. What can I do to help? Or what can I do to avoid blowups?

Trying Hard

Dear Trying Hard: Your letter indicates that you're sensitive and caring. These are attributes that your father has probably noticed and presumably highly respects. A good sense of timing is another skill we all need -- the kind of timing that lets us recognize when another person is angry, sad or stressed out and when we need to give that person extra room and take his or her behavior with just an extra grain of salt.

Then, when someone like your dad appears to be more relaxed and calm, that's a good time to let him know how you feel when he blows up and how upsetting that behavior is for you. Finally, try to remember that we can't always be on someone's good side and that it is very important that we don't act falsely simply to maintain calm.

Jerry Plummer, MSW, MPA, BCD
Child psychologist

Sensitivity, caring and timing are skills necessary when approaching mom or dad about their problems. Be sure to give them extra room when approaching the subject.

It is very possible that the criticism may be your sister's way of trying to establish herself as an individual, rather than just being part of the family. Establishing an identity separate from the family is an important part of growing up. Teen-agers often prefer friends to family, and may not even want to be seen with their family in public.

Considering this, it may help to back off a little. When she criticizes, don't argue with her at length, or respond with a counterattack. The more you rely on your own opinion of yourself and your family, the less upsetting her criticism will be.

Roy Grabow, Ph.D.
Clinical psychologist

Dear FYI: My problem is that my parents don't approve of my having a boyfriend. They think I should wait until I'm out of college so I can concentrate on my school work. I've been managing my time and I'm getting good grades, but they still think I shouldn't get into a deep relationship. What can I do to change their minds?

Discouraged

Dear Discouraged: I'm wondering if you've already met a special friend and would like to spend more time with him.

If so, I suggest you speak about this honestly with your parents and ask what their particular concerns are. Whether or not you have a boyfriend, it's usually fun, as well as informative, to ask your parents what their lives were like at your age, and what their dating patterns were. This will help you understand their values and hopes and dreams. They seem to have your best interests in mind.

Boys are people too, and it's good to have friends of both sexes.

In the family cycle the teen years are the time that children start separating from parents in preparation for adult life. Going out from the family nest gradually and spending a reasonable time with peers is an appropriate expression of growing independence. Perhaps you could make a contract with your parents that you would continue studying a certain number of hours a week, and in return you can invite friends in. As your family meets and gets comfortable with them, it will be easier for them to allow you to expand your social life. If you continue to talk to your family about your problems, "dating" can give you an opportunity to get guidance from them as inevitable relationship problems emerge. Socialization can help make you a well-rounded, self-disciplined individual and guide you toward becoming the loving, mature adult your family wants you to be.

Pat Spake, MFCC
Marriage &
Family counselor

103

Dear FYI: My problem is that my parents won't let me go over to my boyfriend's house. His mom works and my parents think it's improper for me to be there without parental supervision. How can I get them to trust me enough to let me visit him?

Junior in High School

Dear Junior: Trust is an important issue for teens and their parents. It is the developmental task of teen-agers to become independent from their parents, ultimately forging adult identities. It is a parent's job to encourage these steps to gain full independence. At the same time, parents wish to protect teens from experiences they feel they are not ready for.

Parents must constantly struggle with how much freedom to allow. Too little freedom and the teen stays immature and fails to develop the necessary skills for independent living - or becomes resentful and alienated. Too much freedom and teens run the risk of encountering painful experiences which overwhelm them, or which they later regret. All families struggle, sometimes painfully, with these decisions.

Your letter raises some questions.

In general, do your parents consider your behavior trustworthy? How well do your parents know your boyfriend, and what do they think of him? Do you and your parents agree on what is appropriate sexual behavior for people your age?

To discuss this issue with your parents, first pick a time convenient for everyone. Find out everything you can about your parents' concerns. At this stage, you may agree with some of what they are saying or may learn some things you can do to make yourself more trustworthy in their eyes.

Don't lose your cool and do set another time for discussion. Hopefully, you and your parents will get a much clearer picture of what the problem is and a direction for resolution. If you cannot get their cooperation, or feel there is no way to have a reasonable discussion with them, you may need the help of a neutral third party.

Remember, a good, trusting relationship is built slowly.

Barbara Sherwood, LCSW
Psychotherapist

Further Suggested Reading

- Bassoff, Evelyn, *Mothers and Daughters: Loving and Letting Go.* Penguin Books, New York, N.Y., 1988
- Elchoness, Edward Monte, Jane Nelsen and Lynn Lott, *I'm on Your Side: Resolving Conflict with Your Teen-age Son or Daughter.* Prima Publications, Rocklin, Ca., 1991.
- Elkind, David, *All Grown Up and No Place to Go: Teen-agers in Crisis.* Addison-Wesley, Reading, MA., 1984.

- Krementz, Jill, *How it Feels When Parents Divorce*. Alfred A. Knopf, New York, 1984.
- Lansky, Vicki, *Vicki Lansky's Divorce Book for Parents: Helping your Child Cope with Divorce and its Aftermath*. Penguin Books, New York, 1989.
- Marone, Nicky, *How To Father a Successful Daughter*. Fawcett Crest, New York, 1988.
- Nelson, Jane and Lynn Lott, *I'm on Your Side: Resolving Conflict with Your Teen-age Son or Daughter*. Prima Publications, Rocklin, Ca., 1991.
- Pedersen, Anne and Peggy O'Mara (Mothering Magazine eds.), *Teens: A Fresh Look*. John Muir Publications, Santa Fe, N.M., 1991
- Richards, Arlene and Irene Willis, *How to Get it Together When Your Parents are Coming Apart*. Willard Press, Summit, N.J., 1976.
- Rydman, Edward J., *Finding the Right Counselor for You*. Taylor Publishing Co, Dallas, Tex., 1989.
- *Why Can't Anyone Hear Me?: A Guide for Surviving Adolescence*. Monroe Press, Sepulveda, Ca., 1986 (for parents and teens).
- The Scott Newman Center, *Straight Talk With Kids: Improving Communication, Building Trust, and Keeping Your Children Drug Free*. Bantam Books, New York, N.Y. 1991.
- Vedral, Joyce, *My Teen-ager is Driving Me Crazy*. Ballantine, New York, N.Y. 1989. See also: *My Parents are Driving Me Crazy*.

5

School days ... school 'daze?'

I don't know what to think. I've been friends with Diane since we were 5 years old. But two weeks in high school and she's a different person. Just yesterday... I couldn't believe it.

Her new "friends" were going to the mall. Invitations to Diane have always been automatic invitations for me. When she told me what she was doing, I told her "Great. It'll give me a chance to do some shopping for school. Maybe we can stay for dinner and see a movie."

Diane stopped in her tracks, looked me straight in the eye and said: "Oh, you've got it wrong. I'm going with Jackie and Mayleen. I don't think you were invited."

Stuck up? Trying to impress somebody? Did I do something? I'm confused ... and it's only the first month of high school!

Dear FYI: My daughter, a high school senior, has always been what I would call conscientious. Now she doesn't seem to study and mainly watches television (when she isn't on the phone).

It took constant nagging just to get her to apply to college and everything she did was just barely under the deadline. Her father is constantly "on her case" and I'm caught in the middle and about to lose my mind. What's wrong with my kid?

Frazzled

Dear Frazzled: High school seniors have a great many issues with which to deal -- perhaps these days more issues than ever. If your daughter appears less conscientious and motivated than usual, of course you are concerned, even when you know that this kind of response to pressures is very usual. Any marked personality change should be taken seriously, but it is indeed sometimes difficult to sort out what is part of an expected growing up process and what needs further investigation.

You have probably already noticed that constant nagging and "getting on her case" are counterproductive. You may want to ask these questions: Does she feel she has a problem? Does she have non-judgmental adults with whom she can confide in easily? Is she withdrawing from other interests, friends and activities?

Has her pattern of sleeping or eating changed? Is her physical health good? Is she in any real danger of failing to graduate?

The most likely reason for her becoming less conscientious and conforming is that she is making the difficult but essential transition from a good, obedient child to an autonomous adult capable of making her own choices and accepting the consequences of them. In the process she will no doubt make many decisions that are not what you or her father would choose. Both of you are being given one of the hardest and most important challenges of parenthood -- to maintain an open-arms policy.

When she moves away from you into adult independence you open your arms and give her your blessing, and when she moves toward you, your arms and your hearts are open to her, even if she has made choices that you see as unwise, hazardous or shortsighted.

If you feel her changed behavior is an indication of depression, then you may wish to have a consultation with a professional, even if she does not want to participate. Good luck to all three of you!

Nancy Du Bois,
Psychologist

Dear FYI: How do you deal with parents who are over-bearing about grades? My parents are never satisfied, and never give me a lot of support with my work. They tell me how I will never make it into a decent college and I have a high B average! Plus, I do a lot of extracurricular activities.

From Minus X

Dear Minus X: I am sorry to see that while your high school career seems satisfactory, you haven't pleased your parents -- and feel so badly about yourself that you sign yourself "Minus X."

The problem you have is a common one. Tension is often present between teenagers and parents because they do not share the same perspectives, goals or concerns. Frequently parents set high standards and they worry and criticize when the student does not meet them. Unfortunately this is not productive.

In fact, research has suggested that parental criticism may actually casue a decline in grades. Likewise, using money or privileges as rewards does not improve grades either. What works best is lots of encouragement from parents ... and assistance where needed.

Now to your question... What can you do? Have you talked with your parents about this at a time when all of you are calm? Try sharing your hopes, dreams and fears and ask them about their own and their hopes for you.

Sometimes parents have fears or unfulfilled dreams from their own growing up which cause them to over-react to their children. Clarifying this should make it easier for both of you. If you have a hard time talking with them, try showing them your letter.

If none of the above works maybe you could invite your parents to talk with you and a favorite teacher, minister or other person who knows you and whom your parents respect.

Ilana Davis, Ph.D.
Psychologist

Dear FYI: I consistently feel like all I do is go to school, participate in my sports, do my homework, and go to bed late after finishing my homework.

I never have enough time to eat, get rest, talk to people on the phone or be with my friends. I feel like just giving up. I want to do so many things and I don't have the time. I'm sick of remaining on my boring and monotonous schedule. What should I do?

Someone Who Needs a Change

Dear Needing a Change: You are busy! Perhaps you need to look at the time your school work and sports do take, and make sure that you are focusing on your work while you are "studying." You may be able to condense or change the time when you study your priority subjects so that you can slip in fun things and a short phone call or two each day.

You might check with your friends to arrange getting together at lunch-time or on the weekend, rather than during prime study time. Finishing an assignment during school hours might leave extra leisure time. And when assignments are given far in advance, you might think about collecting ideas in a notebook or making an outline of what you will do so you don't feel pressured at the last moment. If you have an efficiency plan for your schedule, you will, over time, find you can include things you really would like to do.

Rather than considering dinner-time an intrusion on your busy day, use it for relaxing and "touching base" with your family so that they know your needs and understand your pressures. Perhaps family members could give suggestions and constructive criticism on your expenditure of time. If not parents, try someone who will listen.

In reality, your task at this age is learning, but high school need not be monotonous and boring. This is a time for discovery. Consider whether you are really challenged to your physical and intellectual limits; if not, you may want to try a new sport or class just for the learning experience. Think about your life goals, and your parents' hopes for you, and see that you have a broad base for reaching these goals.

It often is difficult to balance school work, activities and socializing without feeling one of them is suffering. Hang in there ... look forward to vacations ... share your feelings with those who care about you ... give yourself permission for error ... and try to manage all the activities in your life with flexibility.

Ann Teal, LCSW
Psychotherapist

> *Consider whether you are really being challenged to your limits -- physical or intellectual. If not, you may want to try a new sport or class just as a learning experience.*

Dear FYI: I have a problem with school. I have five solid classes. Two of those are English classes. I'm also playing sports. I get out of school at 2:30 and then back to school for practice at 3:30. That goes until 5:30.

When I get home I'm really tired, but I have to do my homework which sometimes takes more than two hours. It's hard to keep my grades strong and play a sport. I'm also in two clubs. I want to do all these things to put them on my record for college. Is it really worth it to do all these things for my college record?

Burning Out

Dear Burning Out: There are some tough decisions ahead. You're obviously a hard worker and want to go to a good school, so apparently you've taken on a lot -- maybe too much.. While it is important to have a good high-school record, physical or mental exhaustion can undo all the goodwill and impression credits you're building.

You must keep a mental, physical and social balance.

Viewing your situation from afar, it's a good guess that something's got to give. Eliminating a "lesser" activity so the others don't suffer is advisable. Truly relaxing when you have some leisure time is a good idea. If you have a tough time being by yourself, just resting, there are a handful of good books that can help you discover techniques to relax.

What you're up against in high school is just the tip of the iceberg when it comes to college. Keep your goals lofty, but remember to take time out. Don't wear yourself so thin that you have nothing left to give.

FYI Editor

Dear FYI: Do you have any suggestions for relieving the tensions during college-application time. We have watched other families suffer through the process and would appreciate any tips you can give us.

Concerned Parents and Offspring

Dear Concerned Parents and Offspring: Nothing can totally eliminate the stress and tension associated with applying for college admissions, but consideration of the following might help...

1. Plan ahead. Applying to college is a time-consuming process, so don't wait for deadlines; get things in early. Rushing at the last minute can cause major stress and tension;

2. Prepare to file multiple applications. Many colleges cannot admit all applicants -- not even all qualified applicants. As a result, it is not wise to apply to only one college. Consider at least two or three colleges that would be acceptable. Consider one college that is highly selective, one where chances of selection are greater and yet a third in which you are comfortably sure you will be accepted.

(Keep in mind the opportunities available in community colleges where all high school graduates can complete lower division college work and transfer as juniors to four-year institutions. Many have guaranteed transfer contracts that assure admission to the four-year college you prefer. Community colleges accept applications until late in the spring semester);

3. Be realistic in college selection. Colleges have unique qualities and characteristics. So do students. Try to find the best match. Does your daughter function better under pressure or in a less competitive atmosphere? Does your son enjoy large classes, crowded campuses, and the fast pace of an urban

environment, or is he most comfortable in a smaller more rural setting? Do college costs fall within the family's financial situation? Does the college offer a variety of academic programs and majors that suit your son or daughter?

4. Pay attention to detail. Read applications carefully and complete them accurately. If an essay is required, start writing it early and stick to the topic. Well before deadlines, take necessary entrance tests, file application forms, request transcripts and request letters of recommendation from teachers and counselors, if required.

Once you have selected a few colleges, carefully completed your application forms and mailed them off, feel good knowing that you have done your best. Then celebrate!

One caution to your senior sons and daughters ... keep up efforts in your studies throughout the year. Colleges will see and evaluate your final high school transcripts.

Carol Boyer, MA
High school counselor

Dear FYI: I read with interest your question and answer about the pressures of getting ready to apply for college. Now I would like to ask some other questions. What about the kids who are not going to college? How do they make plans? How do they deal with the stigma of not going to college?

Concerned Parent

Dear Concerned Parent: Frankly, each of your questions, while quite related to each other, could take several pages to answer! Here's a broad response.

I suggest the following for the making of all plans for those kids not going to college: Any planning, involving college or not, needs to cover basic needs, both physical and emotional. There is no essential difference in the planning needs for those attending college from those who are not. Concern, affection and support are needed equally in both cases.

The "stigma" to which you refer is both an unnecessary and hugely unfortunate one. Not everyone wishes to enter college (especially right after high school) and not everyone has life plans requiring a formal college education. It is certainly true that college can be rewarding for someone who wishes to be there, but not everyone has that wish and that ability.

Neither of these need to represent a lack of intelligence, personal drive or, for that matter, a lack of ability to enter college later if desired.

One of the most critical things we can teach our kids and ourselves is how to decide what it is we would most like to do in life, and to figure out the best path for getting there. If college is not part of that path -- fine.

Dear FYI College-Bound Readers: If you're swamped with application forms, save yourself aggravation by photocopying all your forms *before* filling them out. Make a trial copy *and* have extras should you need them.

A Practical Parent

Are there other types of classes or courses that would help?

Again, the critical thing is to allow the creation of the most interesting and accessible options available.

My sincere hope is that any stigma created by not attending college is more than compensated for by the development of goals and plans that allow the most fulfilling life possible.

College is not something everyone needs to enter, although it can be highly enjoyable and useful. However, a full and fulfilling life is something we all have a right to enter. Let's help with that.

And just a quick note about *high school* graduation...

Whether or not one is planning to go to college, it is imperative that youngsters at least set their sights on a high school diploma. While not everyone needs a college degree to succeed in the workplace, if one tries to earn a living without a high school degree, he or she is starting with two strikes.

It's important to at least finish high school.

Christopher Bauer, Ph.D.,
Clinical psychologist

Dear FYI: Is it better to go to a large college or a small one?

Can't Decide

Dear Can't Decide: You are wise to know that college size is one of the major questions to address in choosing a college. We suggest that you investigate one or more of the books called "college guides." They can be found in your school's career center, your school or local library and most book stores. Also talk to your school counselor for ideas.

FYI editor

FYI asked students to answer a key question about high school...

Dear Someone or Anyone Now in High School: I am going to start high school next year and I am getting more and more concerned each day. I don't know what to do. I don't know how to act, or how to dress. I'm worried about someone trying to get me to use or sell drugs, finding my way around and making friends. How do I know where I'll fit in or even if I will? Can you help me, please.

Scared

Dear Scared: Going into high school isn't a real big thing. Sure you're going to be scared, but that's perfectly natural. How should you act? Just be yourself - don't try to impress anybody or be like anybody. Dress in clothes that are you, fit your personality and are comfortable. Keep this in mind and you'll do fine.

Sincerely, Someone

Dear Scared: Don't worry about the drug scene. It is highly uncommon that you will be offered drugs, but if so don't take them. No one will say a thing. *The Stud*

Dear Scared: First of all you've got to know you're not the only person just starting high school! Have you got an older brother or sister or friend that's going there or just graduated who could show you around? If you don't find any friends on the first day don't sweat it. You've got plenty of time and if they're snobs they probably weren't fit to be a friend of yours anyway. Peace! *Ms. Ann*

Dear Scared: Whatever you do, don't flunk. It's a drag going to summer school. You can't sleep in, no free time. It tires you out. Don't listen to what other people say, do what you feel is right. *Jesse*

Dear Scared: Try not to be scared, you'll survive just fine. Act normal and try not to make it look as though you are new. Little by little you'll make friends -- they'll come around. *Sue*

Dear Scared.: If doing drugs ain't your style, don't hang around with a crowd that does drugs. Most kids don't even pressure you into drugs. They normally ask you if you want some of whatever drug they are doing. If you say no then they will say fine, more for us. *Joseph*

Dear FYI: I want to get a part-time job for the summer. When should I start applying? How important is job experience in getting a job? I am a senior in high school.

Job Hunter

Dear Job Hunter: There are several sources that you should use to get a part-time job and you should start preparing to use these sources now.

Successful temporary employment is one opportunity that may develop into a permanent part-time job and/or summer position. If you have the opportunity to work and are available during the holiday season, that will be one way you can gain some employment experience.

Some of the sources that you should consider using are the telephone yellow pages, business directories, newspaper help-wanted ads, your city's teen job program (if any), your state Employment Development Department and the

 Work Experience Education office at your school (if it has one). You should begin to develop your plans after the holiday rush. Many employers will be making summer staffing plans between that time and the increased business activity that begins when spring arrives.

A few helpful hints: dress appropriately, go by yourself (no friends), be positive, be prepared (names, addresses, telephone numbers), keep a record (where you apply, when you apply, to whom you spoke and, most important, follow up until you get a yes or no). A resume is recommended.

George R. Fleming,
Work experience coordinator

Further Suggested Reading

• Bingham, Mindy et al, *Choices: A Teen Woman's Journal for Self-Awareness and Personal Planning.* Advocacy Press, Santa Barbara, Ca., 1985, updated 1990. See also "Challenges" for boys.

• Campbell, David, *If you Don't Know Where You're Going, You'll Probably End Up Somewhere Else*, Tabor Publications. Allen, Tx., rev. ed. 1990.

6

It isn't always you

When Karen got home that afternoon, she could barely think or talk she was so tired from her day at school.

No one had yet asked her to tomorrow's dance. Senior kids were picking on her and her friends. She spilled milk on her blouse at lunch and she felt like an idiot -- walking around all afternoon with that big splotch on her front.

It's tough enough just trying to cope with physical changes when you're 15 years old -- braces, growing pains, reactions to new emotions -- but all that other junk at school was too much.

Karen settled back on the couch, stared at the ceiling and began to cry. "Why me? Why *always* me?"

Not that it's consolation to Karen after she's had this bad day, but she shouldn't worry a whole lot about these tough days at school. There are a lot of people Karen's age dealing with the same problems ... and, mercifully, Karen will outgrow many of them while others may turn out not to be as big as they first seemed.

Dear FYI: Why do older students pick on younger students? They were in that grade before, wouldn't they figure that you feel the same way? Just because we are shorter, younger or even look like a toothpick doesn't make us dumb.

A Seventh-Grader

Dear Seventh-Grader: Sure it's the pits being at the bottom of the pecking order. You're wondering why they don't behave in a rational manner. This can really be a useful demonstration to you that people usually do what their feelings dictate and not what is necessarily reasonable.

People (not just older students) pick on other people -- discriminate against them, invade their countries -- most often out of fear. The person who is secure and getting what he or she needs in life has no need to find a scapegoat. When people grow up and feel they are in charge of their lives, they usually give up bullying.

117

However, as the victim of these bullies, it may be some help to remember that their behavior says a lot about them (they're troubled) ... and very little about who or what you are. Also, it will help you avoid the same pattern when you are the bigger or stronger one.

Nancy DuBois,
Psychologist

Dear FYI: Why are girls so bossy?

Annoyed Guy, 12

Dear Annoyed: That's easy to answer.

All girls are bossy because all boys always think that all girls always are bossy. If someone presented you with such a vast generalization, you would probably say, "Don't be silly. Just because you met two or three bossy ones, that does not mean all of them are."

What does the word actually mean to you? What's "bossy" for one, might be prudent for another. For instance, when you were a small child, did your mother give you as many cookies as you wanted? Of course not. At that moment she may have looked mean and bossy to you, but all she did was to keep you from getting a bellyache.

If you look at it that way, you may discover that most girls are really nice to have around. You may even try one of these days to have a date with one of them. I hope you will be pleasantly surprised.

Herbert Bauer, M.D.
Psychiatrist

Dear FYI: Why do people often tease and make fun of people who aren't popular? By "popular" I mean the people with all the "in" clothes who throw parties with lots of booze, have nice cars and lots of money.

What is wrong with nice people who have fun without expensive thrills or booze? Or does it matter what they think?

Eleventh-Grader

Dear Eleventh-Grader: A person who would tease others in the way you imply often feels insecure.

Conformity to the pressures of a group is often used as a method of feeling less insecure. Kids who don't have very high self-esteem have a hard time accepting others who are different from themselves.

They try to make themselves look better by putting others down. I'd say their opinions of you don't matter much. Be true to yourself.

Carol Cotton, MFCC
Marriage & family counselor

Dear FYI: I am a good gymnast ... at least I think I am. But anyway, when I joined a gymnastics training program I thought, wow, this is pretty neat. Not everybody can do this.

Then when I was at school we had to do an oral report on "What's your favorite sport?" When my classmates found out I was in gymnastics they called me "fag," "gay," "girl," "sissy" and all kinds of names. I felt so bad I felt like having no reason to live, for to this day they still call me names, and at night I ask God why those people call me names and act so cruel?

I haven't done anything wrong to anybody. Why do they do that?

Hurting

Dear Hurting: There is never a very satisfactory reason for name-calling. Of the many reasons, the common thread is that the person doing the name-calling somehow feels better at the expense of someone else. Name-calling is often due to jealousy, and perhaps your classmates are envious of your skills. Name-calling can also be the result of some unnecessary but imagined threat. This is often the case when slurs are directed toward others who are "different."

The best thing you can do to stop this is to ignore the silly remarks of your classmates.

If they see that you are not affected by their behavior, they are likely to stop.

Remember, it is awful but true that those most frequently teased are the ones who get visibly upset by it.

Turn your attention to your skills and achievements in gymnastics. You have every right to enjoy and be proud of them.

Christopher Bauer, Ph.D.
Clinical psychologist

Dear FYI: My parents are on a trip and I am staying at home alone. My friends want me to have a party with lots of beer.

My parents left strict orders not to have any parties. If I don't, my friends will make me an outcast. What should I do?

Confused

Dear Confused: These types of pressures can be both confusing and angering. By asking to use your parents' house against their wishes, your friends are asking you to choose between their respect and the respect of your parents -- even, perhaps, your respect of yourself. Being asked to make such a choice is unfair. Hopefully, such a choice is unnecessary.

Your friends are going to be able to find another place to party, if they decide that partying is what they want. You must, of course, decide whether or not you want to join them. In addition, you must decide for yourself whether or not you are going to drink. "Just say no" sounds much easier than it often is. Still, it is the best tool there is.

Taking a stand against one's friends is always difficult. However, a true friend is able to respect a different feeling or point of view.

Christopher Bauer

Dear FYI: I have a best friend who is going out with another good friend of mine. I hang out with them sometimes and I have a lot of fun. It's just that I can't handle it when I'm sitting or standing alone and they're kissing right in front of me. I try not to say anything, but it's hard. What should I do?

Jealous

Dear Jealous: It would be surprising if you *didn't* feel excluded and hurt. Imagine if you were a threesome and the two others kept talking in a language you didn't speak. Do you think you would be comfortable just telling your friend that as much as you enjoy being with them, you feel left out when they do that? It might be something that your best friend is totally unaware of, wrapped up (no pun intended) as she is with her boyfriend.

Nancy DuBois

Dear FYI: My best friend recently started going with a guy and really loves him. We've been getting farther and farther apart. She rarely spends time with me anymore -- and when she does, she goes on and on about her boyfriend for hours.

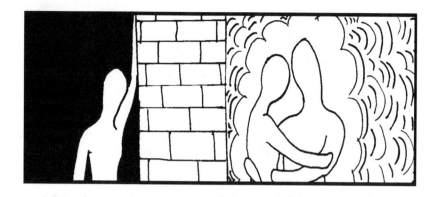

It's frustrating because sometimes I need some advice or just want to talk to her, but she always seems to be in some other world. I'm feeling quite lonely. What should I do to have her know that I'm still alive?

Left Out

Dear Left Out: You are describing a painful experience that happens at some time to everyone from teens to senior citizens. It is natural at this time to feel left out, lonely and confused. We all need our friends, although sometimes we don't realize it. Your friend will most likely be back. Hopefully, when she comes back you won't be so mad that there is no friend for her to come back to.

The most important thing is to talk to your friend about your hurt feelings and the fact that you miss her company. Recognizing each other's feelings can be especially important when relationships are changing. Maybe you can work out some time to be together; time that will feel good to both of you. But for now don't expect your friend to go back to the way things were.

This may be an excellent time for you to expand your important support network or get involved in an activity you've always thought about but never got around to doing.

Most likely, when you find a boyfriend whom you really like, you may also have a hard time balancing your desire to be with this special person as much as possible and finding time for your friends as well. It is important for all of us to remember *not* to drop our old friends when a new romance comes along. We need them. For one thing, the other relationship may break up. More importantly, a healthy, long-term relationship requires that both people be separate individuals with their own friends and interests. If we are there for our friends now, they will be there for us when we need them.

Barbara Sherwood, LCSW
Psychotherapist

121

Dear FYI: I have been a loner most of my life and would like to change. I like people a lot but never seem able to communicate with them or make friends. I see people every day that I would like to be friends with, but I never can bring myself to introduce myself or just say "hi."

My problem started in grade school. There I would try to make friends with other kids or be in their games, only to be left out or ignored most of the time. This led me to adopt an aloof attitude toward them. I thought that if I felt better than them, being left out would not hurt as much.

Unfortunately, this caused me to become stuck-up. I've dropped this negative attitude since then, but I'm afraid that people still think I'm this way. I've tried hard to overcome my paranoia, but it still exists. I would appreciate any advice you could give me to help me overcome my problem.

In Need of Friends

Dear In Need of Friends: You describe a difficult but common problem that can be overcome, but will take a lot of time and constant effort on your part. Your past haughty, aloof attitude is a frequent ploy of shy people in order to protect themselves in advance from expected rebuffs.

First, let me commend you for recognizing your problem and encourage you to work hard at changing this basic attitude. Your life will be much richer and have more meaning if you can enable yourself to become more involved with others.

Second, you must not be discouraged easily. You will experience hurt and frustration as you attempt to change. "Faint heart never won fair lady," nor close friends.

Third, you will be most able to try out new ideas and behaviors if you feel secure. If you enjoy music, auto mechanics, sports, electronics or whatever, use this activity as a setting from which to reach out and make friends. You'll already have something in common. Discuss your feelings with your family and practice your new approach with them.

Often seeing a psychotherapist is helpful. The time, energy and money spent in such an effort is an excellent investment if it enables you to broaden your personal world.

K.H. Blacker, M.D.
Psychiatrist

Dear FYI: My problem is that I cannot relate to people since moving recently to a new town. I have never felt so alone in a group of people. I realize that there are "cliques" in any community, but that's not all.

I have friends but am unable to communicate with them. Everyone seems to be hung up on being "cool," and no one seems able to really express themselves. They seem afraid of discussing their inner feelings. I have yet to have a deep and meaningful conversation with anyone.

I have tried to break the ice, but people are unresponsive. Please give me your advice.

Unrelated

Dear Unrelated: Join the crowd. Many people in communities new to them feel like you. I hope you'll be reassured to know that your feelings are shared by many others.

The size of the community does not matter: you can be lonesome in a tiny village, and you can feel relaxed and in good company in a huge metropolis. What really matters is how you feel about yourself. Even when you are alone with yourself, you should still feel in good company.

There are many ways -- besides verbal -- to communicate: letters, flowers, invitations to share a funny show or an ice cream. Don't start an acquaintance by discussing "inner feelings." Folks normally don't want to be too serious until later in the relationship. Try a little humor and conversations will come easier. Good luck and happy relating!

Herbert Bauer

Dear FYI: I feel neglected by my friends. I think I have nothing in common with them anymore. I can't tell this to anyone. What can I do? What are some good ideas for making new friends that may share some interests with me?

Neglected

Dear Neglected: Before I try to answer your question about making new friends, I'm wondering whether there might be something else going on in your life?

Sometimes when it seems we're being neglected by others, it's a sign of depression. Family trouble or loss of a loved one or other significant problems can reduce self-esteem and interest in things we ordinarily enjoy. If this is true in your case, I can't suggest too strongly that you talk to someone: a school counselor, for example (despite your fear that you can't).

As to ways of making new friends with common interests, the most obvious way is to take a close look at what you enjoy and see if there is some sort of organized group in your school or off campus that you can join. It can sometimes be hard to find a group already made for you, however, and you may need to "advertise."

(Continued on Page 126)

What makes you really angry?

When people won't believe me.

When my parents interrupt me when I'm talking. They always interrupt just after they tell me not to interrupt!

I don't get angry, I get even.

If someone lies to me about something very important, and when someone innocent like a baby or kid dies.

When my mom still treats me like a small child and wants to go to the mall with me. Also, when she expects me to cancel all my plans so we can go on some embarrassing family outing.

When older students pick on us younger ones.

When parents and teachers tell you what is best for you without even asking how you feel.

When I feel I've been treated unfairly.

When grandma favors my little sister.

When my dad drinks. It's one drink after another.

When I think about the homeless. Something should be done about it.

My mother always is nagging me. She repeats everything at least 20 times!

To see discrimination of any kind, and when somebody judges you without getting to know you first.

That money is spent on foreign countries when that money could be used for the homeless and all the people starving in our own country.

124

My mom asks questions about everything. She is really nosy. I know she has the right to know certain things in my life, but I also need my own privacy as well. I tell her that a lot, but she never seems to understand.

When a guy pressures a girl into having sex with him.

When my sports don't get equal treatment or as much recognition because it's a girl's team.

When a friend tells others your secrets.

When everybody is on my case. Parents trying to get me to get straight A's, teachers about everything from assignments to being on time, and friends about going out or getting drunk or high. I hate it all.

To be yelled at or lectured to. Also, I get angry because I can't stop smoking. It is the most stupid thing I have done and I'm angry at myself because I'm the one suffering now.

When my girlfriend flirts with other guys.

Puberty. And when my mom talks to me about going through it.

When a new person comes to school and they don't have a very good appearance but they are very nice, and people won't give them a chance to be friends.

When my parents tell me not to do something and then they do it.

When people start to say something and then say "never mind."

You might start by looking around school for a few people who dress and act pretty much like you do and go up to one or two of them and start a conversation. You might say, "Where did you get that...?" or "Do you know where I might be able to find...?" Give them a chance to feel knowledgeable and comfortable and see where the conversation goes. Then begin to mention your interests and see if theirs match. The conversation should take care of itself. If not, try someone else.

It can be hard to take such initiative, but the person who takes the initiative is the person who gets to do the choosing.

Bonnie Wilson, Ph.D.
Marriage, family &
Child counselor

Dear FYI: This year I suddenly seem to be breaking off from my friends. We don't get along very well anymore. How can I leave that group without having them all hate me?

Breaking Off

Dear Breaking Off: Tastes in friends, like our tastes in other things, change sometimes. It may be that mutual interests have decreased, or that personal needs or values may have changed. All of these can affect the course of friendship. Hopefully, none of these changes requires any angry response from your friends. They may be puzzled or sad about the decrease or loss of your friendship - after all, what kind of friends would they be if they didn't care about your distance or absence? However, talking about these changes, without putting anyone down, significantly reduces the chances of anger.

When we have difficulties with one or two people within a group, it can result in rejection of the whole group. There is probably no problem in keeping up a friendship with one or even several friends from your old group. Remember, friendship groups often overlap. Also, true friends will accept your changing needs even if, at times, it affects their relationship with you.

Christopher Bauer

Dear FYI: Recently I've been feeling really bad about myself. All my friends say I've changed and they don't want to be around me anymore. I don't know what I did or how to change it. All I know is that I spend a lot of time alone. What am I doing wrong?

Down & Out

Dear Down & Out: It is very painful when your friends abandon you, and you find yourself trying to work things out alone. It is especially difficult when you aren't sure why they don't want to be around you. I'm concerned that you, may be blaming yourself when you aren't doing anything wrong.

Good friends who care about someone usually are willing to talk about a problem. Once you have some specifics you'll be in a better position to work things out with your friends. If they aren't willing to talk to you, you should find some other person (like your folks or a school counselor) with whom you can share your concerns or feelings. Talking will help you feel better about yourself.

Kathryn Jaeger, Ph. D.
Psychologist

Dearest FYI: Whenever my best friend has a problem or is in trouble, I am always ready to listen. But when I have a problem or want to talk to her, she seems annoyed and always changes the subject. What can I do?

A Little Hurt

Dear A.L.H.: Ask your friend for attention. Try something like: "I need you to listen to me."

We all forget that people don't know what we need unless we tell them. You might also say, "I don't want you to solve my problem, just hear it and talk about it with me." However, your friend may feel uncomfortable with the idea of your having problems. She might want to see you as the strong one -- problemless -- always ready to listen to her. You could ask her if this is the case.

Finally, your friend may not be willing to play the listener role, and you may not be able to change her. Still, because she is your best friend, it will be worth talking about this instead of just keeping the hurt inside.

Edith Rothchild, MSW & LCSW
Psychotherapist

Dear FYI: What can I do for my friend if I know she is a shoplifter? I have been with her a couple of times when she has done this and I told her how I felt, but she won't listen.

Wanting to Play It Safe

Dear Wanting: You have good reason to be concerned. Shoplifting often is associated with problems of self-esteem, relationship problems and family problems. However, your friend may feel embarrassed or not even perceive her behavior as a problem.

I suggest you talk again with your friend, privately. Reassure her that you like her and value her friendship. Tell her that you are concerned about her taking things from stores, and that you want her to be able to stop, so that she doesn't endanger herself.

Tell her that you don't think her shoplifting makes her a bad person, but that you can see it as a serious issue with which she needs to deal. People who shoplift, or can't stop other potentially self-defeating habits (for example, gambling, over-spending) can receive help from a trained therapist. Suggest that if she can't stop herself, she should get help from a counselor.

Let your friend know that you will not be a part of her shoplifting and will not go to stores with her if this behavior continues. Find other ways to be with her. This will give her the message that not only do you not support her shoplifting, you are protecting yourself.

Stay firm, even if your friend gets angry with you. Yours is a genuine, healthy and caring concern. She is fortunate to have a friend like you.

Renee Dryfoos, Ph.D.
Clinical psychologist

Dear FYI: A friend of mine got really drunk at a party and went upstairs with a guy. I didn't want to go up and stop them because it would be dumb. Now she's not sure if she's pregnant or not and blames me because I was sober and she wasn't. She thinks I should have stopped her. What should I do and say?

Person in Distress

Dear Person in Distress: The situation you describe is not unusual. It is very difficult to know how to handle such an issue and to feel that you have done exactly the right thing. As a matter of fact, there is probably no exactly right way to handle such a situation.

You must realize you are not responsible for the actions of your friend -- in spite of her showing poor judgment. You are not responsible for your friend's drunkenness. She is.

Ditto with having sex (presumably unprotected) with the young man. Most likely she would have spurned your efforts to stop her behavior, and a scene would have erupted.

Please do not allow your friend to place any guilt on you. I am certain that you would have liked to prevent the situation if you could have, and if it was appropriate for you to do so. It is clear that you could not. Remember, you cannot assume responsibility for your friend's actions.

A final note: Whether or not your friend is pregnant, she may want to be tested for sexually transmitted diseases, including the AIDS virus.

Elwood E. Morgan, M.D.
Psychiatrist

Dear FYI: What do I say to a friend who tells me that her divorced parent is getting married again? I don't really think "congratulations" is the proper response, so what is?

Wanting an Answer

Dear Wanting: It would be most appropriate for you simply to ask your friend how she feels about her parent's forthcoming marriage.

This will give her a chance to share the very mixed emotions she may be experiencing. Putting feelings into words is a valuable way to sort out emotions, and sharing with friends is good for everyone's mental health.

FYI editor

Dear FYI: What should you say to comfort a friend when she tells you her parents might get a divorce?

Wanting to Help

Dear Wanting to Help: First let your friend talk as much as she is willing about her thoughts and feelings concerning her parents' marital problems and what she anticipates in the event of a divorce.

Try not to voice your own opinions about divorce, but listen carefully to your friend and offer her as much understanding as you can.

Divorce is a crisis which takes different shapes in different families, and always involves loss. Sometimes the feelings of pain, anger, guilt and sadness over the family breakup are so long-standing and/or intense that people need to seek professional help. Groups for children of divorce are available in some school systems.

You can be of most help if you will listen to your friend throughout the many stages of her family's change.

Renee Dryfoos

Dear FYI: I'm one of those people who regularly does most of their homework. I put in some effort to complete it, and it has bothered me for some time that my friends always ask to borrow it so they can copy it.

I want to keep my friendships, but...

I am upset that they think they don't have to do the work, but rely on me to do it for them. What can I do?

Morally Disturbed

Dear Disturbed: As difficult as it may be, you need to say NO. True friends do not ask to copy or give out their work for copying purposes. The person copying will run into trouble on tests -- and since tests are usually weighted more than homework -- he or she will not benefit in the long run.

Since copying is simply cheating, both students have guilt and worry. Teachers were not born yesterday. Once they know that your friends cheat and you allow it, it will be difficult for you all to regain the trust they had in you previously.

Collaboration is another matter. If you work separately and then get together or exchange papers to check results, there are benefits to both able and less-able students. It takes maturity to walk the line between collaboration and copying.

Ann Studer, BA, MST
High school teacher

Dear FYI: I'm 15. I love looking through magazines and buying clothes and getting really good bargains. I try very hard to look nice and I think I do. My problem is that when someone tells me I look nice or they like what I'm wearing, I always feel embarrassed and usually say something stupid. Do you have any suggestions?

Embarrassed

Dear Embarrassed: You certainly aren't alone in finding it hard to accept a compliment. Many of us -- well over 15 -- still struggle to accept compliments gracefully. For some reason, perhaps because we're afraid we'll appear egotistical, compliments often leave us feeling that we must say something self-effacing in return: "It's really a little tight for me..."

What can you do about it? Practice, practice, practice!

Practice smiling and saying a simple "thank you." The first times are the hardest, but after a while you may even have a real feeling of accomplishment as you realize you have conquered your habit of feeling you have to "put down" yourself or the compliment.

FYI editor

Dear FYI: I was wondering how to become less shy. It interferes with my getting friends and doing things. Another thing ... how do people become shy in the first place?

One Shy Cat

Dear Shy Cat: I want to let you in on a well-kept secret: almost everyone we know is shy about something, whether it's talking in front of a group, meeting new people, going on a date, attending a party, and so on. Shyness usually reflects uncertainty or lack of confidence.

Shyness becomes a real problem when it keeps us from doing something necessary or personally meaningful -- like dating, making friends and being active socially.

Here are some suggestions to help you overcome your shyness:

1. Try to maintain eye contact with the person you're talking to.

2. Be a good listener. You don't need to be the person doing all the talking.

3. Let a good friend know how you feel; and then both of you could go together to the same event you feel shy about.

4. Practice in private to increase your confidence. For example, you might rehearse a speech in front of a mirror or practice dance steps in the privacy of your room.

5. When going into a situation you feel shy about, try to have a plan for yourself. For instance,"At this party I want to meet four new people. Or, "I want to dance at least two times." A plan helps you to focus on your goals instead of your shyness.

Good luck, and remember, you are not alone.

Jerry Plummer, MSW, MPA, BCD
Child psychiatrist

Dear FYI: I can't dance. What should I do?

A Wallflower

Dear Wallflower: The main elements preventing anyone from dancing are fear and self-consciousness. Knowledge helps greatly in changing fear into fun and self-consciousness into self-confidence.

Dance can be self-taught, learned through a friend or by taking dance classes.

I, too, had difficulty getting onto a dance floor at first. I would watch the dancers from the sidelines, learn the step, then go into the men's room and practice the step, return and watch and learn another. After three dances, I finally mustered the courage to ask a girl to dance. I've been enjoying dance, one of the greatest social sports, ever since.

Jere Curry, MA
Dance instructor

Dear FYI: How do you know whether or not your social life is "normal?"

Wondering

Dear Wondering: "Normal" or "average" are probably not very useful standards of measure for a social life. If you are comfortable with the number and quality of the friendships you have, then your needs are being met. If someone tells you that you should be more "outgoing," or that you have too many or too few friends, it's useful to hear them out, but your style of preferred social life is a unique choice that is yours to make.

Nancy DuBois

Dear FYI: I am told by school counselors that junior high is the most difficult time psychologically for young people. How can I help my daughter deal with the changes in friendships, self-criticism and other psychological traumas that occur during this time?

Junior High Parent

Dear Junior High Parent: Seeing our children experiencing stress or pain is one of the most difficult tasks parents encounter.

We want to spare them these experiences and often would gladly assume them ourselves ... if that were possible. But we also know that children develop self-confidence and increased self-esteem as they deal with their challenges and problems.

We can help our children best by acting as resources for them, while essentially allowing them to exercise their own skills (or develop new ones) as they struggle with the demands of this exciting and difficult period.

To be an effective resource for your daughter:

1. Keep communication open. Let your daughter know you are available to listen to her concerns about any areas of life. Then, do just that: listen with acceptance and very little judgment so she sees you as a person she can turn to.

2. Show confidence in her ability to handle difficulties. Convey an attitude that says "I'm confident that you'll be able to work this out, let me know what you decide to do." Be sure to discuss the alternatives available. All this will help give your young person a sense of competence and self-reliance which will stand her in good stead in the daily decisions she faces.

3. Model your own problem-solving and coping strategies. Our children always learn most from what we actually do. If you are one who handles pressures, stresses and even disappointments from friends with some equanimity, you will be providing your daughter with an invaluable model for dealing with these events at any age.

You may also help by staying in close touch with school personnel and with the requirements of her junior high program. By becoming well informed and by remaining her back-up resource, you will be in a good position to help your daughter enjoy junior high.

Marilyn Roland, Ph.D., MFCC
Family therapist

Dear Junior High Parent: I read with empathy your letter to FYI, remembering how difficult those junior high years were with my daughters. With all the physical and emotional changes taking place during this time, junior high girls are so vulnerable. Yet they can be so cruel to one another. And the unstable nature of their friendships just increases their feelings of worthlessness and insecurity.

I'd really like to give you a hug and tell you just be there for your daughter. Listen to her, love her, hug her -- and in every way you can, let her know how valuable she is as a person. Look at this period of time as a lesson in coping. Believe me, it does get better.

Been There

Dear FYI: Why are there homeless people?
V.F.

133

Dear V.F. and R.H.: Right now there are many more people who have only $500 or less a month to spend on rent than there are apartments and houses in that price range. So, just like a game of musical chairs where someone ends up with no chair to sit in, some people end up without a place to live.

It is not a complete game of chance, however. The people who end up homeless, for one reason or another, cannot compete well with other renters. Here are just a few of the reasons people are homeless.

1. A single mother without a high-school diploma cannot make enough money to pay for rent, utilities, food and child care.

2. A family has been evicted for failing to pay rent in the past and landlords are reluctant to rent to them again.

3. A low-income family with an old car has spent too much money on car repairs, insurance and gasoline to be able to pay the rent. The family feels they need the car to function.

4. A single person has lost his or her job because of alcoholism.

5. A mentally ill person has had a mix-up with his or her aid check and doesn't have anyone to turn to for help.

There are two things you can do. First, as a student, learn and educate. Most people approach a problem like homelessness from a preconceived political viewpoint. However, the closer we get to the problem, the more we seem to agree on solutions ... and there *are* solutions.

You can learn by volunteering, for example, at a homeless shelter or food kitchen; by doing a school research paper; or by reading all you can about homeless people and what they face. Once you learn, you can share information with others.

Second, there may be students at your school who are homeless from time to time or who live in garages, cars or motels. The homeless kids we see don't have pencils or binder paper, a place to wash their clothes, this year's styles, blow dryers, and so on. They don't have a place to get a good night's sleep and to get cleaned up in the morning.

So when you hear other kids being critical of someone who isn't clean or stylish, don't join in. Be understanding and help your friends build a value system that isn't based on money and appearances. If homeless kids feel accepted, by even a few others, it may encourage them to stay in school -- and that's important in ending homelessness.

Mary McCurdy, MSW, director
Mission & homeless program

Dear FYI; Can you tell me how to help a friend of a friend who is homeless? He always changes places and sometimes he just sleeps outside. I know he wants to go home, but he hasn't enough money. I feel really sad for him. Give me some help and I'll try to send him in the right direction.

Sad

Dear Sad: Tell your friend about a program called Greyhound and Trailway's Home Free. The number is 1-800-448-4663 (1-800-HIT-HOME) and operates 24 hours a day, seven days a week. If you are on the street and have no charges against you, go to a police station and tell them you want to go home. If possible, contact your parents or another relative first to make sure your name is on the National Crime Information Center Computer as a missing person. If you cannot do this, the police can help you with the process. Once you are on the list, the officer will conduct you to the bus terminal to arrange a free ticket home with no arrest or fine.

FYI editor

Further Suggested Reading

• Lang, Denise V., *But Everyone Looks So Sure of Themselves: A Guide to Surviving the Teen Years*. Betterway Publications, Crozet, VA., 1991.
• Shepherd, Scott, *What Do You Think of You? And Other Thoughts on Self-Esteem*. CompCare Publishers, Minneapolis, 1990.

7

From acne to athlete's foot

I've lived with this condition for three years. Itchy toes, smelly feet, cracking skin between the toes. I didn't know there was a simple step I could take to control the problem ... until a friend told me that he read that athlete's foot was common and easy to stop. I found it helps to read -- and listen to friends...

Dear FYI: I have a friend on the football team and he takes steroids. He doesn't play much but he thinks it helps him. What can I do to stop him? He won't listen to me.

Worried Friend

Dear FYI: Can there be extensive damage to your organs if you take steroids for two months?

Worried

Dear Worried and Worried Friend: Anabolic steroids are similar to the male sex hormone testosterone, but don't have as pronounced masculinizing effects.

They cause an increase of muscle bulk and strength if combined with weight lifting. They are used primarily by weightlifters, bodybuilders and for sports primarily involving strength rather than endurance or technique.

Risks from anabolic steroids include liver damage, liver tumors, heart disease and stroke.

Injecting steroids has the potential life-threatening risks of hepatitis and AIDS.

In men, steroids can cause infertility and impotence. In women, steroids can cause development of male-type characteristics. Also, if steroids are used in the teen-age years before the bones have stopped growing, they can cause premature closure of the growth plates -- leading to short stature. Any drug obtained at a gym or club is illegal and carries the obvious legal risks associated with any illegal drug.

The psychoaddictive potential of steroids is another area of concern. Often people get a steroid high that makes it very difficult to stop taking steroids when they get to the end of a "cycle." The steroid high is characterized by aggressive behavior and a feeling of power. When I read in the sports pages about incidents at college sports dormitories, there is no doubt in my mind that a lot of the date rapes and criminal behavior are related to steroids.

Steroids do not heal injuries faster. They do not increase tendon strength in proportion to muscle strength and may lead to recurrent tendon problems. They do not improve endurance or coordination.

A two-month course of steroids may have severe consequences in terms of psychoaddictive potential, behavioral problems and legal problems. Whether or not it causes extensive organ damage probably depends on the dose and route of administration. You can point out the risks and problems of steroid use to your friend, but he, himself, must face his own illegal drug use and put it behind him.

> ## Only two months with steroids can mean addiction, behavior problems and legal hassles...

Sport is for healthy competition, learning teamwork, dealing with victory and defeat -- and good, healthy exercise. Using a drug for performance enhancement is unfair and risky.

Lansing C. Stenson, M.D.
Sports medicine

Dear FYI: What are the side effects of taking steroids to build muscle?

Just Curious

Dear Just Curious: Besides the physical and psychological effects mentioned in Lansing C. Stenson's reply, there are other effects. For one, the male reproductive system is adversely changed (with decreased sperm production, testicular atrophy and impotence). Other side effects include acne, baldness, enlarged and painful breasts and weakness of the connective tissues (ligaments and tendons), predisposing the athlete to injury.

The bottom line is that some

> ## ...while other side effects include acne, baldness, enlarged and painful breasts.

of the potentially harmful effects of anabolic steroids are irreversible ... others may not come to light until years after the drugs have been stopped.

Proper diet and other training methods may be at least as effective and are far safer.

Ronald Sockolov, M.D.
Family practice/sports medicine

Dear FYI: Why is it that I am still slightly overweight even if I am eating less and exercising a lot?
Curious Flip

Dear Curious Flip: Your dilemma is a common one -- many regular exercisers feel they are eating less than they "deserve." Your energy (calorie) needs depend upon your energy output such as exercise and basic bodily functions like heartbeat and brain function. In theory, when you exercise you expend more energy and eat extra to support your calorie needs. Yet, this scenario may not hold true (or at least appear to) for some individuals.

First, you must examine your food choices. It may appear that you don't eat much in the way of food, but calories, particularly fat calories, are what count. Fat packs over two times the calories per weight as protein and carbohydrate. Therefore, a high fat food provides more calories than low-fat foods of equal servings.

For instance, premium ice cream tips in at 290 calories per half-cup serving, while lower fat ice milk has 100 calories for the same serving.

Additionally, a high fat intake has been linked to obesity independently of total calories.

If you truly are eating fewer calories and exercising more than in the past, you may be facing what researchers call an energy crunch. Studies involving women runners showed they maintained their body weight on 1,400 calories daily (sedentary women typically eat 1,500 to 1,800 calories daily).

Such a discrepancy between calorie input and output can be explained in part by the body's ability to use incoming food energy more efficiently.

This makes weight loss more difficult and reduces the number of calories you need to maintain your present weight, thus less food.

Your best bet to minimize your dilemma is to:

-- Avoid crash dieting which sends a message to your body to store fat;

-- Eat consistently (avoid skipping meals);

-- Eat a high carbohydrate diet, which is heart-healthy and fuels your exercise.

Liz Applegate, Ph.D.
Lecturer in nutrition

Dear FYI: I have a friend who recently stopped doing drugs. Ever since then he's not been eating right. He occasionally drinks and he has a good job. His diet consists of bagels and more bagels, raisin bread, mineral water and corn chips. He races mountain bikes so I don't think this is a good diet for him, but he doesn't listen to me. How can I help him?

Any ideas?

Dear Any Ideas: It's good news your friend has stopped abusing drugs. However, his eating habits are unsound.

Aside from issues relating to past drug use and the influence this potentially can have on eating habits, your friend seems to be "grazing" his way through the day without eating the variety of foods his body needs.

While frequent snacking can be very conducive to good health, it must be done in a way to include foods from the various food groups that supply protein, vitamins, minerals and fiber that are all essential for good health. For instance, his bagelmania is fine as long as he includes a piece of fruit and a carton of yogurt, low-fat cheese, or lean meat, tuna or poultry along with it.

Taking the time to sit down and have a "square" meal once a day will also help to ensure better nutrient intake. An easy fast-food meal of a baked potato topped with chili or steamed vegetable, salad bar and low-fat milk is a speedy way to get what an active body needs.

Your friend's eating style also detracts from his mountain-bike racing and training.

Exercise like biking, running and long distance swimming requires a diet loaded with carbohydrates (breads, cereal, grain, fruits and vegetables), adequate protein from beans and grains or meats and milk, and vitamins and minerals from these foods to make everything work.

I suggest that your friend try to get some type of eating routine going. Perhaps you could meet him for lunch so he will be more apt to eat a more balanced meal. Help him shop for a variety of tasty and easy-to-prepare foods.

He may not be taking any interest in eating, so any way you could get him motivated would better his health and performance.

Liz Applegate

Dear FYI: I currently lift weights, run, swim three times a week and have been for the past year or two.

Since I wanted to bulk up by at least 10 pounds or more (and it is difficult for me to gain a pound more as it is), I was given this product to take (label enclosed). But I have read that too much protein will not help to build muscles and that it could be harmful in some cases. What would be the consequence of taking this weight powder? Already it has given me diarrhea.

Pee Wee

Dear Pee Wee: To gain muscle weight or "bulk up" you must follow a strength training program such as your weight training, and increase your calorie intake from a variety of foods, not just protein. While muscle is part protein, excessive protein intake does not lead to bigger or stronger muscles.

If you are eating a varied diet with good protein sources (lean meats, dairy products, dried beans and grain, fish and poultry), then diet is not limiting your ability to "bulk up." All of us have limitations on maximal muscle size dependent upon heredity.

Like yourself, many athletes try protein supplements such as the weight-gain product you are using. These products can be harmful if taken in large amounts -- they can cause dehydration, nausea, diarrhea and kidney problems. The product you are using also contains vitamins and minerals that can potentially be toxic if you are taking other supplements.

Most weight-gain products and protein supplements cost users $25 to $50 per pound of protein. You are better off eating a diet high in complex carbohydrates (bread, pasta, potatoes, rice) to meet the energy demands of your exercise along with sufficient dietary protein to allow for muscle growth. In this case, more is not better.

Liz Applegate

Dear FYI: What exactly do diet pills do to your body? Are there any that are relatively safe?

Dreaming Thin

Dear Dreaming Thin: The last part of your two-part question is the easiest to answer. No, there are no diet pills that are safe, either relatively or absolutely.

The answer to the first part of your question is more complex. There are over-the-counter diet pills as well as diet pills requiring a doctor's prescription. They are basically the same except that prescription drugs are somewhat stronger. Unfortunately, neither type has proved to be of much help in losing weight ... and all such drugs have significant side effects. They act by stimulating the central nervous system, resulting in nervousness, a faster heart rate, increased blood pressure, dizziness, sleeplessness and, incidentally, a slight depression of appetite.

Scientific tests using diet pills on some people and placebos (harmless, inactive pills) on others have demonstrated that those taking diet pills lost only a fraction of a pound more per week than those taking placebos. When the facts are balanced against the side effects they produce, the use of such drugs cannot be recommended.

To lose weight safely one must adhere to a strict, well-balanced diet. Diet pills are not a substitute for eating less, and the side effects may be very dangerous to your health. They are not worth the risk.

Robert J. Bolt, M.D.
Internist

Dear FYI: My girlfriend wears contacts and when she gets something on them she puts them in her mouth to clean them. My dad wears contacts and he says that it is a terrible thing to do. She says (to me) that she has done it for years and that it has never caused any trouble. Now it *really* bugs me when she does it. Who is right, her or my dad?

Bugged

Dear Bugged: The mouth is a place loaded with bacteria (germs). Putting a contact in your mouth and then in your eye has the potential to cause a serious eye infection that could lead to blindness. Your girlfriend may have gotten away with it in the past, but there is no assurance that she will in the future. Your dad is absolutely correct.

John Keltner, M.D.
Ophthalmologist

Dear FYI: Can you give me an average amount of time that would be dangerous for someone to spend in the sun with no sun protection?

A Sun Worshipper

Dear Sun Worshipper: There is no absolute answer that would apply to all people. However, I can offer guidelines to help you determine how you can safely enjoy the sun.

When natural sunlight strikes the untanned skin it starts the process by which the skin protects itself from sun damage, namely tanning. When you are

> **Excessive sun exposure over a long period of time can lead to wrinkling and skin cancer, particularly in those with fair complexions.**

untanned you burn easily at first, but within a week or two the skin becomes tanned and will burn less severely. Some people with very fair skin or freckles tan very poorly and burn repetitively with each sun exposure. These people need to be more protective than those with darker complexions.

During the spring, summer and early fall months we burn more easily than during the winter because there is more ultraviolet light coming through the atmosphere. Mid-day sun is intense and affects the skin more than early morning or late-afternoon sun.

Some important facts for sun safety:

1. Don't burn (that is turn crimson or blister). Blonde, fair, red-haired, blue-eyed, freckling-type skin is almost always going to require protection during the high-intensity sunlight seasons.

2. Lying still by the water is unhealthy for one's skin even if you pigment well.

3. Excessive sun exposure over a long period of time can lead to wrinkling and skin cancer, particularly in those with fair complexions.

Most kinds of outdoor activities in the sun are encouraged -- if one uses common sense. Know your skin type, protect the sensitive areas of your face and minimize burning and you will enjoy the outdoors.

Cleve B. Baker, M.D.
Dermatologist

Dear FYI: I want to go to a tanning salon but my mom says they cause cancer. My friend goes and she says the bad rays are screened out. Are they?

Pale Face

Dear Pale Face: Unfortunately, there is no such thing as

143

harmless ultraviolet light irradiation. It is true that ultraviolet A (UVA), used in tanning booths, does not cause the acute sunburn reaction that occurs with ultraviolet B (UVB). However, there are other harmful effects from UVA.

UVA penetrates deeper into the skin than UVB, thereby causing damage to collagen and causing premature wrinkling. UVA can cause cataracts in your eyes 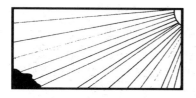 if the eyes are not protected by ultraviolet protective goggles. Also, ultraviolet light enhances the cancer-producing effects of ultraviolet B either from sunlight or from UVA bulbs that have a small amount of UVB irradiation.

UVA, like UVB, can reduce the skin's immune defenses by reducing the number of immune-receptor cells in the epidermis. Without this immune protection system, the earliest changes leading to skin cancer may go undetected by the body's defensive immune system. Finally, if you are exposed to certain types of medications, cosmetics or chemicals, UVA can result in allergic reactions.

In short, UVA can produce long-term damage to the skin and should not be considered harmless.

Cleve B. Baker

Dear FYI: Is it possible to surgically remove freckles?
Curious

Dear Curious: Freckles are very common. Freckling is a genetic tendency occurring most often in those with fair skin, blond- and red-haired characteristics. Surgery is not a feasible means of removing routine freckles. Can you imagine the number of surgical scars that would result if one were to try to cut out one's freckles? The result would be worse than the problem.

Since sunlight darkens freckles, wear sunscreens (sun protection factor 15 or greater) to minimize this, and protect the fair skin that lies between freckles from burning. Chronic burning of fair skin can lead to skin cancer in later years.

There are fading creams containing hydroquinine that are sometimes helpful in lightening freckles, but these creams do not erase one's freckles. The best results are often found when using a combination of fading creams and sun-

> **For the most part, the severity of acne is not a result of a person's diet or even the way they take care of their skin.**

> **Most factors -- genetics, rate of growth, stress -- often are out of the control of the person at the time they're having acne.**

blocking agents. Remember, others may not be turned off by your freckles. Many people find them cute and attractive.

A word of caution: any individual freckle that seems to be growing and changing on its own -- behaving differently from other freckles -- requires a doctor's evaluation. A "freckle" that behaves in this way may not be a freckle.

Cleve B. Baker

Dear FYI: What is the best way to lose acne?
Pizza Face

Dear Acne Sufferer: Your signature, "Pizza Face," shows only too well how hurtful acne can be. Sometimes acne is mild; sometimes painfully severe. The more severe the case, the more the necessity for dermatological care. Treatment varies with the degree of discomfort and disfiguration, but the goal during the acne years is the

145

same -- to minimize the number and severity of pimples and the lasting scars they can produce.

When acne is mild, topical (surface) care may be all that is necessary. When more severe, antibiotics and other internal medications may be necessary. The course of acne is long, usually seven to nine years.

For the most part, the severity of the disease is not a result of a person's diet or the way they take care of their skin. Most factors -- genetics, rate of growth and development, stress -- are out of the control of the individual at the time they are having acne. Treatment controls and minimizes acne but does not cure it. Generally, when growth and development are complete -- usually in the early 20's -- acne will come to an end.

Meanwhile, if you have acne which causes you to feel embarrassed about your appearance, acne which is painful, bumpy, red or pustular, see your doctor or specialist in skin diseases. Above all, don't pay heed to the cruel remarks of those dumb enough to make them.

Cleve B. Baker

Dear FYI: I have athlete's foot. Can you tell me how to get rid of it?
Sign me, A Jock

Dear Jock: Athlete's foot is a fungus infection that commonly affects the web spaces of the feet, particularly when the weather is warm and the feet are sweaty.

The common indentifying symptoms are itching, cracking, moisture and bad odor in the web spaces. However, athlete's foot may also appear as dry scaling on the soles of the feet and occasionally as tender blisters. As "a Jock," it may spread from the feet and cause a red groin rash commonly called jock itch.

Prevention means clean socks, changing shoes and socks when sweaty, drying the feet and between the toes after showers, wearing sandals around public showers and pools and keeping the feet dry with foot powder. Good, anti-fungal foot powders, such as Desenex, Enzactin and Tinactin, have acids or anti-fungal ingredients. Treatment requires anti-fungal agents applied to the clean, dry, web space twice a day. Many former prescribed anti-fungals are now available over the counter, such as miconzole (Micatin) and Tinactin. For stubborn or complicated cases, see a doctor. Sometimes oral medications are necessary. If the foot becomes painful, red and swollen, see a doctor *fast*. Athlete's foot can become infected with bacteria and dangerous infection can move rapidly. Occasionally, what is passed off as "athlete's foot" may be another skin disease. The clue will be lack of response to the above measures, and a specialist in skin diseases may be required to unravel the problem.

Cleve B. Baker

Dear FYI: I am a 17-year-old high school senior. I am fairly attractive but extremely flat chested. My best friend always teases me at school and I feel like the boys aren't interested in me because of this. Even my father makes jokes. I laugh it off so people think I don't care, but it really hurts. What should I do?

Don't Need Bra

Dear Don't Need: There is so much stress and anxiety with growing up it is not uncommon to focus on one thing that seems to be the source of our unhappiness.

Like you, many young people have concerns and questions about the size and shape of the body and its various parts.

Breast size can be a very serious issue for young women. Unfortunately, we have learned to associate self-worth and sexual attractiveness with specific parts of the body. This is largely a result of strong sexual stereotypes presented in popular magazines and other media forms. When we choose to judge ourselves or others by such restrictive standards, it is not surprising so few "measure up."

You need to remember that you are a lot more valuable and interesting than any one body part makes you. When you decide to accept each part of you as simply part of the whole package, you will have taken a big step toward self-acceptance and higher self-esteem. A person's worth cannot be measured in inches.

Honesty will go a long way in solving your problem. Talk to your friend and your dad about how you feel when they make comments or tease you about your breast size. Let them know that their remarks hurt you. I am sure they are unaware of how seriously you take their teasing.

Judith C. Buchholz,
School counselor &
Sex-education teacher

Dear FYI: Do a girl's breasts stop growing when the rest of her does? If not, when do they? If so, how much does a bust job cost and where can it be done?

Flat-Chested

Dear Flat-Chested: The breast gland is under the influence of a number of hormones in the body, most of which are active between the ages of 10 and 18.

It is during this time that females experience a gradual increase in their breast size. By the time they are about 18 years of age, they can notice a gradual decrease in the growth rate of their overall body but not necessarily their breasts. Breast size can increase even when the rest of the body has stopped growing. This is the general rule but there are many exceptions.

The cramps are terrible ... I feel sick.
Some of my family members say it's
only in my head. Is it?

There is a surgical procedure known as a augmentation mammoplasty (a "bust job," as you call it).

The cost for this surgery is around $3,500. It is best performed by a board-certified plastic surgeon and is almost always done at an out-patient facility, using heavy sedation and local anesthesia.

Women who have this surgery usually want an increase in their breast size so they can appear to have a well-developed or what they believe is at least a "normal" bustline. Most do not want to be overly large after this type of surgery.

Jack G. Bruner, M.D.
Plastic surgeon

Dear FYI: When my period comes each month I feel awful. The cramps are terrible, I feel sick and cold and have diarrhea for hours. Some of my family members say it's only in my head. Is it?

The Same Every Time

Dear Same Every Time: No way is it in your head!

Certainly that was the common explanation for years, but it was also one of those examples of "blaming the victim" when the real cause wasn't known. We now know these symptoms are most often caused by an excess of a substance called "prostaglandins." This substance is necessary in large amounts during labor, but excesses each month aren't so welcome.

There are now over-the-counter prostaglandin inhibitors such as Advil or Nuprin which can give dramatic relief. You should consider having a gynecological exam to check for less common causes of painful periods (dysmenorrhea) if these don't stop your symptoms; you may just need a prescription strength of a similar drug.

Please note that you should not take these on an empty stomach ... or if you have ulcers, kidney disease, sensitivity to aspirin or any other problem that the package insert discusses. Also, for maximum effectiveness, start this medication immediately with the onset of your period, before symptoms become troublesome.

Lynn Schimmel, MS, RNC, NP
Women's health nurse practitioner

Dear FYI: I would like to know why my menstrual period sometimes gets delayed. Is there something wrong or is it normal?

I'm not fooling around.

Occasionally Late

Dear Occasionally Late: If you are not sexually active it is not considered a medical problem that needs checking unless you've missed several months. Common causes of missed periods include dropping below your ideal weight or exercising excessively. If these are not applicable to your situation your body should "kick back in" soon.

FYI editor

Dear FYI: Why doesn't your blood clot when you get your period?

C.J.

Dear C.J.: What makes blood clot, among other things, is something called fibrin. Menstrual blood, which is mostly the lining of the uterus sloughing off, is rich in something called "plasminogen activator," which destroys the fibrin before it gets a chance to make clots. Heavy bleeding often does have clots in it because the usual enzymes don't have a chance to act on the fibrin and fibrinogen rapidly enough to affect their action.

> Common causes of missed periods include dropping below your ideal weight or exercising excessively.

Lynn Schimmel

Dear FYI: Sometimes it is difficult for me to insert a tampon. What causes that? Also, does that mean that when I become sexually active, sometimes I will not be able to have sex, or will it hurt a lot?

Help

Dear Help: Many young women share both your problem and your concerns. If you have just removed a tampon, sliding in another over dry tissue can be very difficult. Try lubricating the tube with an oil or lotion that does not contain alcohol. A water-based lubricant such as KY jelly works well. If you are usually using tampons comfortably, sexual activity should not be a problem.

Joyce Wisner
Public health nurse

Dear Stressed Out: First try writing down everything you can think of that is making you feel uptight and anxious. Then, see if you can identify the problem areas where you might be able to change your attitude toward the event or situation that's stressing you.

For example, if it's a relationship problem with a partner (boy- or girlfriend) or a parent, ask yourself if there's some way you might change your attitude to improve the relationship. Often unknowingly, we have certain expectations for people who are close to us, and when they don't live up to them it can be extremely frustrating. Learning to accept our friends and loved ones as they are often lessens the tension in a relationship.

Another example is feeling the stress of maintaining high grades. Reminding yourself that you have a right to feel good about your work in a class if you're doing the best you can, even if you don't eventually get the grade you want, can be helpful in decreasing stress.

Other tips that can help you de-stress your life are the following:

1. Avoid obsessions. Try to substitute obsessions with preferences.

2. Remind yourself when you're stressed to keep things in perspective. Take time each day to enjoy the small but important pleasures in your life such as talking with friends, playing with your dog or taking a bike ride.

3. Avoid continually comparing yourself to others. Try to set goals for yourself that are realistic and then give yourself credit if you've done your best, regardless of what your friends may have accomplished.

4. Think well of yourself. If you find yourself continually putting yourself down with private thoughts such as "I'm stupid," "I'm such a klutz," try to catch yourself, substituting positive thinking such as "I tried and that's what counts." Low self-esteem is a heavy burden to carry around.

5. Before an important exam or other stressful event, take a few minutes to close your eyes and focus on breathing deeply. Also, visualize yourself doing well. This can help decrease tension.

6. Exercise regularly. Swimming, jogging, walking, stretching or dancing help you practice deep, full breathing and are excellent ways to relax.

7. Write a personal journal . A journal can be like a trusted friend (making it possible to express your innermost thoughts and feelings, and also reminding yourself of some of the above tips). It can be very helpful, especially in dealing with anger in a positive way.

Good luck and don't forget to "take time to stop and smell the flowers."

Will Lotter
Senior lecturer in health & physical education

Dear FYI: What is a Pap smear? Do I need one?
Sixteen

Dear Sixteen: A Pap smear is a simple test that can find pre-cancer in a woman's cervix years before it might become a real cancer. A wooden stick, like a popsicle stick, is used to wipe the loose cells off the opening to the uterus; it should feel no different than, for example, wiping along the inside of your cheek.

Certain people are at higher risk for developing this pre-cancer. Those females who start sexual activity in their teens, or who have had more than one sexual partner, are at greatest risk. Women who have routinely protected themselves as much as possible from this and other sexually transmitted diseases by insisting that their partners use a condom, have minimal risk.

As you can see, your age alone doesn't dictate the need for a Pap smear. If you have ever had intercourse, then, of course, yearly Paps are important. Many teens who are not sexually active also prefer yearly gynecological exams since more than just a Pap is done; the rest of the exam can be very informative, interesting and reassuring.

One final note: women whose mothers were given a hormone called DES during their pregnancies should start exams when they start having periods.
Lynn Schimmel

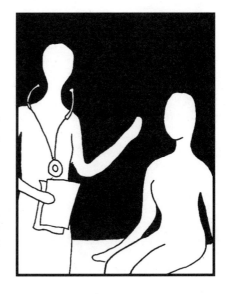

Dear FYI: If you go to the doctor to get a Pap smear, can he tell whether or not you are a virgin?
Interested to Know

Dear Interested: A doctor can observe if a woman's hymen (the membrane that covers the opening of the virginal vagina) is intact -- but that doesn't mean he or she knows if the woman is a virgin. Some strenuous exercises can cause the hymen to break.
FYI editor

151

Dear FYI: I was wondering if you could get on the pill without having a pelvic exam? If not, how much is a "pelvic?"

Not So Rich

Dear Not So Rich: A lot of women wonder about this. Actually, you don't need a pelvic exam before going on "the pill" as much as you need what we call a "comprehensive health visit." Even that visit isn't so much related to "the pill" as it is to the fact that you are considering, or engaged in, sexual activity.

That visit includes a pelvic exam and is a great opportunity to help you learn about your body and how to keep it healthy and happy.

Besides giving you a chance to learn important things for a teen to consider regarding her health, the visit gives you a chance to ask questions that you might have wondered about, but have been afraid to ask. They will be answered in complete confidentiality ... and in a non-judgmental atmosphere.

For this reason, it is important to see a nurse practitioner or physician you feel comfortable with, or you'll be missing an important opportunity to talk, and they may be missing out on knowing significant information about you that would help you receive better care.

Costs will vary (around $100 in many offices) and may be covered by insurance.

Planned Parenthood also offers exams on a sliding-scale fee. Please don't worry about the pelvic exam -- not only are we careful not to hurt anyone, but we routinely hear the surprised comment: "That was interesting!"

Lynn Schimmel

Dear FYI: If you're using birth control pills, can you get addicted to using them?

If you use them for a long time could you become ill? (I'm not using them right now).

Planning Ahead

Dear Planning Ahead: Birth control pills are not addictive.

If you were using them, the only way you could become ill would to be continue using them if you were having problems and not telling anyone about the problems.

Birth control pills are very efficient and safe, but as with any medicine, there are risks and benefits. If there is something in your medical and family history that might cause you problems, The Pill might add to them.

Check with your medical provider if you are concerned about taking them.

FYI editor

Dear FYI: What is semen?

Curious Girl

Dear Curious Girl: Semen is a whitish fluid that is full of sperm. This liquid is from the male and can be found after the male ejaculates. Ejaculation occurs after masturbating or having intercourse to a climax.

FYI editor

Dear FYI: Can you tell me what a "wet dream" is?

Heard Different Things

Dear Heard Different Things: Wet dreams usually occur as you enter puberty. They happen while you are sleeping, and may be caused by a pleasant dream, perhaps about the opposite sex.

This dream results in an erection followed by an orgasm. Girls as well as boys can have wet dreams, but they are usually fewer.

Don't feel embarrassed or get worried about wet dreams. Having them is normal as young men grow up.

Sexual feelings are being aroused in your body for the first time. This is your body's normal, early reaction to those feelings.

FYI editor

Dear FYI: I am almost 16 and I still haven't had a wet dream. Is this normal?

Worried

Dear Worried: Yes -- perfectly normal.

FYI editor

Dear FYI: I have a small penis. Is this abnormal? Will I be able to have sex?

Different

Dear Different: From your question it sounds as though you have compared your penis with those of other young men you know.

A small penis is just fine. Penis size has nothing to do with your or your partner's sexual satisfaction.

FYI editor

153

Dear FYI: I am 14 years old. I have a very long penis and I'm scared. Is this abnormal? (This is not a joke, I am serious).

Very Concerned

Dear Very Concerned: Your family doctor will tell you (if you can get up the courage to ask him or her) that penises come in a great variety of lengths.

Most young men have the opposite concern, that is a penis that is too short, small or inadequate in some way.

I think these worries come from the part of us that has a lot to deal with in the teen years -- much of it concerned with our sexuality, because that seems to be one of the hardest things to talk about.

The body's hormones come on so quickly and so strong, that it is natural to wake up in the morning feeling as if you had a new body, and wonder what next, for crying out loud?

> **Hormones can come on so quickly and so strong, that one could wake up in the morning feeling as if they had a new body.**

First, check with your doctor or other medical authority.

Then find a trusted someone with whom you can discuss some of your deep concerns.

I have a feeling that anatomical measurements are where these worries surface ... and that just reading a medical book on the range of normal penis length really isn't going to do it for you, although that might be a good place to start.

Many girls feel the size of their breasts is grotesque, while others are in acute agony at feeling flat-chested. As you can see, you guys have plenty of company when it comes to body-image worries.

Nancy DuBois
Psychologist

Dear FYI: Could a really huge penis pass through a woman and kill her?

Anonymous

Dear Anonymous: The vagina of a woman who is eager for sexual activity expands to accept any size of penis.

It may be helpful to know that even a nine-pound baby will pass through a woman's vagina quite well (the tissue is amazingly accommodating). On the other hand, a relatively small penis used without love can be as emotionally and physically damaging to a woman as any other weapon.

Please talk with a health care provider if you need specific reassurance.

Lynn Schimmel

Dear FYI: Can you explain something to me? Do I have bone in my penis?

Uninformed

Dear Uninformed: You may have heard the term "boner," which simply refers to an erection (the stiffness that occurs when a man becomes aroused or excited). There is no bone in your penis.

FYI editor

Dear FYI: Can a man with an uncircumcised penis have sex?

Curious

Dear Curious: Good question. You aren't alone in wondering about this. Yes, indeed, a man with an uncircumcised penis can have sex. Vast numbers of people wouldn't exist had circumcision been a prerequisite for sex.

According to Lynn Schimmel of Women's Health Associates:

"Actually, when a penis is erect, you can't tell the difference between a circumcised and an uncircumcised penis. Only without an erection does the foreskin on an uncircumcised penis cover the end of the penis."

You may be interested to know that fewer and fewer babies are being circumcised these days as the risk of the procedure and the pain involved to the baby seem to outweigh the benefits previously attributed to the circumcision operation.

FYI editor

155

Dear FYI: What if one side of my vagina has pubic hair and the other side doesn't?

Lopsided

Dear Lopsided: Most development takes place asymmetrically, resulting in, for example, one breast smaller than the other for a while at least.

New hair growth also does not have an adult's configuration immediately.

If you remain concerned, please have an examination to ease your worries - - you'll learn a lot about other parts of you, too.

Lynn Schimmel

Dear FYI: Does pubic hair turn gray?

Too Young to Know

Dear Too Young: Yes. However, just as some of the hair in people's heads remains without gray, not all pubic hair turns gray.

FYI editor

Dear FYI: Can masturbation hurt your brain in the future?

Afraid

Dear Afraid: There are quite a few "old wives' tales" about masturbation. Masturbation is normal.

It will not hurt your brain now or in the future.

You will not lose your hair or go blind or crazy, nor are you in danger of using up all your sperm. Sperm is constantly reproduced, replacing what you use.

FYI editor

Dear FYI: Is it normal for girls to masturbate?

Extremely Curious

Dear Extremely: Yes. It is normal for girls, and for boys.

There are many people who think that masturbation is wrong or abnormal, however it is perfectly normal.

FYI editor

156

Dear FYI: What is a "G spot?"

Puzzled

Dear Puzzled: The "G Spot,", supposedly located in the front wall of a woman's vagina and greatly enhancing her sexual pleasure, is a spot no one has ever found. It was named after Ernest Grafenburg, a gynecologist who claimed to have discovered it.

While an actual spot has not been found, however, many people report an area of greater sensitivity in this location which, when stimulated, enhances arousal and orgasm.

FYI editor

Dear FYI: How can I stop chewing on my nails? Where is this habit from?

No Nails

Dear No Nails: If this has been a habit from many years, nail biting can take some time and willpower before you are able to stop.

This habit often begins (at any age) when one is under stress.

At your age, you may be biting your nails as a reaction to pressure to do well in school or because of a fear of "failure" (which you put on yourself). Perhaps you need to learn studying or test-taking skills to help you in this area. Other causes could be family problems, finances or your feelings in regard to having friends. You might try speaking to a professional counselor, parent, teacher or a friend you trust.

Dr. Herbert Benson, who writes about stress in *The Relaxation Response* (Avon Books, 1975) has a six-second response:

"Be aware of what is happening (fingers in mouth); smile and say to yourself, 'I can control this'; breathe slowly until you feel in control and you can comfortably put your hands elsewhere."

With practice you should be able to fine-tune your awareness to realizing your hands are in your mouth, and then to the urge to bite your nails. Learn to stop and be in control at each level.

You might also chart the days you do not bite your nails. After a reachable goal, say three days, reward yourself with some little treat. You and your parents may want to discuss larger rewards when you reach your goal of X-number of weeks or months biting free.

There are preparations available in drug stores that taste awful but may be a deterrent or reminder whenever you put your hands to your mouth.

157

Regular hand care -- manicure, hangnail clipping and hand-softening cream -- may help you feel better about your nails.

Ann Teal, LCSW
Psychotherapist

Dear FYI: What if you are too small and are always teased about it? People always push me around.

Shortest in the Class

Dear Shortest: There is much about yourself that you can change, but, not your height. If you are an adolescent who seems to be getting your "growth spurt" later than your friends, don't give up hope.

I also have some suggestions for accepting and handling what you can't change.

You can control your reaction to teasing. Some people continue to tease when they get an angry or upset reaction. If you ignore their remarks, people often stop teasing. If the teasing comes from close friends, you could let them know how you feel about it. You can also consider how you come across to people. You are most likely to get a positive reaction from people when you are friendly and when you believe in yourself and your own good qualities.

Another controlable thing is the type of people with whom you spend time. You might be happier being with friends who are more understanding and considerate.

Cathy G. Neubauser, Ph. D.
Psychologist

Dear FYI: I have a sugar tooth that just won't quit. I am constantly eating foods that contain sugar to satisfy my desire for sweets. When my appetite for sugar isn't fulfilled, I get irritable and annoyed. I want to stop this addiction to sweets so I won't be moody, and eat a better diet. Although I'm thin now, I know that if I continue to eat as I do, I'll be as big as a cow in a few years. Any suggestions?

The Sugar Freak

Dear Sugar Freak: You are wise to think about the future effect of poor eating habits on your health. As a first step to making changes, you could work on eating three balanced meals per day. If you skip a meal, such as breakfast, you may get hungry and snack mid-morning on sweets, or you might end up eating more food, including sweets, at the next meal. When you have a desire for sugar, try substituting a piece of fruit or a whole-grain cracker. Some people find that a pickle can satisfy the desire for sugar.

To gradually reduce your consumption of foods high in sugar, make a specific plan for the week. Pre-plan to have good snacks (vegetables, fruits, rice, crackers, popcorn) ready for when you arrive home from school. Allow yourself to have some sweets during the week so that you do not feel too deprived and become susceptible to binging. Remember that any habit takes time to change, so set realistic goals for yourself.

Carolyn Waggoner, MS, RD
Dietician

Dear FYI: What are some symptoms of some eating disorders?
Confused and Wanting to be Skinny

Dear Confused: There are different symptoms for different eating disorders.

Most often people with eating disorders need guidance in learning how to master the challenges in their lives...

The main symptoms of anorexia nervosa include a fear of being "fat" (even when not overweight), losing weight as a goal in itself by restricting food intake, extreme exercising and loss of menstrual periods.

The main symptoms of bulimia include bingeing or feeling out of control with eating -- and an effort to undo the effects of bingeing by vomiting; fasting or extreme dieting; over-exercising; or abusing laxatives, diuretics or diet pills.

The main symptom of compulsive overeating is obesity.

Body image is just one part of self-image. In contemporary American culture, thinness for women is considered a positive attribute and is over-promoted with the result that at any time about 50 percent of women are "on a diet' (and about 75 percent are dissatisfied with their current weight). However, these women typically have a target weight in mind, and stop losing weight when they reach that target. Also, although a majority may be dissatisfied with their weight, they are not necessarily dissatisfied with themselves and generally have a positive image of themselves as people.

On the other hand, people with eating disorders have poor self-images, and to avoid the discomfort of facing up to this problem and correcting, they focus all their attention on their body image.

They believe they would feel good about themselves if only they were thin. When that magical happiness doesn't arrive along with their thinness, they conclude that they must not be thin enough. They continue to lose weight in a futile search for a positive self-image.

Only facing the challenges in one's life and mastering them will really produce a positive self-image.

Most often people with eating disorders need guidance in learning how to master the challenges in their lives in order to break the powerful spell of an eating disorder.

Sheldon Berkowitz, Ph.D.
Clinical psychologist

Dear FYI: My teen-age daughter has practically stopped eating. She lives on green apples, carrots and celery. I've heard that eating like this can lead to losing all your teeth and other health problems.

I'm worried sick when I wake in the middle of the night, but by day I convince myself that everything will be OK.

Does she need help?

Worried Mom

Dear Worried Mom: Your letter speaks to several concerns that face parents and teen-agers -- and go beyond your daughter's extreme dieting. The first point involves any sudden and extreme behavior changes.

An extreme behavior change in teens or adults is usually an extreme means of coping with a psychologically extreme situation. It is possible that your daughter is experiencing a crisis in her life that is affecting her self-image.

It is not uncommon for teen-age girls to judge self-image by their body image, thinking that they will feel better about themselves if they are thin because "thin is in", and the opinion of peers mightily affects one's self-esteem. Dieting is one means of having some control over self-image.

Most girls diet, lose a reasonable amount of weight, and all is well. However, for some, the initial loss of weight doesn't resolve their self-esteem crisis. They believe that maybe they need to be even thinner to feel good about themselves. They begin to focus most of their energy on weight and avoid positively coping with the normal developmental challenges which genuinely build self-esteem. This can lead to extreme weight loss and a very serious condition known as anorexia nervosa.

The second broad point raised is taking an authoritative position with a teen-ager. You are avoiding this and it is causing you -- and perhaps your daughter -- much grief.

You need to communicate your concern directly to your daughter. Tell her to end her extreme dieting ... and inquire about her concerns. She needs you to be a parent in this situation; to step in and help her.

If she has lost a lot of weight, take her to your family physician to reassure yourself about her health. If this doesn't alter your daughter's behavior, then you should seek professional psychological help to facilitate communication between you.

Sheldon Berkowitz

Dear FYI: Is it possible to be anorexic *and* bulimic at the same time? If so, how can that be?

Completely Confused

Dear Completely Confused: Since anorexia means self-starvation and bulimia refers to binge eating and purging, it may seem strange to find both conditions occurring simultaneously, but this often is the case. In fact, in the last few years the two words are frequently combined to form the term bulimarexia.

Anorexia refers to a pattern of self-starvation to the point of malnutrition and, in many cases, even death. Bulimia is characterized by binge-eating, usually followed by purging in the form of vomiting what has just been eaten. But the purging can also be in the form of laxatives, fasting or exercise to compensate for the excessive food intake. The two disorders share some similar underlying features: low self-esteem, distorted body image, preoccupation with losing fat and perfectionism. The overt goal of the behavior is roughly the same for the anorexic and the bulimic, that is, attaining the perfect body -- as perceived by that person.

Since anorexia and bulimia are so closely related, they often occur together. A person who restricts food intake to the point of excessive weight loss, but who perhaps "gives in" to an occasional binge, could be said to have a combined anorexic-bulimic disorder. Likewise, a person who frequently binges, but purges so thoroughly that an overall trend of weight loss is maintained, might also be said to suffer from a combination of the two disorders.

There are several excellent books available about eating disorders, including one titled "Bulimarexia," by Marlene Boskind-White and William C. White.

Kent Reade, Ph.D.
Psychologist

Dear FYI: What can you do to help your friend if you suspect she's bulimic?
Watching With Worry

Dear Watching With Worry: People with bulimia are out of control. People with bulimia are generally ashamed of it. This further lowers their self-esteem. Few of us are comfortable when others point out our problems, especially if we don't feel we can change them.

The bulimic person desperately clings to bulimia as a way of trying to feel good about herself instead of facing life's complex challenges -- the only genuine path to self-esteem. The bulimic person needs counseling to begin constructive coping once again.

In approaching your friend, you should consider the following:

1. Review your own feelings -- are you concerned as a friend or are there other motives which might not be positive? Sharing love and concern is helpful, but being a "detective" and "catching" someone with bulimia is not helpful.

2. When approaching your friend share your concern about her. Remember that you are powerless to make someone seek help and that his or her response may be defensive and not welcoming. Even if you get a defensive response at first, your friend will know you really care about her. Sometimes it's a relief to share a secret.

Tell your friend that she probably will not be able to overcome her bulimia alone. She needs support from friends like you, her parents and a professional.

If you persist in sharing your concern and are stonewalled, you might consider talking to your parents about how you might approach your friend's parents with the problem.

Sheldon Berkowitz

Further Suggested Reading

- Bell, Ruth, et al, *Changing Bodies, Changing Lives: A Book for Teens on Sex and Relationships.* Vintage Books, New York, rev. ed., 1988.
- Benson, Herbert, *The Relaxation Response.* Avon Books, New York, 1975.
- Boston Women's Health Book Collective, *The New Our Bodies, Our selves: A Book by and for Women.* Touchstone Books, New York, 1984.
- Gardner-Loulan, Jo Ann, et al, *Period.* Volcano Press, Volcano, Ca., rev. ed., 1981 (on menstruation.
- Valette, Brett, *A Parent's Guide to Eating Disorders: Prevention and Treatment of Anorexia Nervosa and Bulimia.* Avon Books, New York, N.Y., 1988

8

Abuse

I always liked going to Terry's house. Her parents were so nice to me. They never fought. I found myself spending more and more time at Terry's. I thought it was going to get to the point that Terry was tired of my coming over ... but she understood.

Then one day Terry's mom took me aside. She said she knew, too, why I was spending so much time away from my house; away from my folks. She said Terry told her about the beatings and the constant verbal abuse. She said she wanted to help, but didn't know what to do -- where to start to help me.

All I could do was cry. Terry's mom held me. If only that could've been my mom. I knew I had to get long-term help; I wasn't sure this was the right place.

Dear FYI: What signs should you look for if you suspect child abuse?
Interested

Dear Interested: Two major factors involved in the determination of child abuse are the age of the child and the type of abuse (physical, sexual, emotional).

In general, children who are abused will frequently show changes in eating, sleeping or academic performance. They may become self-destructive or show a change in personality. For example, a child who was outgoing may become withdrawn. Abused chldren may be overly compliant or become aggressive and defiant. Older children may begin acting out, using drugs or alcohol, or running away from home.

It is extremely important to listen closely to what children say and to watch how they communicate. Young children may not use words to tell they are being abused because they are afraid, embarrassed or feel guilty.

Signs of physical abuse include bruises and burns of a suspicious nature or shape, frequent injuries with a vague explanation, and behavioral changes as listed above. Children who are sexually abused may have a venereal disease and/or a vaginal yeast infection; be preoccupied with masturbation; or be extremely fearful of certain people or situations. They may show an understanding of sexual behavior far beyond that of their age mates or act out sexually.

All abuse leads to problems with self-esteem and trust. Many of the behaviors are warning signs, but may not necessarily mean the child is being abused. Anyone who suspects a child is being abused should call their local Child Protective Services or law enforcement agency. Such a call may be made anonymously and may save a child from further abuse.

Douglas R. Adams, LCSW
Clinical director,
Child sexual abuse
Treatment center

Dear FYI: Are there many cases of date rape in the teen-age bracket? In what age group do most date rapes occur?
Curious But Worried

Dear Curious But Worried: Date and acquaintance rape are common occurrences. There are no statistics specifically among teens, however a 1988 study of date and acquaintance rape on 32 American college campuses found that one in four women surveyed were victims of rape or attempted rape. Furthermore, 84 percent of those raped knew their attackers.

Perhaps one reason there is not more outcry against this crime is that most of the time the victims never tell anyone. Besides feeling fear and shame -- and even responsibility -- many women don't realize that the name of the horrible thing that has happened to them is rape. This is because it is so difficult to believe that someone we know and trust would rape us.

If you would like to talk to someone about rape or sexual abuse, please call your local crisis line or Sexual Assault Center (the front pages of your phone book should have the numbers listed). Your call will remain confidential.

Sexual assault center staff

Dear FYI: I have so many single questions about rape that I don't know which single question to ask. I guess I want to know how I could avoid rape. And what are the signs of someone who is a rapist? Are women with large breasts more susceptible to rape, or is that just a myth?

Bewildered

Dear Bewildered: There is a great deal of misinformation about rape. Here are some common myths:

Myth: Most sexual assaults occur in dark alleys and similar places.

Fact: The majority of sexual assaults occur in places familiar to the victim, that is, at home, some other residence, or in a car. While avoiding certain "dangerous" places may be wise, it does not guarantee safety. Being aware and alert to the people around you, and their intentions, is a better way to prevent assault. If you do need to be in a place that feels unsafe, walk or stand with confidence and assertiveness - not appearing as a frightened "victim" can be a helpful deterrent.

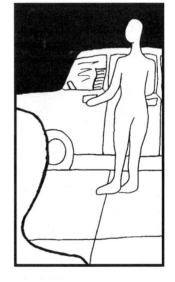

Incorporate prevention strategies into your daily life. Learn to recognize danger signals. Some practical precautions to take with an acquaintance include meeting in a public place, driving yourself, watching your alcohol and/or drug intake (so you can better remain in control), and letting someone know where you will be and when you will return.

Take a self-defense class. It will heighten your awareness, increase confidence, and teach you physical skills to protect yourself.

Myth: Sex offenders are "dirty old men" or sex-crazed maniacs.

Fact: Most rapists are between the ages of 15 and 35, are in a relationship with a woman and appear "normal." They can be of any race, color or economic class. You can't pick them out in a crowd. Fifty to 75 percent of the time the victim knows her assailant.

Sometimes we don't take precautions with someone we know well and trust. We ignore early signals that we might be in danger because we think "I know this person -- he wouldn't hurt me." But even with friends, lovers and partners, we need to be aware of threats to our personal safety. If someone has had too much to drink, becomes verbally abusive, is physically forceful, or unwilling to listen and to respect our wishes, their behavior may indicate a dangerous situation.

With a partner, clearly communicate your sexual limits and expectations. Listen to each other. Both partners need to agree in order for the experience to be a fulfilling one. Above all, always trust your instinct; if you feel that something isn't quite right, it probably isn't.

Myth: Sexual assault is caused by uncontrollable sex drives.

Fact: Sexual assault is an act of physical and emotional violence. Rapists assault to dominate, humiliate, control, degrade, terrify and violate. Studies show that power and anger are the motivating factors.

Myth: Women provoke sexual assault, and sexy women are most often the target of a rapist.

Fact: Sexual assault victims range in age from infants to the elderly. Appearance and attractiveness are not relevant. A rapist assaults someone who is accessible and appears vulnerable.

Sexual assault center staff

Dear FYI: The other day I had a phone call and there was only heavy breathing on the other end. At first I thought it was a joke, but then I realized it wasn't. I wish now I had hung up as soon as the breathing began. Would that have been the right thing to do? Also, it scares me to think this is a sex pervert who knows me. Do you think someone I know was calling?

Kind of Scared

Dear Kind of Scared: Your reaction to such an annoying and frightening phone call is very normal. Believe me, you are not alone in how you feel. How you react to these calls can be a determining factor about whether they persist or not.

Your instinct to hang up sooner was correct. A quick, unemotional response is the best way to discourage such a caller. In most cases the caller is a juvenile with a twisted sense of humor. Some, however, can be more serious. This is why all such calls should be treated the same way.

Most annoying or obscene callers are looking for an emotional response such as crying, panic or fear.

Quickly hanging up the phone without responding to the remark or breathing is denying the caller the response he wants.

Another method is to blow a whistle into the mouthpiece ... leaving the ringing in *the caller's* ears!

Either way, you should report the incident to the police.

If the calls persist, the police can give you more detailed advice.

Police department staff

Dear FYI: I think a friend of mine is being sexually abused by her father. I've seen the way he explodes if she goes out with a boy, and once she started talking about the "strange way" her father touches her. Also, she started asking if my dad ever touched me in some personal areas. I want to help but don't know what to do.

Concerned

Dear Concerned: Sexual abuse hurts. It is painful and traumatic, and the victim may require years of counseling to resolve these events in her life.

Sexual abuse is wrong and against the law. If you suspect that your friend is being abused, trust your intuition. There are several steps you can take to help her. First, tell your friend that you are concerned about her. Then ask her if she wants to talk to you more about her father. If she chooses to confide in you, remain calm and listen to what she is saying. Offer her your understanding, concern and support without passing judgment.

The abuse is not her fault. Tell your friend that it is good she talked to you, and that what her father is doing is not OK. Help is available. You or your friend can call anonymously your local Child Protective Services for assistance. You could also talk to a school counselor or teacher.

If your friend does not wish to talk to you, you might show her this letter with a note telling her that you care. Your concern and willingness to get involved are a wonderful gift to your friend.

Sexual assault center staff

Dear FYI: What happens when you tell the authorities that your father has raped you? How do you get protection if your father has found out you told the authorities?

Scared

Dear Scared: I know from your question that you are going through a difficult time right now. What your father did to you was wrong. It is also a crime. No one has the right to hurt you in the way he did.

Reporting your father to the authorities is an important way of getting the abuse to stop and of getting your father the help he needs. If you have younger sisters or brothers, reporting your father to the authorities may save them from going through all the pain you are having to deal with now.

To report your father to the authorities you need to call Child Protective Services and/or your local police department. A child protective services worker and/or police officer will make arrangements to talk with you about the rape in a place (for example, a school) where you feel comfortable and where your father is not present. The authorities' main concern will be for your safety.

If your father has made any threats to you, they will make sure you are protected. The authorities will probably talk with all the members of your family -- including your father -- in order to decide how best to help you and your family through this difficult time.

I know that reporting your father is not easy. I imagine that you are going through a lot of different feelings right now: fear, guilt, shame, anger, depression. You are not alone! Many children and teen-agers -- girls and boys alike -- have gone through what you have and survived. The key is not keeping a secret that does you -- and the rest of your family -- harm. There are people who care about you and are willing to help.

Sexual assault center staff

Dear FYI: I feel very uncomfortable around a certain relative. He has molested someone before and he is always touching me. What should I do? It really angers me.

Ick -- Lay Off

Dear Ick -- Lay Off: Your feelings of discomfort are justified and legitimate. No one has the right to touch you in a way that makes you uncomfortable. Tell an adult you trust about the problem, and ask for help in telling your parents. Perhaps your school counselor, doctor or minister could be helpful. You can also call a trained sexual abuse counselor to discuss your fears and what you can do. I know that reporting a relative is not easy, but it is important not to be silent about this problem.

Nancy Hanks, Ed.D.
Sex therapist

Dear FYI: Are sexual relations more common between fathers and daughters or mothers and sons?

I.

Dear I: Research indicates that sexual relations are more common between fathers and daughters than between mothers and sons. Sadly, the statistics for sexual abuse in one form or another are very high. One of every three girls and one out of every seven boys in the United States is the victim of some type of sexual assault.

According to the Sexual Assault Center, "sexual relations of any sort between a parent figure and his or her child are known as incest. This includes step-parents and live-in partners of parents. Incest is probably the most difficult form of abuse for a child to report to someone else, since it often occurs with a previously trusted parent figure.

"In addition, adults who are sexually abusing a child will often make threats if they feel the child might report the abuse. These threats may include causing harm to themselves, the child, other siblings, or blaming the child for the abuse. However, sexual abuse, like any other form of abuse, is *not* the responsibility of the child."

To Our Readers: If you have ever experienced incest it is important that you talk about it with someone. It may be difficult to feel an adult can understand, or be trusted, but taking the step toward talking about incest is *the first step toward ending it!*

FYI editor

> # One out of three girls and one out of every seven boys in U.S. is sexually abused.

Dear FYI: Is mental abuse just as bad as physical abuse? It feels like it.

Fed Up

Dear Fed Up: If it feels bad -- it is bad! Everything that is painful "hurts," and is damaging to the self. It makes us feel helpless, vulnerable and decreases our sense of worth.

By calling yourself "fed up," you appear to be ready to do something about it. If possible, speak to the abuser(s), telling them how you feel and what exactly makes you hurt. Speak about your own feelings: use "I" statements (give an example) rather than accusatory language.

If this does not work, do see a counselor to help you with action plans and to hasten healing.

Hanna Bauer, Ed.D.
Psychotherapist

Dear FYI: What do you do when an oppressive male continuously threatens you and sometimes carries out those threats? Telling someone, a grown-up, will only make it worse.

Continuously Threatened

Dear Continuously Threatened: Everyone has the right to live in a safe environment. Unfortunately, the violence and abuse will not stop on their own. They will only get worse. That is why, as scary as it may be, telling someone about what is happening is very important.

You say that telling a grown-up will make it even worse. You can start off by talking to someone anonymously to find out what you can do in your particular circumstances. Two places that you can call safely are your nearest crisis line or Sexual Assault Center, and Child Protective Services.

When it is your parent, or a friend of the family that is hurting you, the thought of telling someone is frightening. You may be afraid that the abuse will get worse, or that you won't be believed, or that somehow you are to blame for the situation. Even with all those worries, you should tell someone you trust: another relative, the school nurse, or call one of the places we have suggested.

If it is a boyfriend who is threatening you, do consider talking to your parents. They may be more supportive than you think. If you can't talk to them, call one of the places mentioned above.

Each situation of violence and abuse is different. Please speak to someone. No one has the right to threaten or hurt you.

Sexual assault center staff

Dear FYI: What do you do when your stepfather beats you and you tell your mom but she doesn't care? Who can I turn to? I don't want anything to happen to me when and if he finds out who wrote this. I need help. If you print this, please don't use my name.

Just sign me "Nameless"

Dear Writer: Your letter states two problems: your stepfather beating you and your mother apparently not caring. Let's talk about these separately.

Your stepfather probably thinks that he is only disciplining you and thereby helping you to behave differently. But discipline is by no means the same as punishment, and even when punishment is indicated, it must never include beating.

Of course, it depends on what you call "beating." If it is an occasional spanking (not a desirable form of discipline), no great harm would be done by it. However, if this is done with instruments such as a belt, if it includes slapping your face, and certainly if it leaves marks on your skin, this is an entirely different matter.

I understand, of course, that you are afraid to become involved in reporting, but you can play it safe. If you have any visible marks on your body as a result of physical punishment, all you have to do is to show them -- as soon as possible -- to your school nurse, teacher or doctor, and he or she will contact the Child Protection Agency, where immediate help is available. Don't be afraid to do this, it is your right to ask for protection.

Now, about your mother... Does she really not care?

Did you ever tell her that you were unhappy and ask her to stand by you? Could she be afraid of your stepfather?

Are you the only one whom he beats? It is of great importance for your mother to know how you feel. She may be quite unaware of it and thereby give you the impression that she does not care. Please talk to her -- you have nothing to lose.

I wish I could tell you that you are the only one in such a situation, but unfortunately that would not be true since a great many children are being treated, or rather mistreated, by their parents.

Again -- your parents have the duty to educate you and the right to discipline you.

Nobody, I repeat, nobody has the right to beat you.

Herbert Bauer, M.D.
Psychiatrist

Dear FYI: Why do parents have to be rough on their kids?
Just A Kid

Dear Just A Kid: Based on the wording of your question, I would like to speak to the issue of parents who physically hit their children.

Spanking children as a form of discipline has a long history but some major drawbacks.

First, it models the use of violence to obtain one's goals. Children learn from what their parents do much more than from what they say.

Second, the persistent use of physical discipline tends to force a child to avoid the pain. Avoidance can take the forms of being emotionally distant, actually running away, or the use of evasion or lying. Finally, the use of corporal punishment makes some parents feel very guilty, a feeling their children can sense, and undermines the effectiveness of the discipline.

Unfortunately, physical abuse is a fact of life for some children and adolescents.

How do you know if you're being physically abused?

If you live in a constant state of fear that you will be hit, or have been hit persistently and with force many times in the past, you probably are a person who has been physically abused.

Why do people abuse?

The reasons may be numerous. In moments of passion parents frequently misidentify their children as miniature adults who are deliberately frustrating them, much as their own parents may have done when they were children. In this way, physical abuse gets transmitted across generations. The children begin to accept the message that they are very bad - and act accordingly. They often feel guilty and take the blame for the punishment, justifying their parents' act.

The most important contributing factor for child abuse is alcohol and other drug use. The loss of inhibitions with alcohol allows the crossing of the line between control and losing control -- often with disastrous results.

What do you do if you are being physically abused?

The first thing you do is get rid of the idea that it is your fault.

No one deserves to be hit and injured. Talk to an adult you trust, perhaps a teacher or counselor. Get advice, *don't* keep it a secret. If your parent is the abuser, he or she may have a problem which needs addressing before the abuse can stop. Social workers will investigate your report, often coming to the home and offering counseling services. In extreme cases, where there is continuing threat of injury, they will take a child from the home (or have the abuser removed) to ensure safety before any counseling begins. Reports can be made by *anyone* aware of the physical abuse occurring, even anonymously.

No one deserves to live in terror!

Stewart Teal, M.D.
Child psychiatrist

Dear FYI: We would like to comment on the discussion of physical abuse by Dr. Stewart Teal. Our children are grown now and we did "spank" them. We thought we were doing this because we loved them and wanted them to become better people. We now see that there is a very fine line between "spanking" and abuse.

If we could turn the clock back we would not ever hit our children. Dr. Teal's answer made several very good points which applied to us. We did hit our children because that was the way we were treated. We did often feel guilty, but did not understand why. Hitting did promote worse behavior in our children which in turn required more punishment. We are now somewhat estranged from our children, mostly because of this problem.

We live in a violent society. "Spare the rod and spoil the child" is much more prevalent than "never hit your child for any reason." We are writing to ask to you print the following message: "If you are a parent -- no matter the age of your children -- vow never to hit them again. If you need help to fulfill this vow, call for help.

"If you are a child who is punished by hitting, show your parents this letter and ask that together you find a way to change this pattern of discipline. If you plan to have children, vow that you will never use physical punishment at all and discuss it with your future spouse."

The only way we can really have a gentler, more peaceful nation is by starting *now* and in our own homes. We may have learned too late, but we hope that others can learn from our mistakes.

Regretful Parents

Further Suggested Reading

• Finney, Lynne D., *Reach for the Rainbow: Advanced Healing for Survivors of Sexual Abuse.* Changes Publishing, Park City, Ut., 1990.
• Forward, Susan and Craig Buck, *Betrayal of Innocence: Incest and its Devastation.* Penguin, New York, rev. ed., 1988.

9

Drinking & smoking: hardly 'in'

Dear FYI: I am in high school. A lot of the students at my school go out and drink and party every weekend. I have one friend, though, who goes home at lunch and drinks by himself. I'm wondering if he is considered a real alcoholic and what kind of help he should get?

A Scared Friend

Dear FYI: How can I tell if I am an alcoholic?

Dear FYI: Does a drink a day mean I'm a drunk?

Dear FYI: What are the signs of being an alcoholic?

Dear Writers: As you can see, the most commonly asked questions of FYI remain "How do I know if I am an alcoholic?" and "How do I know if my friend is an alcoholic?." The first step in understanding yourself and your behavior with respect to alcohol is to ask "in what ways has alcohol been a problem in my life?" You might want to ask yourself the following:

1. Have I ever endangered lives while operating a vehicle while under the influence of alcohol?

2. Have I ever embarrassed myself while under the influence of alcohol?

3. Have I ever hurt my family or others as a result of alcohol?

4. Has my academic performance suffered as a result of alcohol?

5. Has anyone ever lost trust or faith in me due to my drinking?

6. Has my drinking ever gotten me into trouble with the law?

175

7. Have I ever worried about my physical health as a result of my drinking?

8. Have I ever noticed that my drinking is to get drunk?

9. Do I frequently drink more than I plan to drink?

10. Has my sense of self-worth ever suffered as a result of my drinking?

A "yes" response to any of these questions will indicate problem drinking at least on some level.

The next step is to consider how problems are solved. If we assume that alcohol causes you problems, the only logical way to get rid of the problems is by abstaining from alcohol. Alcohol is not a nutritional need; our bodies can function well without alcohol ever touching our lips.

The third step, actually not drinking, is critical to understanding your personal relationship to alcohol. If after deciding that alcohol causes serious problems, you quit drinking and are no longer in trouble because of alcohol, the case can be considered closed. If you acknowledge that drinking causes you serious problems and you find it impossible to quit, then the possibility of alcoholism must be seriously considered.

Nearly all definitions of alcoholism include or mention a pattern of pathological use: blackouts, repeated attempts to go on the wagon, and continuation of drinking despite a physical disorder.

In other words, the drinking is a whole lot more than "social drinking."

Secondly, there is generally impairment on the job or school front as well as with peers, friends and community. Violence, absenteeism, legal difficulties and strained friendships are but a few of the ramifications.

Lastly, the definitions address the concept of addiction. Is there a physiologically binding need for alcohol?

If you have developed tolerance you will observe a need for markedly increased amounts of alcohol to achieve the desired effect. At the same time, the body may respond to the absence of alcohol with a reaction called withdrawal. Symptoms vary, but there can be very serious medical dangers associated with the withholding of alcohol from an addicted individual.

Contrary to popular myths, alcoholics don't necessarily drink every day, nor do they always drink in the morning.

Alcoholics can be beer or wine drinkers, rich or poor, any nationality and either sex.

There is a growing body of evidence suggesting a genetic link to alcoholism. Having alcoholic grandparents or parents makes it statistically more likely that you will become alcoholic. Fortunately, help is available. Alcoholics Anonymous has group meetings in almost every town in our country. Your local drug abuse clinic can also help. Please don't wait; alcoholism is a terminal disease.

Kristine A. Rominger, MS, MFCC
Licensed marriage, family &
Child therapist

Dear FYI: If you have a glass or maybe two glasses of wine almost every night to calm you down before you go to bed, is that a kind of alcoholism?

Thinking

Dear FYI: I drink alcohol. I know many students at the high school who do. I drink with my friends on weekends, but sometimes I drink when I'm alone. I sometimes even feel like I *need* a drink. I feel this way when I'm in a situation where I feel nervous, depressed or not in control.

I know that there are other ways to deal with these feelings and I don't want to really start to depend on the alcohol. My parents drink, but they're not heavy drinkers. I like the alcohol because it makes me feel relaxed and I feel better. I want to know who I can talk to about trying to stop.

A Student

Dear Thinking and Student: I would not call drinking one or two glasses of wine in the evening "a kind of alcoholism" if that is the total extent of the drinking, but I definitely consider it cause for concern for a couple of reasons.

Learning to relax or "calm down" is an important skill. If we use alcohol or another drug to accomplish that effect, we are not learning this valuable skill. As soon as we must have a drug to accomplish a task we could do ourselves, we have become dependent on the drug.

I would worry about such a dependency because it may lead to bigger problems later as more and more alcohol is needed to accomplish the calming effect. Whether full-blown alcoholism develops or not, this kind of drinking is neither harmless nor social. You should talk to your school outreach counselor or look in your phone book for the number of your local drug and alcohol clinic.

Learning to relax is a skill we all need. The use of alcohol just prolongs the learning.

Joan Parnas, director
Drug & alcohol program

Dear FYI: Could you please tell me the symptoms of an alcoholic? I think a member of my family might be one. I also would like some advice on what I can do for myself because I feel very ashamed and extremely angry.

A Twelfth-Grader

Dear Twelfth-Grader: The symptoms of alcoholism are specific, but because alcoholics are so clever at hiding them it's often hard to know with certainty if someone is an alcoholic or not.

Alcoholics might drink openly, get drunk, act nasty or passive or excessively sentimental (or all of these), get sick, pass out, then start all over again. Alcoholics may also sneak drinks, pretend they are sober (and carry it off pretty well), continuing to participate as family members and to deny that their drinking is not normal.

Since your own perception and sense of things is probably the best source of assessment, if your response is yes to any of these questions, there is likely to be a problem:

1. Are you embarrassed at the way the person acts when drinking?

2. Do you feel scared about what will happen if the drinking continues?

3. Do you not have friends over because the person might be drinking?

4. Are you afraid of the person when he or she is drinking?

5. Do you think that if you work harder at school or at home, things will get better?

6. Are things at home sometimes fine and then suddenly, for no reason, they're not?

Alcoholism is a disease that affects the entire family; it is not a moral issue. It is treatable and the treatment is total, lifelong abstinence.

You need to know that the drinking is not your fault, and the anger and shame you understandably feel are normal. You need to know that the drinker does not mean to hurt you and drinks because of the disease. And you need to know that no one can control the alcoholic's drinking, including the alcoholic, who *must* seek help.

Alcoholics Anonymous for the alcoholic is the most successful treatment program to date. Al-Anon is the program for adult family members and friends and Alateen is for teenagers. Alateen is a place for you to share your feelings with others who have lived and are living through the same things you are. The idea behind Alateen is that you can't change the alcoholic but you can learn to take care of yourself. Alateen is anonymous and everything said at meetings is confidential. If there is no Alateen group in your community, you can attend Al-Anon. To seek help is courageous. Good luck.

Joanne Evers, Ed.D.
Psychotherapist

Dear FYI: What am I supposed to do when my father starts yelling at and fighting with me and I'm stuck yelling back at him but he won't listen because he's drunk? I know I could go to a friend's house, but what if he wants to know where I'm going and I don't want to tell him? What am I supposed to do?

Desperate

Dear Desperate: As you probably know, yelling and fighting with a person who is under the influence of alcohol usually makes matters worse. The best thing to do in this situation is to not engage your father in a fight. If he starts yelling at you, try to ignore him or speak calmly. Many people who get angry when they drink feel bad about themselves and try to bring others down, too. Find other things to do with your anger. You might try writing your feelings down, listening to music, exercising, calling a friend, doing some deep breathing exercises or drawing.

If he continues to yell, you can call one of the many crisis lines available in your community. There are people there who will listen to you. The important thing is that you are safe. If at any time you feel your safety is threatened, call a crisis line or leave. Go to a friend where you can get support and be safe.

> **Alcoholism is a disease. You didn't cause it, you can't cure it, you can't control it, but you can learn to cope with it.**

You may wish to seek out a trusted adult to whom you can talk about your situation. You are certainly not alone. Many schools have support groups on campus for students who are concerned about another person's use of alcohol or drugs. Check with the counseling department and ask to speak with a counselor. Although it may be hard to ask for help at first, by "breaking the silence" you're actually helping yourself and your family.

Remember -- you and only you are in control of your feelings. With help and support from a support group at school or Alateen you can learn to detach yourself from your father's illness. Alcoholism is a disease. You didn't cause it, you can't cure it, you can't control it, but you can learn to cope with it.

Magdeline Winkelblack, MS, .ADC
Youth outreach counselor
Alcohol & drug counselor

179

Deal head-on with the impacts and influences of an alcoholic family life...

Dear FYI: I am the product of a pair of alcoholics who happened to be my parents. I am now 40 years old, and I am paying my own penalty for having endured alcoholism in the way my family, and so many other families, chose to accept it -- with silence.

I grew up in a small, upper-middle-income household. While all my basic living needs were met, alcoholism prevented my parents from developing an interest, or participating with me, in any activities. Although excessive drinking by both my parents occurred almost on a daily basis -- frequently accompanied by domestic violence -- there were no support groups, no outlets available for confronting and dealing with alcoholism. It simply was not discussed, since any discussion of adult behavior was a sign of serious disrespect.

So, at the earliest opportunity I took flight by becoming involved with activities outside the house, including sports, photography, cars, part-time jobs, etc. Home was not a place to grow as a person, it was a place to sleep, change clothes and grab a quick bite to eat.

While activities outside the home occupied my time and allowed me to avoid dealing with alcoholism during evening hours, I was still subject to the daily uncertainty about what I would find on arriving home from school. Communication with my parents was eliminated, I became somewhat of an overachiever at school and stopped expressing any personal needs in order to avoid compounding the problem situation at home.

Today my own marriage is strained to the breaking point by the effects of my parents' alcoholism on my self-esteem, inability to communicate ... and inability to accept love from others. I am currently seeing a counselor, trying to understand and correct the negative effects my parents' alcoholism has had on me. It is the first positive step I have taken in my life to deal with alcoholism.

I encourage anyone who is in an alcoholic environment to seek support from friends, family, school counselors, other support groups such as Alcoholics Anonymous, or anyone with whom you feel comfortable discussing your situation. Ignoring alcoholism may avoid an uncomfortable situation in the short term -- but will be paid back many times over in lost self-respect over the long term.

An Adult Child of Alcoholic Parents

Dear FYI: My mom drinks and smokes a lot. I know smoking causes cancer but our teacher told us that drinking can cause cancer, too. Did I hear that right? Is that really true?

Concerned About My Mother

Dear Concerned: We don't know how much "a lot" is, but according to Dave Stoebel of the Yolo County Department of Alcohol and Drug Programs:

"The Fifth Special Report to the U.S. Congress on Alcohol and Health cites evidence for a 'strong association between chronic alcohol consumption and cancers of the mouth, larynx and esophagus.'

"It also describes studies showing that alcohol may play a role in cancers of the liver, digestive tract, pancreas, breast and skin. The link between alcohol and cancer is particularly strong among people who both smoke and drink."

Dr. Paul Donald of the UC Davis Medical School specializes in treating cancers of the head and neck. According to him, the link between excessive alcohol use and head and neck cancer is very strong.

You may want to put this answer where your mom will see it, perhaps adding a note of love and concern. Remember, it doesn't mean your mom doesn't love you if she doesn't stop. Addictions are very difficult to overcome, but they can be overcome. Good luck.

FYI editor

Dear FYI: My mother and both my grandfathers are alcoholics. Is alcoholism genetic, and if so, how likely am I to become one?

Worried

Dear FYI: Do children who have alcoholic parents grow up to be alcoholics? Do they go to prison?

Wondering

Dear Worried and Wondering: About one person in 10 in the general population will become an alcoholic, but a much higher percentage of children of alcoholics (COAs) will develop the disease. This is probably due to the fact that they have inherited a tendency to have the disease, but the magnitude of this tendency is not fully understood by researchers.

The problem is that people not only *inherit* biological factors that could make them prone to alcoholism, they also *learn* attitudes and values from their parents. Children who grow up with alcoholic parents are likely to learn that excessive drinking is "normal." It is important for COAs to realize that the alcoholic parent has a very abnormal drinking pattern, one which should not be imitated by the COAs when they become old enough to drink.

Since COAs may have inherited a body chemistry that makes it easier for them to become addicted to alcohol, they should be very careful if they choose to drink when they become adults. It is particularly important for them to avoid excessive drinking or to become intoxicated.

As to the question about prison, alcohol often leads people to lose control and do things they later regret. Sometimes they break the law and imprisonment can result. Usually the consequences aren't this drastic, although they are often unpleasant.

Dave Stoebel, Ph.D.
Prevention coordinator

Dear FYI: My son is driving now (and not drinking), but I worry that he will be hit by a drunken driver if he is out late at night. Are there any statistics on the hours drunken drivers are most frequently on the road?

Worried Parent

Dear Parent: National statistics show that the highest percentage of drunken drivers are on the road Friday and Saturday between 12:30 and 3 a.m.

But that doesn't mean drunks can't be out there in the afternoon or morning. Make sure your son buckles up and drives defensively.

FYI editor

Dear FYI: I know some people who attend parties which are not sponsored by my high school. According to them almost everyone there drinks. The people I talked to don't drink or get drunk at the parties, so they must resist the peer pressure. Why do the others drink and get drunk?

Baffled

Dear Baffled: It is difficult to pinpoint a single reason to explain why some people drink to the point of drunkenness. Ann may not have drunk alcohol before and is unaware of the amount that will cause her to become intoxicated. Tom may do it to be "cool" and to show that he is grown up. Neal may have a false sense of power that leads him to believe that he won't lose control if he drinks. Tracy may have difficulty in saying "no" and thinks that her friends won't like her if she doesn't join in. Shawn may drink to excess as a sign of rebellion against his parents.

Almost all teen-agers feel awkward in some social situations, and some may mistakenly believe that alcohol will diminish their feelings of shyness and insecurity. Often these people end up feeling embarrassed the following day when they realize how foolishly they acted the night before.

An important thing to remember is that you don't have to use alcohol to have a good time at a party. If one of the people at the party does drink alcohol and is acting differently than normal, be a true friend and make sure that he or she does not drive an automobile.

Communication between parents is also important. Teenagers may pressure their parents to serve alcohol at private parties because "all the parents do it". If the parents of teenagers attending a party call the parents of the host or hostess and express their feelings about alcohol being served, it may provide mutual support and reinforcement among the parents.

Eva Peters Hunting, Dr. PH
Psychotherapist

Dear FYI: Some parents buy alcohol for their kids' parties and brag about it. Why do they do this?
Mad and Confused

Dear Mad and Confused: This is a hard question to answer. I have to guess that parents buy alcohol for their kids and brag about it because they want the kids to like them and see them as one of the crowd. They have forgotten that they are needed as guides, not buddies.

Some parents actually believe buying alcohol for their kids keeps the kids safe because they will drink at home instead of in cars, but I'm afraid I'm not convinced that's the lesson taught. Although it might keep kids at home, it seems to me to give the message that parents agree that alcohol is very important to having fun and needs to be available for any successful social situation.

Joan Parnas

> **If one of the people at the party is drinking and acting differently than normal, be a true friend and make sure that he or she does not drive an automobile.**

183

Is there a drinking problem in your family?

My father is an alcoholic. He drinks at a pretty steady pace. He works outside. But when I come home and find him inside on a sunny day, I have a pretty good idea what is happening. I usually go to my room until my mom comes home, but that's when the action starts.

All I hear is screaming and at night my mom will be crying. She takes me to my friend's house so I can get some sleep, but who can sleep when your dad and mom are at home fighting like mad?

Over the past two years my mom has been saying my dad will get help, but he *never* once has followed through.

My dad drinks and when he drinks he becomes a whole different person. He acts like he knows everything, and anything I do is wrong. I hate him when he's a drunk...

I know my father has a drinking problem, but he's stopped drinking for seven months. I confronted him about it and so did his girlfriend. She's the one who got him to stop.

My father has a drinking problem. I deal with it by just staying out of his way. But when I can't go any-where and he's drunk I just yell at him. I talk all my hurt and sadness out with my two little sisters or my friends and my boyfriend. I really wish I could hold it in because I don't want to hurt my friends. My sisters always ask why I'm mad at them and all I can do is hold them and say I'm sorry and that I love them and will try harder.

My mom's boyfriend has a drinking problem. I used to deal with it by avoiding him and staying in my room a lot. After a while though I got sick of having to be punished by staying in my room. I went to my mom and told her I was scared and stressed out from *his* drinking problem. We had a long talk and it did a lot of good. After two weeks he moved out.

My dad has a drinking prob-lem. I think he gets stressed out at work. He goes to a club and drinks for an hour and then comes home. I just ignore him by going to my room to play Nintendo. But I would like to say that if my dad doesn't drink one night he is a real cool guy.

Or do you know someone affected by alcohol?

I don't have parents with a drinking problem but I used to drink (not heavily). My two friends who don't drink are runners and they challenged me to run with them. I soon found that drinking doesn't work for me. I am now an exceptional runner. If I had a friend in the position I was in I would do the same for him as my friends did for me.

My best friend's mom is an alcoholic and she tells me that her mom blames it on her all the time and that sometimes she does think it's her fault.

My friend's parents are both recovering alcoholics. The main thing my friend worries about is becoming an alcoholic herself. Because of this, she stays away from alcohol completely.

I do have a friend whose father is an alcoholic. Because he drinks so excessively, her family suffers quite a bit. She took it upon herself to get a family counselor.

How do you deal with it?

I get mad at my folks, but I don't show it.

I go into my room and blast my stereo.

Ignore it. That might not solve the drinking problem, but it does avoid a lot of stupid fighting.

I deal with it by just sitting and watching TV or by doing my homework. If he gets real bad I just try to avoid him.

I have a friend with a drinking problem and he handles it pretty poorly. It probably started with social dinners, a bunch of us would get together almost every night and there would always be some kind of alcohol.

He was always the one who drank too much and ended up stumbling around, making no sense whatsoever, and then passing out.

He still drinks more than he should and when he does, he always gets out of control. We, as his friends, have tried to get him to stop drinking, but there's not much you can do for an alcoholic who doesn't want to help himself.

185

Dear FYI: We are all concerned about our junior high and high school students drinking, but until parents get the message that serving liquor to under-age students is deadly, we will never solve the problem. Any ideas?

An Irate Parent

Dear Irate Parent: We wish we had a solution for you, but we can pass on suggestions from the Safe Homes Project. Parents of a minor invited to an activity are encouraged to call the person in charge: to verify the occasion and location; to check on adult supervision; to be sure that there will be no alcohol or other drugs served.

If the activity seems inappropriate, express your concern, keep your teen-ager home and seek alternate activities.

FYI editor

Dear FYI: Hi. Last year I often went to parties and got drunk, and then I would mess around with my friends' boyfriends. They always found out, and then I would lose my friends. I don't know why I do this, but for some reason it makes me feel wanted. Last year I left to another place to escape this problem, but this year I'm back, and things still haven't changed. What should I do?

Always Sorry

Dear Always Sorry: What a problem it must be to do something you do not want to do! However, many of us do things which we regret or which lead to undesirable outcomes; in your case, loss of friends. Mostly, we learn from these experiences, and after a few repetitions of such painful behavior, find ways to stop or avoid continuing it.

Clearly, you tried to eliminate the problem by going to another place. Did the behavior continue there? I assume not, since you did not mention it.

Well, what to do now? Leaving was not enough; indeed it revealed that this activity may only occur here, suggesting you might look for hidden factors which promote drinking and "messing around." Sometimes school or family pressures are inappropriately dealt with by drinking, which diminishes your control and impairs your judgment and "messing around" follows.

However, you may also look within yourself, not just outside. Many teen-agers feel awkward socially and fear being left out by the crowd. Many times, drinking then becomes a way to feel more comfortable and "be part of the group." Unfortunate acts occur, but why "messing around?"

All of us wish to be wanted, admired, loved; perhaps you feel this particularly keenly and then are willing to risk your friends' rejection for their boyfriends' attention! Complex!

If these suggestions do not ring true for you, or if they do but nothing changes, consider talking it over with your parents, friends, minister, teacher or school counselor. Sometimes seeing a mental health counselor can be particularly useful to help sort out complex problems such as yours.

Joe P. Tupin, M.D.
Medical director

Dear FYI: If you are pregnant and you have an occasional glass of wine, could that hurt your baby?

Curious

Dear Curious: We don't know how much alcohol it takes to cause fetal damage, but most people in the health field agree it is best for the baby if the expectant mother doesn't drink at all.

FYI editor

Dear FYI: Does drinking coffee get rid of the effects of alcohol quicker?

An Inquisitive Kid

Dear Inquisitive: No. Give a drunk coffee and you get a wide-awake drunk. The only way to rid the body of the effects of alcohol is to let the liver break down the alcohol and dispose of it. That takes about one hour for each drink consumed (a "drink" is five ounces of wine or a 12-ounce can of beer or a mixed drink with a shot of alcohol).

FYI editor

Dear FYI: Can a sauna help a hangover?

Slightly Hungover (sometimes)

Dear Slightly Hungover: Lucky you to have access to a sauna. But unlucky you if you combine the sauna with a hangover. Alcohol can relax the blood vessels, which lowers blood pressure.

Heat lowers blood pressure too. Combining the two (alcohol and sauna) may lead to hypotension and fainting. If you are in a sauna with a hangover, be sure to have someone with you who isn't hungover.

FYI editor

> **Dear FYI:** I went to a party Saturday night and there was a lot of alcohol. A couple of kids drank a lot real fast and passed out. One girl was unconscious and throwing up. I really got scared they were going to die.
>
> Other kids took care of them. Everyone was afraid to call parents or take them to the hospital because we would all get in trouble. I feel terrible because I didn't do anything. What should I have done?
>
> _Really Scared_

Dear Really Scared: I am sure you, and others, were very frightened.

You should have been, because alcohol can kill, especially when ingested quickly or in excess. Alcohol is a chemical similar to ether, a drug used to put people to sleep and paralyze them for operations. Drinking a little alcohol can change vision, balance and reactions.

Remember the basketball players who chug-a-lugged at their motel in Ukiah one Christmas and died? Healthy, young people were found dead in their rooms because the alcohol rushed to their brains and stopped their breathing -- as effective as a shotgun blast to the brain.

Walking or sleeping it off usually works when the alcohol has been consumed slowly over a prolonged time. When "gulped" alcohol is a lethal drug. It doesn't matter if it's beer or vodka or...

Fast drinking often causes a very rapid rise in the alcohol content of the blood, then the brain ... and before anyone knows it the drinker is "anesthetized." The fast drinker quickly goes past "drunkenness" and passes out. He or she is:

1. Deeply asleep and at risk of vomiting and sucking the vomitus into his or her lungs and choking to death.

2. In a coma, which may stop breathing altogether.

3. In a coma, experiencing poor breathing and heart irregularity that could cause death.

4. In danger of having his or her heart stop altogether.

It is true that many lucky ones "sleep it off", but as we see more and more "toss it down fast" macho drinking we see more "coma" deaths in 12- to 20-year-old people. If the drunk person cannot be kept awake by talking or walking, place the victim face down, head turned to the side, keeping the mouth clear for air.

Your fear and denial may tell you to wait to call for help, not to cause trouble. Your fear and denial may add another fatality. Call for help immediately.

Do not allow rapid drinking. Stop these potentially fatal experiments.

Anytime a person passes out from alcohol and shows erratic breathing or begins to retch, there is a death risk and emergency assistance should be sought. Dial 911, your physician or someone experienced.

It is better than dialing the coroner...

E. Jack Benner, M.D.

Dear FYI: Can small amounts of alcohol (a half a beer, etc.) be good for your body?

P.T.

Dear P.T.: For a long time people have suggested that moderate alcohol consumption might help prevent coronary heart disease, but the evidence in this area is controversial. The most recent U.S. Department of Health and Human Services summary of alcohol effects on health concludes that "it is premature to assume that moderate alcohol consumption provides protection against coronary heart disease".

Dave Stoebel

> **'It is premature to assume that moderate alcohol consumption provides protection against coronary heart disease.'**
> **-- U.S. government report**

Dear FYI: Can alcohol keep you from growing normally?
Already Short

Dear Already Short: The only thing alcohol keeps from growing normally in teen-agers may be their intellectual, emotional and spiritual development .

E. Jack Benner

Dear FYI: I drink beer. My mom and I are having an argument about whether alcohol depressed you. Does it?
Beer Drinker

Dear Beer Drinker: Depression can have several meanings. One is the short-term "down feeling" that all people get from time to time. If you're talking about this kind of depression, the answer is yes and no. It all depends on how you feel when you start drinking. Alcohol is a depressant drug and one of the first effects you feel when you use it is a reduction of your normal inhibitions. When that happens you begin to experience whatever feelings your inhibitions have been covering up.

If you are normally a restrained person who would like to be the life of the party, alcohol can strip away your serious side. Conversely, if you are covering up some sadness, booze can bring that sadness out and make it even more pronounced. As you drink more, however, alcohol's depressant effects become even more pronounced and your whole body slows down.

It is important to remember that alcohol is a potent drug that has far-reaching effects on the mind and body. Well over half of all suicides are tied to alcohol. That is hardly the image of happy, successful young people that beer companies would like you to swallow along with their products.

Dave Stoebel

Dear FYI: What is the most dangerous, long-lasting drug available (the one that can do most damage)?

Curious

Dear Curious: My vote goes to alcohol. It is the drug most readily available, it can be addictive, and once addicted, few alcoholics ever recover. Beyond that, alcohol can cause more physical problems than any other drug I know. The disease we think of most often is cirrhosis of the liver, an irreversible breakdown of this vital organ. In the United States alcohol is the leading cause of cirrhosis, and cirrosis is the ninth leading cause of death.

Alcohol can also cause damage to the stomach and intestinal tract, impair the intestines' ability to absorb nutrients and lead to malnutrition. Heavy alcohol use can cause heart disease and high blood pressure. It can affect the hormones, particularly the reproductive hormones -- leading to reproductive failure and sexual dysfunction. If used by expectant mothers, it can lead to Fetal Alcohol Syndrome (permanent metal retardation and/or physical deformities in the baby).

Alcohol is also known to cause brain damage -- particularly a kind of amnesia known as Korsakoff's syndrome. It has been linked to certain kinds of cancers and to an impairment of the immune system. When you add all this to the fact that alcohol is linked to a large proportion -- if not the majority -- of automobile, boating and domestic accidents, homicides and incidents of domestic violence, I don't think there is any doubt about alcohol being the answer to your question.

Dave Stoebel

Dear FYI: I am an active member in the "It's OK Not to Drink" group at my high school. I just wanted to let people know how much of a difference one person can make in saving a friend's life.

Recently I was at a party where some alcohol was involved. A good friend of mine arrived at the party drunk and later passed out. Since most of the people had been drinking, none of them realized how sick she really was.

After months of training with my group, I knew what to do. I turned her on her stomach, thinking that if she got sick, she wouldn't choke to death on her vomit. After about 20 minutes, I went to check on her and found that she had gotten sick. I'm just so thankful, because if I hadn't done the simple task of turning her onto her stomach, she could have died.

I want everyone to read the letter my friend sent me after she realized what went on. It reads:

"Dear _____ :

"I really want to thank you for helping me Saturday night. My mom told me that you saved my life by turning me over. I feel really stupid, but I learned a lesson. Drinking can kill people and I never will drink again. If it wasn't for you, I might not be here today. Thank you for helping me and cleaning up after me. You are a very special person.

"Love Always, _____ "

She learned a lesson, and I really learned mine. It takes two seconds for someone to stop breathing; don't 'risk it! If someone is that sick, get help immediately or at least call that person's parents. They would rather be grounded for a year or two than be dead.

Thankful

Dear FYI: Forget, for a moment, the legality of minors drinking and please comment on this situation:

There are minors getting drunk and there are responsible teens who offer to take care of them and take them home. What do you do with an intoxicated friend? What would I do if my son brought two kids home who were drunk?

Another Parent

Dear Parent: If I were you, I'd commend my son for his concern for his friends, and then enlist his help in taking them home. Although we often make jokes about drunkenness and see it as a relatively harmless state that most people experience, it is, in fact, a drug overdose and can be life-threatening.

Unless my son's friends were so ill as to need to go to the hospital, or so abused by parents that they were in physical danger, I'd want them home in their parent's custody rather than in mine ... and I would want my child home in my custody as well if he or she were drunk.

If we do not return a young person home, one effect is to buffer that person from the response of his or her family. While the response may not always be pleasant, it is a necessary first step toward recognizing potential problems and toward clarifying that family's values and responses to such problems.

Joan Parnas

Dear FYI: Is it wrong if, when your friend is drunk and wants to drive, to take the keys and drive yourself, even if you have no driver's license, when that is the only way home?

High School Student

Dear Student: Unfortunately, it is illegal for you to drive a vehicle without a license, even if you seem to have no other alternatives. Yet I would suggest that there are alternatives. Have you ever talked with your parents about calling them for help if you find yourself in this situation?

Also, do you have any other friends with driver's licenses? If so, keep their phone numbers in your wallet or purse. Talk with them before such a situation occurs, to see if they would be willing to help.

In addition, there is always the police department, which is much more concerned about keeping someone out of trouble or from being injured, than about putting them in jail. Unless the minor is so intoxicated he or she would be a danger to himself or herself or to the public, there would be no violation of the law (this shouldn't be confused with possession of alcohol by a minor in public, which is against the law). You may have to wait if the officers are busy, but it would beat your other alternative.

The fact that your friend has been drinking is something he or she will have to resolve with his or her parents, but at least you both would be alive and not injured or in jail.

Drinking to the point of becoming a "drunk driver" could be an indication of alcohol abuse. This is especially true for someone under the age of 18. If you care about this person, have an honest talk with him or her. Explain your concern about the excessive drinking and the predicament you were forced into. Try to get your friend to see a professional.

Lt. Leo G. Sackett
Police officer

Dear FYI: If someone you know who is not a close friend but a little more than an acquaintance brings alcohol to school, what can you do besides telling someone (the administration) who will get him in trouble?

Want to Help

P.S. This guy drinks with his father when his father is in town.

Dear Want to Help: I am concerned that your friend is bringing alcohol to school and see this as an indication that the person may be developing a problem with alcohol. He is drinking during the week (not just occasionally on the weekends) and brings alcohol to school despite the fact that he may be caught.

Bringing alcohol to school is something not to be taken lightly. The person may get hurt or hurt others while under the influence, and telling the administration is not necessarily getting him or her into trouble.

For some, having the administration find out allows the student to break silence about the drinking, and this may be what is needed for a person to recognize he or she is developing a problem with alcohol. Many people deny they have a problem or are afraid to ask for help. Some schools refer a student to counseling and the consequences of the alcohol abuse are reduced if the student participates in alcohol/drug counseling.

Since your friend drinks with his father, there may be some concern on your part that telling about your friend's drinking at school will cause problems in the family. You are not responsible for what happens in the family. The important thing is that you feel your friend needs help. Have you talked to your friend about his father's drinking?

There is a support group in many communities, Alateen, for children and teenagers who are concerned about someone's drinking. At Alateen your friend can feel free to talk about his feelings or just listen to others who have the same feelings.

Another option for you to consider is to seek out a trusted adult: a parent, relative, neighbor, minister, etc. Find someone with whom you feel comfortable who will listen and help you develop a plan of action.

Your friend is lucky to have you. Not everyone is willing to help a person who is not a close friend. Remember, you don't have to act alone. There are many people who can help you.

Magdeline Winkelblack

Dear FYI: If I smoke and don't inhale, can I get cancer?

G.

Dear G: The logic behind the ban on smoking in airplanes, restaurants and other public buildings is that passive inhaling from other people's cigarettes is associated with an increased incidence of lung disease, cancer and heart disease.

E. Jack Benner

Dear FYI: What exactly are clove cigarettes? Are they dangerous?

Concerned Parent

Dear Parent: Clove cigarettes are made up of about 70 percent regular tobacco and 30 percent ground cloves.

Clove cigarette smokers run even more risks than cigarette smokers, for smoking machine tests show that the tar and nicotine content of clove cigarettes is more than double that of regular cigarettes. In addition, cloves contain the chemical eugenol, which is used as a local anesthetic.

Because of this anesthetic effect, it is easier for the beginning smoker to smoke clove cigarettes than regular ones, increasing the chance of becoming addicted to regular cigarettes. Clove cigarettes are dangerous, and there have been some incidences of serious illness.

Dave Stoebel

Dear FYI: How long would it take for a person to develop mouth cancer from chewing tobacco? What's a usual length of time -- two years, 10 years or does it depend?

Just Interested

Dear FYI: How long do snuff users have before they get lip cancer?

Very Worried

Dear Just Interested and Very Worried: The chances of developing mouth cancer from smokeless tobacco and the length of time to develop it would depend on the frequency of use and the amount used. Because no two bodies have identical reactions, there is much biological variability.

As little as a year or two of moderate smokeless tobacco use can produce precancerous changes in the tissues. Some people believe that smokeless tobacco causes a greater risk for mouth cancer than cigarettes because of the continuous contact with the tissues.

It is critically important for smokeless tobacco users to see a dentist at least every six months so a biopsy can be done if tissue changes look suspicious. The dentist should be informed of frequency of use and exactly where the tobacco is placed in the mouth.

Chewing (sucking a wad that is a mixture of tobacco and molasses) and dipping (putting powdered or crushed tobacco -- snuff -- between the lower lip and gum) do not only increase the chance of cancer, they cause bad breath, tooth discoloration and decay. Teeth may become loose and even fall out.

Dippers and chewers should examine their mouths, lips and tongues often. They should look for sores that bleed easily or don't heal. A sore throat, pain in chewing and swallowing, or sore and red gums may also be danger signals. A doctor should be consulted if any of these signs are present.

Once a person starts using tobacco, it is very hard to stop as addiction can occur. As a matter of fact, this form of tobacco use is more addictive than smoking. Quitting is possible -- it has been done. The best answer is not to start.

Jeffrey Light, D.D.S.

Special note to coaches: Because the use of smokeless tobacco is prevalent among athletes, and considered "macho," we encourage you to share this information with your teams.

Dear FYI: I've been smoking since sixth grade. I'm in the 10th now and my lungs burn real bad. Do you think I have a good chance of getting cancer?

Getting Really Worried

Dear Getting Really Worried: Lung cancer is now the most common cause of death from cancer in both men and women, and most cases are due to cigarette smoking. About one smoker in 10 will eventually die from lung cancer and an almost equal number will die from emphysema, which is a destructive disease of the lung. In addition, smoking markedly increases the chance of having a heart attack, which can be fatal. Although these conditions do not develop until the person has been smoking for many years, you are still wise to be concerned about smoking at your relatively early age. Smoking is a drug addiction, and the longer you smoke, the harder it is to break the habit. It will be easier for you to quit now than later. There are medicines, available on prescription, which have helped many people to quit smoking.

Glen A Lillington, M.D.
Internist

Dear FYI: I don't like it when my mom smokes. She says she's in the midst of quitting, but hasn't. Do you have any tips for me to help her stop?

Concerned Kid

195

Dear Concerned Kid: You are wise to be concerned about your mother smoking, both for her health and your own. Unfortunately, there are no sure-fire ways to persuade another person to stop smoking, even one you love as much as you obviously love your mom. Smoking is an addiction to a drug, and quitting is not easy.

With that awareness, there are still some recommendations I can make.

1. Encourage your mother's efforts to stop whenever you notice them, and let her know you appreciate them.

2. Give her lots of approval and appreciation in other areas as well, so that you don't get into a position of always being critical of her.

3. Let her know occasionally that you realize how hard quitting smoking is, but you also know she can do it if she gets the support she needs, which might include such things as stop-smoking classes and/or ex-smoker support groups. Your local Lung Association sponsors classes, and they also have materials for smokers to work with on their own.

Your mother is lucky to have such a caring supporter. Why not show her this letter?

Joan Parnas

Dear FYI: Is it true that smoke from cigarettes or cloves stays in your lungs for a few weeks?

Rumor Hearer

Dear Rumor Hearer: Yes, dangerous chemicals from smoke do stay in your lungs for a few weeks. There are over 4,000 chemicals in cigarette smoke, including many toxic substances.

Tobacco smoke impairs the lung's primary mechanism for expelling dirt and waste products. As a substitute for this action, the lung produces mucus to trap the pollutants. This can be a problem, however, because the pollution containing mucus stays trapped in the lung until forced out by the "smoker's cough".

Because a smoker's lungs are not fully able to cleanse themselves of pollutants, smoking can lead to lung cancer, emphysema or chronic bronchitis.

April Roeseler, R.N., M.S.P.H.
Health-education consultant

Dear FYI: Is it possible for a child to start smoking because he's been around one of his parents who has been smoking all of his life?

A Smoker's Son

Dear Smoker's Son: There is no evidence suggesting that children raised by smoking parents will become addicted to nicotine because of the smoky environment. However, children learn by example -- and those with smoking parents may try to imitate their elders as they grow up.

On the other hand, there is very good evidence that children of smoking parents have more colds and respiratory infections, an increased risk of heart abnormalities, and the potential for future heart disease.

Cynthia Reeves Tuttle, MPH,ACCE
Health educator

Dear FYI: If children eat raw tobacco can it be a life-and-death situation?
A Curious Parent

Dear Curious Parent: I am somewhat confused as to what you mean by "raw" tobacco. However, after consulting with the Regional Poison Center, I may be able to offer some helpful information.

Consumption of as little as one cigarette, three cigarette butts, one pinch of snuff or *any amount* of nicotine gum is considered toxic and the child should receive medical attention immediately. Symptoms of toxicity may include restlessness, irritability, nausea, vomiting, drowsiness, weakness or seizures. Home administration of ipecac syrup is not recommended. Contact your nearest Poison Center for instruction whenever accidental poisoning is suspected.

Cynthia Reeves Tuttle

Further suggested reading

- Dorris, Michael, *The Broken Cord.* Harper Perennial, New York, N.Y., 1989 (on fetal alcohol syndrome).
- Ferguson, Tom, *The No-Nag, No-Guilt, Do-It-Your-Own-Way Guide to Quitting Smoking.* Ballantine, New York, 1987.
- Klaas, Joe, *The No-Nag, No-Guilt, Do-It-Your-Own-Way Guide to Quitting Smoking.* Ballantine, New York, N.Y., 1987.
- Robertson, Nan, Getting Better: Inside Alcoholics Anonymous. Fawcett Crest, New York, N.Y., 1988.

10

Sex is never an emergency

Sex is never an emergency? Try telling Bill that. Between school and football practice he wanted to do it. While I was doing homework he got all excited. On the way to school, he suggested we cut first period and go to his house.

There was pressure 24 hours a day, seemed like seven days a week.

Well, I finally figured it out. While he wanted to go all the way, I didn't. Our sexual desires were very different and I used a very old line on Bill -- I simply told him "no."

He was disappointed. In fact, we broke up. But guess what? I met a nice guy named Greg, and he feels like I do. I like the relationship a lot more, we do some neat things together and the pressure's off. I still don't get a lot of homework done when Greg's around, but at least now it's my decision...

Dear FYI: I have a boyfriend and he doesn't pressure me into having sex. He says whenever I'm ready. My question is -- should I go ahead and have sex with him? He's also two years older (17). I want to because we don't see each other that much. He lives in another town.

Thinking About It

Dear Thinking: I am glad that you are giving this important decision careful thought. Having sex with someone, especially the first time, is a powerful emotional experience and can have many different consequences. You need to consider carefully your reasons and those of your boyfriend, so that you know what it means and can anticipate some of the problems.

People have sex for many reasons; some have little to do with expressions of love and devotion. Examples: to keep the boy or man interested; to "prove" they are grown up; out of curiosity; because they think it will give them love...

Usually when people, especially girls and women, are sexual they become more intensely involved in the relationship and often put their needs and interests second, or even stay in bad relationships. Having sex for the wrong reason can have tragic consequences -- like unplanned pregnancy.

Even though you say he doesn't pressure you, your letter suggests that you would do it "for him" -- not because you are truly ready.

I see this in the fact that you are hesitant, that you see him as older and that you don't see him often. Why does not seeing him often make you want to have sex? Do you think he would like you more and see you more often if you had sex? Are you worried that he will find an older girlfriend who will?

You shouldn't have sex until you love someone deeply and are willing to have an even deeper involvement and commitment ... and when you truly desire the experience for yourself. It would be ideal for you to talk this important decision over with someone who knows you and your individual situation.

Ilana E. Davis, Ph.D.
Psychologist

Dear FYI: I'm 15 years old. I want to have sex with a boy but I'm afraid I'm going to get pregnant or get AIDS. I don't know what to do.
Scared

Dear Scared: I applaud you for stopping to think about how your decision to become sexually active may affect your future. The fact that you question having sex with your boyfriend indicates that you are an informed and thinking person. Pregnancy, AIDs and other sexually transmitted diseases are possible negative consequences of sexual intercourse. Unless you are honestly prepared to deal with these possibilities, *wait!*

You might also consider the potential loss of parental and peer approval. Most people would tell you that you are risking too much, too soon in your life. Choosing to be sexually active at this age invites additional emotional turmoil, and who needs that? It is interesting and important to know that when young people decide to discuss their feelings about having sex openly and honestly with each other, they discover that it is not sex that they want as much as they want to feel closer to each other.

When two people are able to discuss their feelings of attraction for each other and their sexual sensations, they often find that they do feel closer, trust each other more, learn to show affection in very caring and playful ways and develop a much deeper and more meaningful relationship. Feeling close and intimate with someone does not necessarily include sex.

If you really care for this young man (and he cares for you) consider putting your energies into developing this kind of friendship, which rarely results in feelings of remorse or disappointment.

Judith Buchholz,
School counselor &
Sex-education teacher

Dear FYI: I have a big problem! It all started when I was in sixth grade. Me and this guy messed around a little bit. Well, everyone found out. Ever since then people have been calling me a slut! Which I'm not! We didn't go that far. Anyway, when I got into seventh grade I messed around with another guy. But this time we went kind of far. Well, no one found out except for my pastor and my parents. Now my mom calls me a slut. My life is in a big mess. Please help.

Hopeless

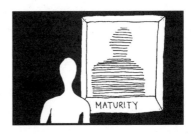

Dear Hopeless: I'm worried less about your mother calling you a slut than I am with you calling yourself "hopeless." Your mother may simply have expressed her anger and disappointment that her young daughter did not postpone sexual involvement until later years, as most girls of your age do. Give her some time. Both of you will get over that part of your story.

But why are you calling yourself hopeless? Because you got carried away? Because you did something you may not really have wanted to do? Because you did not use any precautions and exposed yourself to the possibility of pregnancy? Because you think you will "have to" do it again? All of the above?

Think of it this way: your experiences have taught you the pleasures and displeasures, the advantages and disadvantages of early sexual activity.

You can now weigh them against each other and then make your choice. In that respect, you have gained some maturity. If you had the will to say yes before, you now have the strength to say no, if that is what you decide. You are not a slut, and you are not hopeless. In time, most of your bad feelings should be gone.

Herbert Bauer, M.D.
Psychiatrist

Dear FYI: I've heard of a lewd sex act called "S and M." What is it? Is it illegal?

Uninformed

Dear Uninformed: The "S" stands for sadism, which in a sexual context means inflicting pain on one's partner in order to get sexual pleasure. The "M" stands for masochism, which means getting sexual pleasure from being on the receiving end of that pain. S and M performed between two consenting adults in the privacy of their home is not illegal, but it does involve certain physical and psychological risks.

FYI editor

Dear FYI: I have a problem. My boyfriend and I are very sexually active. We have been going out for a very long time, but now my boyfriend is getting bored with "the same old stuff." He has started doing really gross stuff that I am not comfortable with. But I don't want to lose him. He is the only good thing in my life now ... and I've grown to really love him and depend on him. Sometimes I think I would die if I lost him. But, I mean, sometimes I feel I could just die when he does some of these things to me. He's even gotten into whipping and being abusive -- he says it turns him on. What should I do? Help!

Hurt But In Love

Dear Hurt: It's wonderful to be in love and to want your relationship to grow and survive. However, an important element of any friendship is to be honest and express your feelings. It sounds like you understandably dislike some of your boyfriend's sexual preferences and behaviors. My concern is that his behavior may become even more extreme and demanding.

At this point it's important to give him a strong, clear message that "whipping" is *not OK* and that you want it to stop immediately! If he loves you he will respect your feelings. Since your feelings are so intense, it would be advisable for you to discuss your problem with a counselor on your local crisis line or at your area sexual assault center. Your call/visit will be kept confidential.

Nancy Hanks, Ed.D.
Sex therapist

Dear FYI: I'm 15 years old. I love my boyfriend very much ... and I really want to have sex with him. But before I do, I'd like to know a couple of things. First, does it hurt a lot the first time? Also, if it does hurt the first time, how many times does it take before it doesn't hurt anymore?

Nervous

The *very* first time a girl or woman has sexual intercourse does she bleed? Why?

Afraid to Ask

Dear Nervous and Afraid to Ask: Pain is intensified by fear. When you are comfortable enough with a decision to have sex, your fears, and consequently any pain, will be minimized. Biologically, some women do experience pain in having sexual relations the first time. There may be bleeding from where the hymen (the skin around the opening of the vagina) is stretched and separated at its edges. This varies from woman to woman; often there is no bleeding at all.

Debbie Davis
Newspaper editor

Dear FYI: Is it true that females can't have sex while they are having their period? Why or why not?

A Baffled Guy

Dear Baffled: Women can have sex while they are menstruating. Some women and/or their partners prefer not to have sex because of the "mess." Others, particularly in some other cultures, find this the most desirable time to have sex.

Some women find that having sex during their periods is more uncomfortable because they have more dryness from lack of natural lubrication, although the blood is flowing. It's a matter of personal preference.

Anne Seeley-MacLeod, M.Ed., BFA
Planned Parenthood

Dear FYI: Why do guys use girls for their bodies, then act like they hardly know them?

Disappointed

> **Some of the most basic questions about your new body often go unanswered, but...**
>
> *Experts believe you should know as much about what's going on as you can find out.*
>
> *Many experiences are less traumatic than you may think. Armed with correct information, even tough times smooth out.*

Dear Disappointed: It sounds as though you became involved in a sexual relationship where you weren't clear about his motivation and commitment to the relationship. He may be embarrassed that he wasn't "in love" or committed. He may be scared of talking with you because he then has to face your hopes and disappointments.

Hopefully, next time you will not have sex until you know that the other person's involvement and motivation are up to your expectations.

Ilana E. Davis

Women can have sex while they are menstruating. Some women and/or their partners prefer not to have sex because of the 'mess.' Others, particularly in some other cultures, find this the most desirable time to have sex.

Dear FYI: My boyfriend won't wear a condom. He says he doesn't like how they feel. What should I say?

In a Quandary

Dear In a Quandary: You should say, "If you won't use it, I won't do it." You might add that you don't like how morning sickness, labor, sexually transmitted diseases or an abortion might feel, either. His acceptance of condoms will skyrocket when he realizes you are serious about taking care of yourself.

Lynn Schimmel
Nurse practitioner
Women's health associates

Dear FYI: How come everyone says that it only takes one time and you can get pregnant? Me and my boyfriend have had sex a number of times and we haven't used any protection. We both are the first person that each other has had sex with. Are we just lucky or what?

Just Lucky?

Dear Just Lucky: Have you just been lucky? So lucky it takes my breath away!

All I can picture as I try to answer this is you sitting in the rocking chair across from me. I'm either spending hours trying very hard to prepare you for labor and parenthood or the relinquishing of your baby. Or we're working through the tremendous grief that's involved if you decide that termination of your pregnancy is best. Neither is the joyous journey I would wish for your pregnancy.

Look at it this way — there are cold viruses around all the time, but you don't catch one every time you are exposed. It's the same with pregnancy. Although every exposure doesn't lead to a conception, the fact is that you have between a 90 and 100 percent chance of being pregnant before the year is over. Is that *really* what you want?

I know it is very tempting for teen-agers to want to push their luck, as a pregnancy is an unquestionable assurance of the perfection of their bodies "working." But please consider getting this assurance from looking at other body systems that you take for granted; just as surely as you breathe, your reproductive system works.

One last comment — I meet many young men who come in to accompany their partners for support during the above-described visits. Does your partner care enough for you that he would do that? If so, why doesn't he care enough to wear a condom now? It may not be easy for him to buy them, but it sure is easier than labor!

Lynn Schimmel

HOW DO YOU HAVE FUN ON A DATE WITHOUT GETTING SEXUALLY INVOLVED?

HOW DO YOU SAY NO TO SEX?

Students try to meet the challenge

If my date asked me to have sex I would say no because I'm too young to have a baby. I would have to get up at night and give it food and he wouldn't be there to help me. And one thing I would not want is an abortion.
Female, age 13

If you see she wants to do something or get closer you might want to start a conversation about another friend. Just act normal but start talking.
Male, age 14

If you're not interested in this activity then lots of body movement can explain this *clearly*. And if you *have* to, just plain let that person know that you are not interested. If they do not stick around they are not worth it -- not to me, anyway...
Female, age 16

If your partner thinks sex is the only thing to do on a date you better take a second look at who you are going out with. "No" isn't hard to understand.
Female, age 17

If you go to someone's home, make sure their parents are there.
Girl, age 12

On a date you can go to the movies or play miniature golf. If you are worried about sex, maybe you should bring another friend along.
Female, age 16

Knowing about all the harmful diseases you can catch can help a lot in saying no to sex.
Female, age 17

My girlfriend and I have gone out for two months and we have avoided sex for special reasons. One is the fact of respect and honor, the other is to make it really special when the time comes. One of our techniques is to just do something to keep our minds off it - sports, homework, watching TV and talking. **Male, age 17**

It is not true that guys want or need sex more than girls. Both males and females enjoy sex. However, girls and guys are taught different attitudes toward sex. And don't forget, the consequences for sexual behavior can be much more negative for a girl.

Dear FYI: Why do guys want sex so much? Do girls want sex as much as guys?
Super Curious

Dear Super Curious: Good questions! It is a myth that guys want or need sex more than girls. Both males and females enjoy sex. However, girls and guys are taught different attitudes toward sex. And don't forget, the consequences for sexual behavior can be more negative for a girl.

In our society, guys are allowed to be overt about their interest in and need for sex, whereas girls often are encouraged to be passive.

For example, a boy may feel pressured by friends to prove his masculinity by "scoring." He may therefore pressure his girlfriend. A girl may be fearful to be sexual, afraid to be labeled "fast," to become pregnant, or to contract a disease (such as herpes or AIDS). She could also deny she is interested in relating sexually and could therefore neglect to contact the appropriate sources for help (such as information about birth control) until after intercourse has occurred.

Being aware of, and responsible for, your feelings is a key to enjoying sex. Each person has to develop his or her own set of rules regarding when sex is OK. This takes some time, thinking and usually discussion with a trusted adult.

Some questions to think about:

-- Am I doing this for me or to prove something?

-- How well do I need to know this person first? Am I comfortable with short alliances or do I need a committed love relationship to develop first?

-- Am I comfortable enough with this person to ask tough

questions like, "Do you use birth control?;" "Have you been exposed to any diseases?;" or to say, "Let's use a condom for protection."

-- How will I feel if this person never speaks to me again or it becomes known that we had sex?

Caution: If you are not ready to ask these particular questions, slow down and give yourself some time to be prepared.

Finally, most people find sex is at its best within a love relationship based on mutual respect and trust. Good luck in finding yours.

Carrie Schucker, Ph.D
Marriage, family &
Child counselor

Dear FYI: Why are people labeled?

Don't people have anything better to do? Girls that go and make one "mistake" by either getting pregnant or just fooling around once are "sluts," whereas the guy is "cool" or a "stud."

Why does this happen?

It's Unfair

Dear It's Unfair: What you've identified is an example of using double standards to judge male and female behavior. In this case, it's in relationship to their sexual experience. That's unfair and you are justifiably disturbed.

Negatively labeling a female for her sexual experience is not new to this generation. The attitudes, values and beliefs that feed into this kind of thinking are solidly grounded in powerful cultural, social and religious standards.

Historically, great value has been placed on the female's virginity and purity. She has been responsible for saving her virginity until marriage in order to ensure the legitimacy of her children and her social position. When she broke the rules, she was often publicly punished or labeled as a social outcast.

On the other hand, the man's illegitimate children may have caused him some embarrassment, but seldom affected his position in the social order. Sexism may be a new word, but it is not a new idea.

Quite honestly, it is unlikely that a girl will be judged a slut because she has sex just once. That term is more likely to be applied to a girl who is too active, too soon with too many partners. A more appropriate term for her might be troubled.

Furthermore, with the serious concern over sexually transmitted diseases, like herpes and AIDS, promiscuous behavior that might have been thought cool for the fellow can now be considered simply foolish.

Judith Buchholz

Dear FYI: Is it wrong to have a baby at 15?

Wondering

Dear Wondering: Let's look at the reasons why I think it's better to be older before taking on that responsibility...

At 15, the body hasn't finished growing and developing and it isn't ready to take on the task of nourishing a baby. Therefore, the mom and baby both get short-changed. We know that babies born to women under 16 are more likely to be premature or have other problems.

Then, at age 15, there are a lot of things you want to do and should be doing in school and for fun. Babies have a way of being extremely demanding of time and energy.

There is a lot of truth in the saying, "Having a baby is like being grounded for the next 18 years."

Caring for a little baby is not easy, but in many ways it is easier than meeting the constant demands and needs of the 2 year old, and on it goes... Will you have the maturity and judgment to meet the child's and your own needs?

Naturally, there have been some young mothers who have been able to meet all these demands and be very successful parents.

Usually, this has been with good support from the father of the baby, parents and others. So it is very important to evaluate your support system. Is the father of the baby mature enough to meet his responsibility to his child and is he going to be there for you?

Finally, I would like to suggest that you think what you want to be doing with your life five or 10 years from now. How would a baby affect your plans and dreams?

Women who don't complete high school often end up with poor-paying jobs and are twice as likely to remain dependent on public-aid programs.

Carol Wolfe, RN, PNP
Public health nurse

Dear FYI: I have a friend who wants to get pregnant just to be a rebel and go against her parents. Well, what advice would you give her besides not doing it?

Upset

Dear Upset: As many as 2 million teen-age girls in our country get pregnant every year. It would indeed be tragic if your friend became one of those -- not because she wants a child, but because she wants to get back at her parents.

What she does not seem to understand is that such a "planned" pregnancy would not only wound her parents, which is her intention, but would hurt her much more by burdening her young life with a full time job called *baby care*. More importantly, she probably hasn't considered that she would be using a baby not as a new family member, but as a worthless means to an end which has no further value after the goal -- to hurt her parents -- has been achieved. Unfortunately, this also is often the background for later child abuse.

Your friend's parents may be completely unaware of their daughter's resentment, be it justified or not. It is of great importance to get the family together and help them look into each other's eyes and vent their feelings. Maybe you could enlist the help of a person who could arrange such a family meeting.

If your friend refuses to do that, maybe a visit to Planned Parenthood would be of value; the counselor would not make any decisions for her but would outline what options are available allowing her to make her choice.

A warning: Do not accept any kind of responsibility for her behavior, and do not feel the least bit guilty if things don't work out in the end. She is responsible for her own behavior, just as you are responsible for yours. You are a good friend, but being friends includes setting limits. Set those limits ... and then be satisfied and let go.

Herbert Bauer, M.D.
Psychiatrist

Dear FYI: My friend is 13 and she is pregnant. But she is scared to tell anyone and she's scared to have the baby because she's afraid it will kill her. Will it kill her?

A Frightened Friend

Dear Frightened Friend: Having the baby will not kill your friend. However, it is important for the health of the mother and baby to get medical care and counseling as early in the pregnancy as possible. But first she needs to make sure she is really pregnant. Sometimes periods are missed for reasons other than pregnancy. It is important for your friend to have a pregnancy test (not a home test) immediately. You could go along with your friend if she would like that. Although teens are often afraid to talk to adults when they have problems, it is important for your friend to get the help of a trusted adult quickly. All she has to say is "I need help, I'm pregnant," and she'll find understanding and assistance.

FYI editor

Dear FYI: Does sex before a game really make you not prepared?

A Jock

Dear Jock: No, but depending upon the game, time of the game and the intensity of the sex, you could be really tired.

FYI editor

Dear FYI: What are the pregnancy symptoms besides not having your period?

A Little Uneasy

Dear A Little Uneasy: About the time of the missed period, most women find that they have to urinate more than normal. Their breasts feel larger and/or more tender all the time. Nausea and vomiting may be a regular part of their morning, or even their whole day. They may also feel tired, hungrier than usual, or alternatively lose their appetite completely.

Some women have no symptoms other than the missed period.

Planned Parenthood

Dear FYI: How long do you have to be pregnant before it shows up on a pregnancy test?

Wondering

Dear Wondering: Doctor's office urine tests may be positive as early as nine days after conception. The test kits you buy in the store are very accurate at the time of your missed period, especially if you use a concentrated urine specimen.

If you wonder, please get an exam.

Lynn Schimmel

Dear FYI: What's the exam for "The Pill" like?

Curious

Dear Curious: Easy, painless and informative. Actually, the exam for the pill is no different from any woman's annual exam. Since the birth control pill has more positive than negative effects, nothing extra is done specifically because you are taking it.

First, you talk with the health-care provider who will answer questions and thoroughly explain the exam. Then a general checkup, including a pelvic exam, is accomplished. The pelvic exam should never be painful, but rather, quite interesting, as you can use a mirror to see up inside you while a speculum is in. While some young women expect that might be "gross," the contrary is true -- demystifying that part of one's body is what patients often tell us they most appreciate.

By the way, a virgin can have a comfortable pelvic exam, and her body is not changed by the exam.

Lynn Schimmel

Dear FYI: How long does it take for the pill to work?

Just Curious

Dear Just Curious: A birth control pill is effective immediately, if started correctly, although many couples choose to use condoms also for the first month until the woman remembers to take her pill every day.

According to one women's health nurse practitioner, "To say that you need to be on the pill for awhile before it is effective implies that it 'builds up' in your system. This is not true. The pill is out of your system in a day or two, which is why you take a fresh pill every day."

A woman can become pregnant if she misses a few pills, even if she's been taking birth control pills for years. If you miss a couple of pills, call your health-care provider.

FYI editor

Dear FYI: Are there condoms that are better than others?

A Reader

Dear Reader: The best condoms are prelubricated, latex condoms that

211

contain the spermicide Nonoxynol-9.

There are several brands to choose from today. These condoms are also more effective in preventing the spread of sexually transmitted diseases.Condoms will break if they are used with baby oil or Vaseline as these products cause the rubber to deteriorate. Condoms should be used only with water based lubricants like KY jelly.

Remember that safe sex (for avoiding sexually transmitted diseases and pregnancy) only occurs by abstaining; being 100 percent sure that both you and your partner have only been with each other; or having a condom in place before intercourse begins. Using a back-up method with the ingredient Nonoxynol-9 in it (foam, diaphragm gel or spermicidal suppositories) is even better.

Because casual and unprotected sex has become a life-or-death matter, great attention is being focused on condoms.

Planned Parenthood

Dear FYI: I can't decide if I want to carry a condom in my wallet or not. If I don't I might get a girl pregnant, but that would give me a reason not to have sex if I don't want to. What should I do?

Unsure

Dear Unsure: Your concern is very common among teen-agers. It is advisable to carry the condom not only because of the risks of an unplanned pregnancy, but also as protection from venereal disease and AIDS. However, your question brings out an important issue -- the social and peer pressure to have sexual experiences at an early age.

Most adolescent males are curious about sexuality and are eager to have experiences. They usually have a great deal of anxiety and concern about sex as well. Fear of early sexual experiences, and worries about the unknown, are usually difficult to admit or discuss with others. The decision to become involved in sexual activities is very personal and private. Both males and females need to feel comfortable saying no to sex because of the complex emotional feelings and relationship issues that must be considered.

Gordon Ulrey, Ph.D.
Psychologist

Dear FYI: Does alcohol have some kind of effect on the risk of becoming pregnant?

K.C.K.

Dear K.C.K.: Alcohol has no direct effect on the risk of becoming pregnant. However, it does lower inhibitions, which makes it more likely that people may do things they wouldn't normally do if they weren't drinking, such as having intercourse without a birth-control method.

You should also know that alcohol can have a harmful effect on a developing fetus.

Your safest option is to stay away from drugs or alcohol.

Jean Mackin, BS
Planned Parenthood

Dear FYI: If you are already pregnant and you mess around again, can you get pregnant again?

Heard It's True

Dear Heard It's True: This is a great question because many people assume the answer would be no...

Well, only about one in 1,000 women ever get pregnant more than once from having sexual intercourse or from sperm deposits that have been left at the opening of a woman's vagina (that's what I understand is meant by "messing around").

Double pregnancy does occur in the case of fraternal (not identical) twins, so it is possible to become pregnant "twice" in that one instance.

What happens in that very rare occurrence is that the woman's ovaries release more than one egg into her fallopian tubes where they are fertilized by a man's sperm. Both eggs are then attached to the uterus, where the egg travels for development.

The second pregnancy doesn't happen a week or a month later; it's very quick, the whole process occurring in a time span of about 24 hours. The woman therefore discovers she is pregnant with both babies at the one time.

Anne Seeley-MacLeod

Dear FYI: Can a girl get pregnant during her period?

Serious Question

Dear Serious Question: Since a woman's body runs on a continuous cycle of getting ready for pregnancy -- and sperm can live in the vagina for up to five days -- the answer is *yes*.

FYI editor

Dear FYI: Is using more than one condom at a time a better protection against pregnancy?
Cautious

Dear FYI: If you use foam with nothing else and sperm live three to five days, can you get pregnant?
Planning Sex

Dear Cautious & Planning Sex: Condoms have a 3% failure rate in the first year of use when used every time and with care. Among typical users (people who don't use condoms regularly), the failure rate is 21%.

According to *Contraceptive Technology* (1990), foam, has a failure rate of 2% for perfect users in the first year. Among typical users the failure rate is about 12%. The spermicide in foam supposedly kills sperm on contact, if the woman uses the foam correctly.

Instead of using more than one condom at a time, we suggest that the man use a condom and the woman use contraceptive foam. Foam and condoms used together have failure rate of about 2.5% -- comparable to the birth control pill. They will also give some protection against sexually transmitted diseases, including AIDS.
Jean Mackin &
Anne Seeley-McLeod

Dear FYI: My two friends and I are 14. One hasn't started her periods, one has hers every few months, and mine is very light. Can we get pregnant?

Need to Know

Dear Need to Know: Yes, yes and *yes!* Pregnancy can occur almost anytime, but is especially likely about two weeks before a period is due -- even your first one! Young women often have unpredictable cycle lengths; these often become more regular as they get older. How heavy or light your period is doesn't matter.

If you are old enough to have periods, you are old enough to get pregnant, though your body won't make the healthiest baby until you reach your 20s. Talk to an adult you can trust for more information.

Lynn Schimmel

Dear FYI: When is the best time to have sex according to menstruation so that you won't get pregnant?

Being Cautious

Dear Cautious: The "rhythm method" of birth control involves abstaining from intercourse during unsafe times when pregnancy is most likely to occur.

A woman can more accurately determine these times by plotting her temperature and checking for certain changes in her cervical mucus daily, but even then the pregnancy rate is not acceptable to most teens.

Why isn't it very effective?

Ovulation often occurs about 14 days before the next period starts, but this isn't predictable. Also, sperm live five days in a woman's system, so you could have sex on Wednesday but get pregnant Sunday! To confuse the issue even further, bleeding just like a period can sometimes be because of ovulation.

Sex is never an emergency. Learn what all your options are and choose ones that offer high effectiveness against both pregnancy and sexually transmitted diseases.

Lynn Schimmel

Dear FYI: I would like to know, is there more of a chance that you will become pregnant the first time you have sex or later on?

Need An Answer

Dear Need An Answer: Anytime sperm meets egg, a pregnancy can occur. Your body doesn't know if it's the first time you've had intercourse or the 100th time.

Jean Mackin

Dear FYI: Can you get pregnant from anal sex? If so, are the chances of getting pregnant the same?

Uninformed

Dear Uninformed: No, you cannot get pregnant by having anal sex, but anal sex has other risks associated with it -- like sexually transmitted infections, including AIDS.

FYI editor

Dear FYI: I am a 17-year-old sexually active girl. My friends are also sexually active and talk about their orgasms. I don't believe I have had one. Am I weird? Just sign me...

Seventeen

215

Dear Seventeen: Not at all; in fact, I hear the same question from women many years older than you.

Assuming that other things aren't interfering with your peace of mind (lack of birth control, lack of protection against sexually transmitted disease, lack of comfort with your relationship's level of caring or honesty), you probably just need some basic information, as does your partner.

You can get this information from a wonderful book called "For Yourself" by Lonnie Barbach.

Barbach starts with basic anatomy lessons, including the fact that you have something called a clitoris above the opening of your vagina. This organ has exactly the same nerve endings in it as does the male's penis -- in fact, if you had been scheduled to be a boy, it would have turned into a penis.

One of the implications of this is that intercourse is perfect for stimulating a male to orgasm, but not necessarily a female.

Do yourself a favor and buy the book. If you still have concerns, talk to a health care provider you can trust.

Lynn Schimmel

Dear FYI: Must a woman have an orgasm in order to get pregnant?
Wondering

Dear Wondering: No, there absolutely is no connection between orgasm and pregnancy.

FYI editor

Dear FYI: My friend has been having sexual experiences with her boyfriend. Her parents are very strict and I'm worried about her getting pregnant. They use condoms once in a while but usually use the withdrawal method. How can I help her?

Worried

Dear Worried: Your friend needs information on sex and birth control. The withdrawal method is not a method of birth control. There already is sperm at the tip of the penis before ejaculation and men have a difficult time knowing when they are going to ejaculate, making it difficult for them to pull out in time.

Direct your friend to the nearest Planned Parenthood clinic for information. The clinic's services are confidential, and her parents will not be informed, though she will be encouraged to talk to her parents.

If she is afraid to go alone, offer to go with her.

You might also suggest that she take her boyfriend -- it's important for him to have the information, too.

Your friend needs help *now* before she gets pregnant and is faced with some *very* difficult decisions.

Jean Mackin

Dear FYI: I heard that if a man ejaculates in a spa that the sperm will live and a girl can get pregnant. Is this true?

Wondering

Dear Wondering: If a man ejaculates in a spa and there is no penis/vagina contact, his sperm will die and there is no danger of pregnancy.

FYI editor

Dear FYI: Is it possible to get pregnant if you have sex in a swimming pool?

Different Dude

Dear Different Dude: Yes, absolutely.

FYI editor

Dear FYI: What happens when you have sex standing up?

A Kid

Dear Kid: Sex standing up has the same pregnancy rates as sex in any other position.

FYI editor

Dear FYI: Can jumping up and down after intercourse prevent pregnancy?

Confused

Dear Confused: No, this will not help -- and neither will douching with Coca Cola, which some young folks believe will work.

Besides total abstinence or sterilization, the pill, condoms and foam, the IUD and norplant are the most effective methods.

Talk with your health care provider for further information.

Planned Parenthood

Dear FYI: Does any abortion or the pill cause birth defects later in life?

Sixteen and Worried

Dear Sixteen and Worried: Studies agree that one early abortion is something that a woman's body can handle. More than one early abortion can increase the risk of miscarriage when a woman plans to have a baby. In order to prevent problems when people plan to have a family, people having sex should use birth control or abstain until they are ready for these responsibilities.

Birth control pills cause very few babies to be born with birth defects.

Women who use the pill prevent pregnancy, have regular periods, less frequent gall bladder disease and less anemia when used over a four- or five-year period. They actually decrease the chance of ovarian and uterine cancer. There is still some question as to whether prolonged use of the pill increases the risk of breast cancer.

Anne Seeley-MacLeod &
Jean Mackin

Dear FYI: Can you suggest a good way to ask someone that you're getting involved with if they any venereal disease?

Concerned

Dear Concerned: Although your idea to ask is a good one, it contains a basic flaw -- and that is the assumption that your potential partner, even if he is scrupulously honest, would *know* if he is carrying a sexually transmittable disease.

Unfortunately, the carrier often does not know that he or she has a sexually transmittable disease. Be on the safe side and practice saying "no glove, no love," with conviction until it's automatic.

Lynn Schimmel

Dear FYI: I was wondering if you can get VD any other way than from sex?

Can you get it through drugs or holding hands?

Very Nervous

Dear Very Nervous: People get sexually transmitted diseases most often during genital sex. However, sexually transmitted diseases can also be exchanged during oral sex. A person can get AIDS or hepatitis B from sharing needles to use drugs and may be more likely to get a sexually transmitted disease because he or she didn't use condoms when having sex.

Kissing and holding hands have not been ruled out for the passing of all diseases, although many diseases die when exposed to air.

Holding hands is still considered to be fairly "safe" at this time, you'll be glad to know.

Planned Parenthood

Dear FYI: If you have never had sex and neither has your partner, can you still get a sexually transmitted disease if you have sex without a condom?

A Virgin

Dear Virgin: The only sexually transmitted disease you could get would be AIDS. If one of you had contracted AIDS from a blood transfusion, or from sharing dirty needles, you could pass on the disease. Otherwise, no.

FYI editor

Dear FYI: A couple of weeks after having sex with my new boyfriend I started noticing some bump-like warts near my vagina. They're getting bigger now and I'm scared. What should I do?

Scared

Dear Scared: It sounds as though you might have "condylomata acuminata," also called "venereal warts." They are caused by the sexually transmittable "human papillomatous virus." The only way to know for sure is to see a health care provider who has experience with this and other sexually transmitted diseases.

219

This virus is very common, easily spread and can be quite troublesome. It is usually treated by touching the lesions with a substance that makes them go away after several weekly applications.

We often can't tell by looking at a woman's cervix if the virus is there, but luckily, Pap smears will suggest its presence. This is important, for untreated, the HPV may lead to cervical pre-cancer (which Pap tests are looking for).

This infection usually doesn't cause obvious warty growths on the male. If you are diagnosed as having condylomata, your partner should be checked by a health care provider who uses magnification as part of the exam; otherwise, the flat lesions that typify the male's infection can be missed.

As with other sexually transmitted diseases, the use of condoms would have greatly decreased your chances of contracting this. You have the right and the responsibility to protect yourself; insist on them.

Lynn Schimmel

Dear FYI: I have an active sex life right now and about six months ago I thought I had the symptoms of gonorrhea. I don't completely remember the symptoms. What are they?

Active and Worried

Dear Active: If you have gonorrhea, you may have no symptoms.

If you are a male, you may experience some discharge from your penis, have pain when you urinate and some pain in your groin or your testicles.

If you are a female, you may have some vaginal discharge, pain when you urinate, pain in your lower abdomen, a fever and more painful menstrual periods.

If you are sexually active and worried, you should visit your nearest health clinic for treatment right away.

FYI editor

Dear FYI: I heard that there is a sexually transmitted disease that makes part of your penis fall off. Is this true?

Troubled

Dear Troubled: Sure, but their rarity makes them the least of your worries. There is such a thing, for example, called "erosive balanitis" which, if severe and neglected, can cause extensive tissue destruction. A sexually transmitted virus, called HPV for short, is probably a major cause of squamous-cell penile cancer, which also destroys tissue.

Of more immediate concern should be the many other sexually transmitted diseases which are quite common among teens, and which cause as much heartache as your original worry. A partner who contracts chlamydia because you didn't always use a condom, for example, will not view the destruction of her fallopian tubes and subsequent infertility any less intensely.

Even less serious infections, like most of the ones from HPV ("warts"), result in the need for numerous time-consuming and expensive visits to the doctor, and certainly stress a relationship. Herpes lesions leave no scars, but occurrences can be trying to live with.

Keep your penis and her tissue safe for years to come -- wear a condom.

Lynn Schimmel

Dear FYI: I heard that I can avoid AIDS if I always use condoms. Then I heard that some condoms aren't any good. Is that true? Help!

Curious About Safe Sex

Dear Curious: Your question is life-saving, both for you and for others. When in doubt about what is or is not safe sex, abstain. Condoms *are* helpful in preventing the spread of the disease. They are *not* foolproof.

First of all, condoms must be worn *before* the penis enters the vagina -- no foreplay without them. They should be made of rubber/latex, as animal-skin condoms are porous and can allow the AIDS virus to pass through them..

If other types of sex are taking place, rubber/latex protection should be used. Remember -- the AIDS Foundation labels anal, fisting and rimming as very high-risk behaviors for AIDS and other sexually transmitted diseases.

Oral sex is in the possibly unsafe category and the general advice is to abstain from it.

Historically, condoms have a reputation for breaking. Testing during manufacture has not routinely taken place. Wearing a condom, *if* you are going to have sex with someone, is much better than not wearing one. Using a back-up method with the ingredient Nonoxynol-9 in it (foam, diaphragm gel or spermicidal suppositories) is even better in helping fight AIDS from the very start. If a man is having sex, with another man, they should both wear condoms.

Think twice about having sex with someone new before you do it. Don't necessarily take the person's word for it if he or she tells you "I don't have any diseases." Look at the person's body parts before you leap -- and if you can't ask about his or her previous history, abstain until you can.

Your life depends on it.

Anne Seeley-MacLeod

Dear FYI: What is the incubation period for the AIDS virus?

Interested

Dear Interested: The incubation period is about 10 years on the average. This means that a person can be infected and pass the virus on to others through sexual intercourse or needle-sharing without feeling sick or not even knowing that he/she is infected.

A pregnant woman who is infected can pass the virus on to her baby and then the baby will get AIDS.

Since many teens are experimenting with drugs and sexual activities, they are considered extremely vulnerable to infection with the AIDS virus.

Christine Cipperly
AIDS public health
Program director

Dear FYI: If two people are gay, and haven't ever had sexual encounters with anyone else but each other, can they create AIDS?

Ever-Confused About AIDS

Dear Ever-Confused: No, they can't create AIDS. As long as the two people remain in a monogamous situation, they are safe from the sexual transmission of AIDS.

FYI editor

Dear FYI: Can men get AIDS from women?

Curious

Dear Curious: Men can definitely get AIDS from women in the same way they can get gonorrhea, syphilis, herpes or other sexually transmitted diseases.

Christine Cipperly

Dear FYI: Can AIDS be gotten through a kiss?

AIDS Avoider

Dear AIDS Avoider: According to the San Francisco AIDS Foundation guidelines, dry or social kissing, which is any kiss with the lips closed, is safe because no infected fluids can be passed during the activity. French, or deep,

222

Dear FYI: How are people now-a-days supposed to have sex without having a good chance of getting AIDS?

Very Bummed

Dear Very Bummed: They're not -- or if they do they should use condoms.

Unless you have had sex with the same person -- and no one else -- in the last 10 years, and unless you are 100 percent sure that the same is true of your partner, you could contract AIDS.

AIDS takes so long to manifest itself that if you have had sex with someone new in the last 10 years you are essentially having sex with that person's partners for the last 10 years! If you have other questions about AIDS, call the AIDS hotline at 1-800-342-AIDS.

Anne Seeley-MacLeod

kissing is believed to be risky, but because there is no absolute proof, it remains in the "possibly safe" category.

In the words of a spokesman for the Foundation, "saliva is not suspected as a route of transmission for the AIDS virus. If the virus were transmitted by saliva, we would be seeing many more cases than we are, and they should be appearing far outside the normal risk groups, which they are not."

The question of kissing is complicated, however if one or both partners have bleeding gums or cuts on the mouth or on the lips, blood as well as saliva would be passed and the activity would be considered risky.

FYI editor

Dear FYI: A lot of people have or have had mono. I heard that mono may be the first stage of AIDS; so will people with mono get AIDS?

Concerned

Dear Concerned: No. A virus (a tiny organism that lives inside a cell) causes mono. Most mono cases occur by the time the person is a young adult. AIDS is caused by a completely different virus (as influenza is caused by another virus, polio by another, etc.).

These viruses are *not related*. Mono has no relation to AIDS and can't become AIDS; nor can polio or influenza cause or become AIDS.

E. Jack Benner, M.D.

Dear FYI: Can you get AIDS from a mosquito, like malaria?

Bugged by the Thought

Dear Bugged: According to Dr. Murray Gardner, an AIDS expert at the UC Davis Medical Center, there is absolutely no connection, as far as anyone knows, between AIDS and mosquitoes.

FYI editor

Dear FYI: I'm here from Sweden for a few months studying, and I'm worried about catching AIDS in the swimming pool. What if someone would go to the bathroom in the water? Also, is there a danger if one of the food people in a restaurant cuts his finger or something?

Worried and Hungry

Dear Worried and Hungry: You are not in danger of "catching" AIDS in a swimming pool, nor from getting AIDS from food handlers with AIDS.

We spoke to Dr. James Carlson, director of the AIDS Virus and Diagnostic Laboratory at UC Davis.

Carlson reports that there is no evidence (after six years of research) that the virus can be transmitted by casual contact.

The only proven transmission of AIDS is by intimate sexual contact, by the direct transmission of blood through use of needles contaminated by intravenous drug users, or from mothers infected with HIV to their newborn babies.

So enjoy eating out and swimming. We hope that the rest of your stay in the U.S. is pleasant; have a safe journey home.

FYI editor

Dear FYI: I had hoped to go into the field of medicine. Now because of AIDS I am wondering if I should. What do you think?

Frightened of Dying of AIDS

Dear Frightened: I suggest you consider two things. First, there are many fields of medicine in which the risk of exposure to the AIDS virus is zero. These can be as rewarding as the fields of medicine in which the risk is small, but real.

Second, physicians and nurses have risked their lives throughout history to provide compassionate care to suffering people. AIDS is merely the latest example of risk to medical personnel.

Neil M. Flynn, M.D.

Dear FYI: If you know a person has AIDS, should you be afraid of that person?

Wondering

Dear Wondering: No. There is no reason to fear a person with AIDS, since the only way you could catch the disease would be by sharing syringes for drug use, or unsafe sexual contact, or contact that would or could exchange body fluids. AIDS is *not* transmitted by casual contacts such as touching, talking, eating together: things that friends do. People with AIDS need support of family, friends, doctors and nurses. It would be very frightening to know that people are afraid of me because I have a disease for which there is no known cure.

A 36-year-old man with AIDS

Dear FYI: Can a girl get an infection or a disease by giving a male oral sex?

Looking Out For No. 1

Dear FYI: Can a girl get pregnant from swallowing semen? I don't do this, but I'm not sure.

Dumb Question?

Dear Looking & D.Q.: A girl cannot get pregnant from swallowing semen, but oral sex in general can be very risky. She can get some very serious infections from a male, but only if he had one before her contact with him.

Among these diseases are AIDS, genital warts, gonorrhea, syphillis, chlamydia -- and *more!* Some of these diseases are treatable. You can die from lack of treatment of some or late treatment of others.

It's also important for you to know that people can get some very serious infections from anal sex, too. Often it is painful to have anal sex, but people use this opening to prevent pregnancy. Sometimes the rectal skin can get stretched and torn and if one of the partners has an infection, the other can get it, too.

Anne Seeley-MacLeod

Straight talk about AIDS...

There are so many questions about AIDS. Here's a quick reference regarding the most frequently asked AIDS queries...

1. What symptoms reveal AIDS? Remember that people can be infected with the AIDS virus and have no symptoms at all, or an individual infected with the virus may have mild symptoms of fatigue, weight loss, diarrhea, and may develop shingles or a yeast infection of the mouth called thrush.

These symptoms in an infected person are not AIDS. The diagnosis of AIDS requires that an individual: a) have evidence of infection with the AIDS virus and; b) develop one of the serious infections, called opportunistic infections, or *Kaposi's sarcoma*, a cancer, in addition.

Symptoms of this opportunistic infection include persistent fever, night sweats and symptoms related to the location of the infection in the body. The most common infection is called *pneumocystis carynii pneumonia*, or PCP, and is a lung infection that causes increasing shortness of breath and breathing difficulty. The Kaposi's sarcoma appears as a brown to purple discolored area on the skin.

Remember that almost all people who develop AIDS have a risk factor in their background, such as multiple male homosexual partners, blood transfusions, intravenous drug abuse or hemophilia.

2. Would contraceptive use (like a condom) prevent AIDS virus infection? It is believed that barrier methods of contraception such as a condom will provide a measure of protection from transmission of the AIDS virus from one sexual partner to another. Remember that a condom provides no protection unless it remains in place.

3. Is it true that the AIDS virus will kill a victim within a year? The majority of individuals who develop full-blown AIDS die within one to three years of the diagnosis. However, some patients with Kaposi's sarcoma are still doing well three to five years after diagnosis. Opportunistic infections appear to have the worst outlook for long survival.

4. Is it true that the AIDS virus lives in the back of the brain near the backbone? There is disturbing evidence accumulating that the AIDS virus preferentially infects brain and nerve tissue. Researchers are concerned that people infected with the AIDS virus may develop degenerative brain disorders many years after infection with the virus. Many AIDS patients are beginning to show evidence of brain dysfunction. Early treatment with anti-HIV agents may prevent the development of brain disease.

An added warning: Everyone should be very careful about casual sex.

This has become a heterosexual disease, so I caution heterosexuals not to become complacent. Promiscuous heterosexuals are exposed just like gay men.

Neil M. Flynn, M.D.
Infectious disease specialist

Dear FYI: Can you get AIDS from public bathrooms?
Panicked

Dear Panicked: The only way you can get AIDS from public bathrooms is if you are engaging in some act of sexual intercourse or sharing dirty needles in the bathroom. AIDS is not transmitted from toilet seats or drinking fountains.
FYI editor

Further suggested reading

- Arthur, Shirley, *Surviving Teen Pregnancy: Your Choices, Dreams and Decisions.* Morning Glory Press, Buena Park, Ca., 1991.
- Blake, Jeanne, *Risky Business: How to be AIDS-Smart and Stay Healthy. A Guide for Teen-agers.* Workman Publishing, New York, N.Y., 1991.
- Gale, Jay, *A Young Man's Guide to Sex.* The Body Press, Los Angeles, 2nd. ed., 1988.
- Gale, Jay, *A Parent's Guide to Teen-age Sexuality.* Henry Holt, New York, 1989.
- Kelly, Gary F., *Learning About Sex: The Contemporary Guide for Young Adults.* Barron's Educational Series, New York, 3rd. ed., 1987.
- Somers, Leon, *Talking to Your Children About Love and Sex.* Penguin Signet,New York, 1990.
- Voss, Jacqueline, and Jay Gale, *A Young Woman's Guide to Sex.* The Body Press, Los Angeles, 1986.

Douglas Adams, L.C.S.W. has been with the Yolo County Child Sexual Abuse Treatment Center since 1985. He has a broad background in both inpatient and outpatient settings with a special emphasis on children and adolescents. He maintains a private practice in both Davis and Sacramento.

Beulah Amsterdam, Ph.D. is a licensed clinical psychologist in private practice and a clinical associate professor in the Dept. of Psychiatry at the U.C. Davis School of Medicine. Formerly a pediatric psychologist at the New York Hospital, Cornell Medical Center, she also worked at Boston Beth Israel.

Staci P. Anderson is a reproductive health outreach educator at the Davis Community Clinic. Her work takes her to schools and to the community, where she talks to both teens and parents about reproductive health, and to parents about how to talk to their teens about sex. Previously she was an HIV counselor at Planned Parenthood.

Liz Applegate, Ph.D. is a nationally recognized expert on nutrition and performance and is author of Power Foods (Rodale Press, 1991). She is currently a lecturer at U.C. Davis in the Nutrition Department and in the Medical School. Dr. Applegate is a columnist and advisor for a variety of national publications, international corporations and organizations. She has appeared on numerous nationally televised health and fitness programs, and is a member of the NTTC professional triathlete team based in Los Angeles. She is the mother of two young children.

Cleve B. Baker, M.D. is a dermatologist with the Woodland Clinic Medical Group in Woodland, CA. A California native, Dr. Baker was educated at Stanford University. He has been a general practitioner of dermatology for 25 years. Tropical medicine and infectious disease, because of their skin involvement, led him into specializing in skin disease. Traditional jazz and jazz piano are his avocation, as well as history and historic preservation. He is happily married to Irene, and they have four wonderful, non-medical children.

Christopher Bauer, Ph.D. is a licensed clinical psychologist in private practice in Davis, CA. He has previously worked in a variety of mental health agencies in Arizona and New York. He aspires to juggle more effectively his simultaneous full time careers in clinical psychology and music.

Hanna Bauer, Ed. D. is a psychotherapist and a published poet who usually writes from her beloved cabin on Gabriola Island, British Columbia. She was director of psychological services and special education, and established a continuum of pupil services and staff consultation from preschool through senior high school, in Davis, CA. She's optimistic that her devoted marriage of fifty years "might work out."

Herbert Bauer, M.D. is a child psychiatrist with a public health background. He has held positions as Public Health Director, Mental

Health Director, and Clinical Professor at the U.C. Davis Medical School. He is involved in many community activities, especially those promoting peace, which he declares as his "hobby."

Bonnie Beffa, M.S.W, has been associated with Suicide Prevention of Yolo County, CA, since 1984. For two years as Volunteer Coordinator, she was responsible for scheduling the 24-hour crisis line. In addition, she was the facilitator for a Suicide Survivors Group for individuals who have lost friends or family members to suicide. Currently, Bonnie is the Program Director for Safe Harbor Crisis House, a 24-hour short-term residential program which is part of the Yolo Community Care Continuum.

E. Jack Benner, M.D. is an internist who gravitated south from Washington to Oregon to Northern California - as far south as he's willing to go. An avid sailor, he enjoys caring for a broad range of patient problems, including alcoholism and AIDS.

Kent F. Bennington, Ph.D. is a psychologist in private practice (next to the beach) in Encinitas, CA. He is a Diplomate of the American Board of Family Psychology, and a clinical faculty member of the Department of Psychiatry at U. C. San Diego, and the California School of Professional Psychology, San Diego.

Sheldon Berkowitz, Ph.D. is a clinical psychologist in private practice in Davis. He is an Assistant Clinical Professor of Psychiatry in the School of Medicine at U.C. Davis. His special expertise is in the treatment of eating disorders.

K.H. Blacker, M.D. is professor and chair of the Dept. of Psychiatry at the U.C. Davis School of Medicine, and supervising and training analyst at San Francisco Psychoanalytic Institute. His professional activities include administration, teaching, research in psychoanalysis and anxiety disorders, and treating private patients. Father of four and a doting grandfather, he is an avid skier and tennis player.

Kathy Blankenship is counselor at Wolfskill High School in Winters, CA. Her undergraduate training was at U.C. Davis and at C.S.U. Sacramento. She did casework and volunteer training for three years at Diogenes Youth Services and outreach drug counseling for one year for Yolo County.

Dale Blunden, Ph.D. is a clinical psychologist in private practice. She works largely with adults, a significant number of whom have eating disorders. Ms. Blunden is also an ardent mom, gardener and cat lover.

Robert J. Bolt, M.D. is certified and recertified by the American Boards of Internal Medicine and Gastroenterology. He was Professor and Chair of the Department of Medicine at U.C. Davis for 24 years, and prior to that was Professor of Medicine at the University of Michigan for 15 years. He has been visiting lecturer at universities in Colombia, Belgium,

Iran and medical schools and centers in the U.S. Dr. Bolt is the author of 90 scientific publications and four medical books.

Carol L. Boyer, M.A. graduated from U.C. Davis and taught Home Economics and English before moving to high school counseling over 20 years ago. As Head Counselor at Davis Senior High School, she finds her work both challenging and satisfying.

Jack Bruner, M.D. received his training in plastic surgery in Los Angeles and in New York City. He has practiced in Sacramento for 22 years, is active in the U.C. Davis Medical Center training program, and is an Officer of the California Society of Plastic Surgeons. His love of skiing has led him to combine work and play as a medical officer for the U.S. Ski Team, and he spends winter weekends in ski patrol on the slopes of the Sierra Nevada.

Judith C. Buchholz, school counselor, is still married to her high school sweetheart. She lives for her family, friendships, cafe lattes and gardening, and finds working with adolescents stimulates positive middlescence.

Nancy Chadwick, L.C.S.W. has been in private practice for 14 years, working with individuals, families, couples, children and adolescents. Her first experience in this kind of work was in the U.C. Davis Medical Center psychological crisis clinic. In working with longer term clients she prefers an interactive approach, with much instruction in psychodynamics, coping skills and communication.

Christine Cipperly has held the position of AIDS Program Director for Yolo County Public Health since 1988. Prior to that she was the Director of the Davis Community Clinic Drug Treatment and Counseling Services Program for over 10 years. She is the mother of five boys and four girls including five teens and a new baby. She is a fourth generation California native and loves rock and roll.

Gina Coffman, illustrator, is a 22-year-old graphic artist at *The Davis Enterprise* newspaper. She has studied art and comparative literature at U.C. Davis and at Sacramento City College. She dreams of one day designing her own publication. In addition to her artistic pursuits, Ms. Coffman serves as the President of Venture Club of Davis.

Barbara Colletto, M.S.C., M.F.C.C. Intern, originally trained as a teacher, and serendipitously found her professional niche in the chemical dependency field about 3 years ago. Her primary area of interest at this time is women's recovery issues.

Carol Cotton, M.F.C.C. is a licensed marriage and family counselor who practices in Davis and Berkeley. She is a former high school teacher and college teacher and counselor.

Jere H. Curry, M.A., is an instructor in the Dance Department at U.C. Davis. Over the years he has been there, the number of students has risen from 30 to over 800. He has also taught private classes in tap and ballet to children from aged 8 to teen-agers for many years. Earlier in his career he toured with Miya Slavinska and Natasha Krisofska, and studied under jazz dance teacher Matt Maddox.

Sue Curry, publisher, *Terra Nova Press,* came to Davis, CA., from Australia in 1977. For several years she owned and operated a bookselling and publishing company specializing in Australiana. The present book marks her move into publishing on mental health and family issues. Married and the mother of three children, she hopes the information in this book will be as useful to other families as it has already been to hers.

Debbie Davis is managing editor of *The Davis Enterprise,* the newspaper in which the "FYI" column first appeared. The mother of two young children, she is looking forward to the day when she can draw on the advice presented here.

Ilana E. Davis, Ph.D. received her professional training at the University of Oregon and at U.C. Berkeley. She has been in private practice for 13 years, specializing in long term insight oriented psychotherapy. She is also an Assistant Clinical Professor in the Psychiatry department at U.C. Davis. Her favorite activity is the Sister Cities Project with the U.S.S.R., and she dreams of consulting with Soviet psychologists.

Pat Donlon, M.D. is clinical professor of Psychiatry at U.C. Davis. His wife Patti served as executive director of the Yolo County Mental Health Association at the time the FYI column was launched. They were raised in small communities in N.E. Iowa, and have one son.

Joyce Bezazian-Dovelli, M.F.C.C. currently works in private practice. Originally from San Francisco, she has worked as a therapist in a variety of agencies including Youth Advocates, Pyramid Alternatives, Family Service Agency, and Sacramento Mental Health Center. Her personal interests lie in the arts, music and entertainment.

Renee L. Dryfoos, Ph.D. is a licensed clinical psychologist in private practice in Davis, CA. She also supervises U.C. Davis Medical Center interns and residents in both departments of Psychiatry and Family Practice. Formerly she lived and worked in Los Angeles and Philadelphia. For 11 years she has trained professionals in family therapy, and is continuously learning from her own children and husband.

Nancy DuBois has been enjoying the practice of psychology for 47 years. She has had the privilege of watching and helping children, adults and families grow, in several states - New York, Michigan, Kentucky and California- and in many settings - hospitals, colleges, schools, clinics, churches, and in private practice. She has supervised therapists in training, and is the founder of Yolo Hospice. She is most proud of raising a daughter and two sons to fine adults.

Bob Dunning is 44 and loves pizza. He is a columnist for "The Davis Enterprise" where he has worked forever. A town celebrity, each year thousands of people support a charitable cause by accepting his invitation to join him for "Dinner at the Dump."

Candice M. Erba, R.N., L.C.S.W. is currently in private practice as a psychotherapist in Davis, CA. She has been a public health nurse in Rochester, N.Y.; an instructor of nursing at University Hospitals in Cleveland, OH.; a Family Education Coordinator at Family Service Agency in Sacramento, CA.; Clinical Director of Yolo Family Service Agency in Woodland, CA.; and a faculty member at C.S.U. Sacramento.

Joanne Evers, Ed.D. is originally from San Francisco. Her training was received from U.C. Berkeley, C.S.U. Hayward, and the University of San Francisco. She has been in private psychotherapy practice for over 20 years.

Jay Feldman, M.D., a graduate of University of Illinois Medical School, did his psychiatric residency at Herrick Hospital in Berkeley, CA. He has been in private practice in both Berkeley and Davis for almost 20 years. Currently, Dr. Feldman is doing intensive psychotherapy with individuals and couples, with a special interest in the psychodynamics of the mating relationships in our changing society. He is married and has five children ranging in age from 1 to 30 years.

Daniel J. Ferrigno, M.D. is a specialist in Internal Medicine-Diagnosis who has sub-specialized in Addiction Medicine. He has been involved in the treatment of adolescent and adult patients in both inpatient and outpatient treatment situations since 1974. He is currently the Medical Director of Chemical Dependency Services, CPC-Sierra Vista Hospital, Sacramento, CA.

George R. Fleming is Work Experience Coordinator at Davis Senior High School, and has worked at the school for 20 years. In his free time he enjoys sports.

Neil Flynn, M.D. is Associate Professor of Internal Medicine at U.C. Davis, and Medical Director of the AIDS and Related Disorders Clinic at the UCD Medical Center. He received his training from U.C. Davis, Loma Linda University, and Ohio State University.

Christine Fry is Youth Outreach Coordinator for the Yolo County Department of Alcohol and Drug Programs. Her travels have taken her to the Netherlands, Ghana, Guatemala, Japan and, most recently, Micronesia. She is currently studying to be a Unitarian minister.

Bruce Gallaudet, book designer, is a longtime California newspaperman who now owns and operates Gallaudet and Associates, an advertising and public relations agency in Davis. He is the father of two young children.

Roy Grabow, Ph.D., is a clinical psychologist in private practice. He also works with Yolo County Mental Health, and Suicide Prevention of Yolo County.

Jean M. Grandi, RN, PHN, SN has practiced nursing for 11 years in a variety of settings: State and County Health Departments; U.C. Davis Medical Center; and other hospitals and clinics. She is currently district nurse in the Natomas Unified School District, CA. She enjoys using her knowledge and skills to improve the health of children and young adults.

Nancy Hanks, Ed.D. is a Diplomate of the American Board of Sexology; her doctorate is from the University of San Francisco. Her area of expertise is in women's sexuality and she has practiced in both private and public agency settings. Dr. Hanks is currently a Family Consultant in Salinas, CA.

Ted Hoffman, M.D. has been a therapist for children, adolescents and families for 20 years. After "Dr. Ted" earned his M.D. at UCLA he completed his traning at Brentwood V.A. Hospital and at U.C. Davis. As important as this education was, his own family and clients have been the best aid in "getting it right."

Eva Peters Hunting, Dr. P.H. is currently with Omnibus Mental Health Group, specializing in assessment, evaluation and psychotherapy with children, adolescents, adults, couples and families. She also serves as counseling psychologist to residential facilities for disturbed adolescents. Dr. Hunting is a former Peace Corps volunteer.

Kathryn Jaeger, Ph.D. is a psychologist in private practice in Davis, specializing in evaluating and treating children, adolescents and families. She has worked for various public agencies including school districts before establishing a practice. She provides consultation to several residential treatment homes. In her free time she enjoys sports and travel with her family.

John Keltner, M.D., Professor and Chairman of the Department of Opthalmology at U.C. Davis, came to the west coast from the faculty of Yale University. Happily married to the "FYI" Editor for almost thirty years, he has cheerfully shared his wife, phone, and most available table tops with the "FYI" column and book.

Nancy Keltner, "FYI" Editor, combined backgrounds in English, publicity and mental health to originate the "FYI" column. A "professional volunteer" and the mother of three grown sons, she dreams of becoming a computer literate grandmother.

Guille L. Libresco, Ph.D. is a mother, lover, music student, world traveler, gourmet cook, community activist, and sea-lover. She is a Diplomate in social work, and a psychologist with 35 years' experience as a therapist, consultant and professor.

Jeffrey Light, D.D.S. received his training from U.C. Irvine, Loyola University in Chicago, and Wadsworth V.A. Hospital in Los Angeles. He has practised dentistry in Sacramento since 1984. He enjoys outdoor sports and hiking in his leisure hours.

Glen A. Lillington, M.D. is a physician, a professor of Medicine at the U.C. Davis Medical Center, a writer and a well-traveled lecturer. "Generally speaking, he is generally speaking." He was born in Canada, trained in Internal Medicine and Pulmonology at the Mayo Clinic, and has been a true-blue Californian since 1960.

Will Lotter has taught and coached at U.C. Daivs since 1952. For the past 16 years he has taught a popular holistic health course to over 1,000 students each academic year. He also teaches a health education course for teachers in which he emphasizes teaching young students how to manage stress. He is a former Peace Corps director (Malawi, 1965-7), and since 1975 has made 15 trips to Central America as a member of Davis Religious Community for Sanctuary.

Gary McConahay, Ph.D. received his Ph.D. from the University of Illinois and has worked professionally in California, Oregon, and Washington. He does his best community mental health program planning from the end of a fly-fishing rod throughout the western United States.

Mary McCurdy, M.S.W. is Director of the Yolo Wayfarer Center, a Christian mission to the homeless in Woodland, CA. She was educated at U.C. Berkeley in the late '60s. The mother of three, wife of one, she loves her work but would rather be biking, hiking, swimming or sail boarding.

Jean Mackin, B.S. is currently Medical Administration Manager at Planned Parenthood of Sacramento Valley. A graduate of Eastern Michigan University, she has previously been Area Director for Planned Parenthood of Central and Northern Arizona and Planned Parenthood clinic manager in Davis, CA. She lives in Davis with her husband and son.

Carlos G. Matos. M.A., has served for 14 years as an Alcohol and Drug Counselor in Yolo County, CA.

Stephen Mayberg, Ph.D. is a clinical psychologist and Deputy Director of Yolo County Mental Health Services. A graduate of Yale and the University of Minnesota, he has been recognized for his involvement in the development of policies, legislation, and treatment programs for children with mental health needs.

Cheri McElwee is a Chemical Dependency Specialist who has completed an alcoholism and drug abuse program at California State University, Sacramento. Her interest in this field comes to her naturally as she is a recovering alcoholic/addict. She enjoys being able to facilitate in her clients self-awareness which can lead to change, and ultimately increased self-esteem.

John Meyer, Ph.D. is a clinical psychologist in private practice in Davis, CA. He is a graduate of Gettysburg College, PA., and CSPP-L.A. Dr. Meyer is married and has two daughters.

Ellwood Morgan, M.D. is currently Medical Director of an inpatient drug and alcohol treatment center in Spofford, N.H.

Sumner Morris, Ed. D. received his training from Simpson College, Iowa, the University of Iowa, and Stanford University. He was on the counseling center staff at U.C. Davis for 30 years, serving as director for nineteen. He retired in 1988 and, as a licensed psychologist, maintains a limited private practice in Davis, plays tennis, does yard work, and is an aspiring writer.

Robert L. Neal, M.F.C.C. is a therapist in private practice. His counseling experience stretches over 20 years; previous to that he was a church pastor. He received his graduate education at Texas Christian University, Fort Worth. When not counseling, Mr. Neal enjoys his family, golfing, and traveling.

Cathy G. Neuhauser, Ph.D. is a native of Pennsylvania, now solidly based in California due to some important loves - her husband, her children, and the mountains. Although currently with the Woodland Clinic Medical Group, she has also worked in day treatment programs with seriously emotionally disturbed children.

Robert Ogner, M.S.W., L.C.S.W. is a psychotherapist in private practice in Davis, CA. He serves as Clinical Instructor of Psychiatry at the U.C. Davis Medical School.

Joan Parnas, Director of Alcohol and Drug Programs for Yolo County, California, has been a counselor and administrator for 18 years. She also trains and consults in substance abuse issues, interfaith marriage and assertiveness. In her leisure hours she enjoys traveling, hiking, gardening and reading.

Jerry L. Plummer, MSW, MPA, BCD is a Diplomate in Clinical Social Work and a California licensed clinical social worker and marriage, family and child counselor. He is a managing partner in the Omnibus Mental Health Group. He also enjoys the pleasures of scuba diving, flying, and cycling, and being the parent of a bright, 16 year old son.

Kent Reade, Ph.D. currently lives and practices in Seattle, specializing in the treatment of eating disorders. He also supervises graduate students in psychology at the University of Washington.

Michael H. Robbins, M.D. received his training at the Medical College of Ohio, University of Louisville Hospitals, and at U.C. Davis. He is currently in private practice and is Clinical Professor of Neurosurgery in

Sacramento. Dr. Robbins is also Director of Medical Affairs for the Northern California Center for Rehabilitation Hospital.

Carol Rodgers, M.F.C.C. is a counselor for Yolo County Alcohol and Drug Programs, and is Clinical Director of Suicide Prevention of Yolo County, serving also on its mobile crisis team. The interactive nature of these jobs exposes her to the full range of mental health clients and services. She enjoys her work but shares the frustration of limited financial support and services in mental health programs.

April Roeseler is employed as a Health Education consultant in the State of California Tobacco Control Section, where she oversees approximately 25 projects. As the prior Chief of Planning with the State Office of AIDS, Ms. Roeseler had lead responsibility for the development of a comprehensive state plan on human immunodeficiency virus disease prevention and treatment.

Marilyn W. Roland, Ph.D., M.F.C.C. is a family therapist in private practice, following a 25 year career as a psychologist with the Davis Schools. Her continuing fascination with families grew out of these experiences, as well as from her own challenges as a wife, and mother of two.

Kristine A. Rominger, M.S., M.F.C.C., has been in private practice as a therapist for 4 years. Her previous work experience was with Planned Parenthood, Suicide Prevention (where she worked in the adolescent school program), and with the Yolo County Drug and Alcohol Program. Her own personal therapists are her horses; she also enjoys her part-time farming activities, swimming, reading, cooking and gardening.

Edith Rothchild, M.S.W., L.C.S.W. enjoys working as a psychotherapist with children, adolescents and families, and has worked in California and Virginia, as well as in Kenya, Uganda, Zambia and Ghana. She finds that similar human questions arise within these many different cultures.

Martin C. Ruiz is a Sergeant in the Davis Police Department.

Leo G. Sackett is a Lieutenant in the Davis Police Department, and Division Commander of Technical Services. He has 25 years of law enforcement experience.

Ethel Sassenrath, Ph.D. is Associate Professor Emeritus in the Department of Psychiatry, in the U.C. Davis School of Medicine. She was one of the early investigators of the effects of marihuana (ie. THC) and stress on endocrine systems, reproduction, and social behavior in test systems utilizing rhesus monkeys.

Lynn McCreery Schimmel, M.S., R.N.C., N.P. is a perinatal clinical nurse specialist, a nurse researcher, a long-distance bike rider, a feminist, mom of two wonderful little boys, wife of an obstetrician, granddaughter of two energetic 90 year old grannies, and a women's health nurse practitioner committed to tender, respectful care for all women.

Carrie Schucker, Ph.D. is a licensed Marriage, Family and Child Counselor who practices in Davis and Sacramento, CA. Her specialties include treatment of sexual abuse of children and adults, family and couple therapy, job stress and insight-oriented therapy with adults.

Anne Seeley-McLeod, M.Ed., B.F.A. former Center Manager of Planned Parenthood in Davis, CA., is currently Executive Director of the Camp Fire Council of the Greater Dayton, OH. area. Her most rewarding times are spent sharing fun and love with her husband, Roger and daughter, Marissa.

Elanna Panter Sherman, M.F.C.C. has been in private practice for over 7 years. Originally from the east coast, she has lived in Israel. Her extensive travel abroad has enhanced her appreciation of cultural diversity. Ms. Sherman has lived in Davis for the past 12 years with her husband and two children.

Barbara Sherwood, M.S.W. received her training at U.C. Berkeley. She has worked as a psychotherapist in community mental health, and as clinical director of Yolo Family Service Agency. Currently in private practice in Davis and Sacramento, California, she is also a lecturer and consultant on dysfunctional and healthy families. She lives in Davis with her husband and two teenage children.

Ronald Sockolov, M.D. received his medical degree from U.C.L.A. and a master's degree in exercise medicine from U.C. Davis. He is a team physician at U.C. Davis and Sacramento State University.

Lansing C. Stenson, M.D. is currently in private practice in Davis, CA., and is an Assistant Clinical Professor of Family Practice at the U.C. Davis School of Medicine and a team physician at U.C. Davis.

David Stoebel, Ph.D. Originally from Seattle, Dave now coordinates prevention, public information, and planning for the Yolo County Alcohol and Drug Program. He also teaches in the U.C. Davis Extension Alcohol and Drug Studies Program. In his free time he enjoys gardening, swimming, and being a father.

Marjorie Ann Harley Studer was raised in Sterling, Colorado. She received her training in chemistry and science teaching from the University of Colorado at Boulder, and at Cornell University. She is married and the mother of three daughters. As a chemistry teacher at Davis Senior High School for 14 years, Ms. Studer's life intersects with more than 150 teens each year. She enjoys movies, theatre, walking, and attempting to bloom orchids.

Ann E. Teal, L.C.S.W. works in private practice, specializing in the management of stress and chronic pain. She enjoys teaching young people how to care for themselves physically and emotionally. Her three children were once busy teenagers. During "off hours" she likes to hike, ski and read.

Stewart E. Teal, M.D. is a Clinical Professor at U.C. Davis. His search for a place for an academically oriented Child Psychiatrist in community mental health has led him along interesting paths, including consulting to Sacramento County Probation Department, Welfare Department, residential treatment programs for children, adolescents and young adults; the maintenance of a private practice; the teaching of students at all levels; and chairing the California Psychiatric Association Children's Committee. He has also helped raise his own three children.

Linda S. Tell, R.N., M.F.C.C. works in private practice as a counselor to individuals, couples and groups. She has 17 years experience as an intensive care nurse and counselor in New York City and Sacramento. Her training concentrated extensively on death and dying issues. As a therapist, Ms. Tell has been a Drug and Alcohol Counselor with Yolo County. She is the step-mother of two teenage daughters, and loves hiking and cycling in country areas.

Captane P. Thomson, M.D. is immediate past President of the California Psychiatric Association. A community psychiatrist who has directed the Yolo County Mental Health Service for the past 26 years, Dr. Thomson received his training at U.C. San Francisco, at Massachusetts General and McLean Hospitals, and at the Harvard School of Public Health. He has taught at the University of Edinburgh and at U.C. Davis. His other loves are swimming, running, and banjo-guitar playing of folk tunes.

William J. Treguboff, M.F.C.C. is a former surveyor, truck driver, and campus minister who is now a family therapist and crisis clinician in Davis, CA. He has raised three children, four cats and one springer spaniel. He spends his weekends working on his car and listening to baseball games.

Joe P. Tupin, M.D., Professor of Psychiatry and Medical Director at the U.C. Davis Medical Center, came to California from the University of Texas Medical School. He enjoys his family (especially a grand-daughter who, miracle of miracles, lives nearby), cooking, fly fishing, reading mysteries, the performing arts, and California Aggie football.

Cynthia Reeves Tuttle, M.P.H., ACCE received her training at the University of Hawaii and has worked as a health educator in Hawaii, Alaska and California. She is currently completing her Ph.D., and is working part time as a Lamaze childbirth educator and as a health instructor for two local community colleges.

Gordon Ulrey, Ph.D. received his psychology training in Boston, MA. He has worked in New England, Colorado, and is now teaching psychology and working with children and families in Davis, CA. While in California he has been director of an inpatient adolescent treatment center which confronts extremes of teenage behavioral and emotional issues.

John L. Vohs, M.A. is Chair of the Department of Rhetoric and Communication at the University of California, Davis.

Carolyn Russ Waggoner, M.S., R.D. is chief of the Agency and Nutrition Services Unit of the Department of Health Services, State of California, Special Supplemental Food Program for Women, Infants and Children (WIC). Her work experience includes counseling teenagers and adults on issues related to weight control, fad diets, eating disorders, and disease prevention. Her interests include bicycling, water and snow skiing, horseback riding, hiking, and spending time with family and friends.

Bonnie Wilson, Ph.D. is a marriage, family and child counselor in private practice in Davis, CA., and is currently completing work toward her psychologist's license. She enjoys observing and facilitating continuing development throughout adulthood. Developmental transition phases, such as college age and mid-life, are a special interest.

Magdeline Winkelblack, M.S., C.A.D.C. has worked in the chemical dependency field for the past seven years in inpatient, outpatient and school based treatment facilities. She balances her life by playing piano, scuba diving, and spending time with her husband and animals.

Joyce D. Wisner, Public Health Nurse reentered the school nursing field 7 years ago and continues as school nurse at Davis Senior High School. Her love of teens and her ability to network on their behalf has been reflected in several community awards: Davis Citizen of the Year and the "Woman of Distinction" award from the Soroptimist International of Davis.

Carol Wolfe, R.N., P.N.P. is now, after 21 years of service in public health, a supervising public health nurse in Yolo County. In her leisure hours she enjoys horse-packing in the High Sierra, and spending time with her three grandchildren.

Lynn Zender, L.C.S.W. is currently Director of Social Services at CPC Heritage Oaks Hospital, an acute psychiatric hospital in Sacramento. In the past she has been Executive Director of Suicide Prevention of Yolo County, and is the proud parent of two young adults.